An Apocryphal God

An Apocryphal God

Beyond Divine Maturity

Mark McEntire

Fortress Press
Minneapolis

AN APOCRYPHAL GOD

Beyond Divine Maturity

Copyright © 2015 Fortress Press. All rights reserved. Except for brief quotations in critical articles or reviews, no part of this book may be reproduced in any manner without prior written permission from the publisher. Visit http://www.augsburgfortress.org/copyrights/ or write to Permissions, Augsburg Fortress, Box 1209, Minneapolis, MN 55440.

Cover design: Alisha Lofgren

Cover image: Thinkstock / PaweÅ Aniszewski

Library of Congress Cataloging-in-Publication Data is available

Print ISBN: 978-1-4514-7035-2

eISBN: 978-1-4514-7238-7

The paper used in this publication meets the minimum requirements of American National Standard for Information Sciences — Permanence of Paper for Printed Library Materials, ANSI Z329.48-1984.

Manufactured in the U.S.A.

This book was produced using PressBooks.com, and PDF rendering was done by PrinceXML.

For Marie,

the guardian of my solitude

Contents

	Acknowledgments	ix
	Abbreviations	xi
1.	God Moves On	*1*
2.	God of the Defeated and Scattered, Part I	*31*
3.	God of the Defeated and Scattered, Part II	*67*
4.	God of the Defeated and Scattered, Part III	*95*
5.	God of Revolt	*125*
6.	God of Dreams and Visions	*161*
7.	God of the Future	*193*
8.	Where Do We Go from Here?	*225*
	Bibliography	*239*
	Index of Subjects	*255*
	Index of Authors	*265*
	Index of Ancient Texts	*269*

Acknowledgments

There are always many people to thank at the end of such a project. I completed much of the manuscript during an academic leave from Belmont University, for which I am grateful. I spent much of that time working in the Vanderbilt University Divinity library, and I appreciate all of the resources offered to me there. An academic leave places a burden on colleagues, beyond their usual acts of support and encouragement, so I thank the faculty of the College of Theology and Christian Ministry at Belmont University. The staff of Fortress Press, particularly Neil Elliott and Marissa Wold Uhrina, have been enormously helpful as always. To these, and others unnamed, thank you.

Abbreviations

Bar.   Baruch
En.   Enoch
Esd.   Esdras
Jth.   Judith
Jub.   Jubilees
Macc. Maccabees
Sir.   Sirach
Ws.   Wisdom (of Solomon)

1

God Moves On

When the narrative plot of the Tanak and the Protestant Old Testament comes to a close, the divine being readers have followed through the long story that began at the creation of the world has become a complex, multifaceted character. The setting of the end of the story is the ancient Near East, which was politically controlled and culturally influenced by the Persian and Greek empires. The Jewish people, whose legendary origins had begun with a single family, and who eventually became a small nation, were scattered about these empires that overran them, living in a wide variety of social and cultural situations.[1] Most of the literature produced in these disparate settings never gained the full canonical status of the twenty-four scrolls of the Tanak, but the Jewish people of this period wrote a great deal of material, much of which is unfamiliar to contemporary readers of the Bible. This study will examine the literature of the last

1. The broad picture of Jewish society during this period that I will assume is similar to the one George Nickelsburg sketches. See George W. E. Nickelsburg, *Jewish Literature between the Bible and the Mishnah*, 2nd ed. (Minneapolis: Fortress Press, 2005), 14, 41–43. Matters of greater detail and precision will be raised below when necessary.

three centuries before the Common Era to discover what kind of divine characterization it produces when brought together.

In *Portraits of a Mature God: Choices in Old Testament Theology*, I traced the narrative character development of Israel's deity, from the beginning of the story in Genesis to the ends of the story in restored/Persian Judah and diaspora Judaism. The plot line of Israel and its God becomes more obscure after that point for a number of reasons, but perhaps it is still traceable. The primary conclusion of my previous book was that by the end of the story in the Tanak or Protestant Old Testament, the divine character has become significantly more complex and more hidden. Israel's God is no longer the "mighty actor" that so much traditional Old Testament theology loved, but a more obscure character who works within human beings, both ordinary and powerful, to make a variety of paths available to God's people as they make their ways in a complex world. But where does the divine character go from there?

For a long time, Christian understandings of the Bible, especially in Protestant contexts, have included the idea of an "intertestamental period." This notion presumed that the production of biblical literature stopped sometime in the late Persian period, and only resumed with the writing of the Christian New Testament. There are several problems with such an understanding, a few of which can be identified here at an early point of this study, while others will become apparent as it progresses. First and foremost, a proper placement of the production of Daniel in the early to mid-second century BCE cuts the presumed "silent time" about in half in a single stroke. Second, evidence from the Dead Sea Scrolls indicates the book of Psalms continued to be in a state of flux, perhaps even into the Common Era, which fills most of the rest of the "intertestamental" time with activity still related to the production of the Bible.[2] Third, recent studies on the formation of the Hebrew canon indicate a continuing sense of fluidity until sometime after the destruction of Jerusalem.³ Finally, the idea that a clear boundary exists between the production of biblical books and their transmission and reception is disappearing as we learn more about the history of these texts and the scribal activity that produced them.⁴ Most importantly for this study, all of the evidence points to the conclusion that for people living during and before the first century CE, our own easy lines of division between canonical literature and noncanonical literature would not have been operative. All of these factors point toward a greater sense of continuity between the books whose literary origins lie in the last three centuries before the Common Era and those already completed or significantly developed by this time. It is time to leave behind the assumption that the literary material produced during this time period was fundamentally different in terms of authority and use than the literature that eventually made it into the Jewish and Protestant canons. Whatever the reasons for inclusion and exclusion of particular works in the various canons, the lines they drew were always externally imposed from a later time and were somewhat artificial.⁵

---

2. For a fuller discussion of the shape and significance of the Dead Sea Psalms Scroll (11QPsa), see William L. Holladay, *The Psalms through Three Thousand Years: Prayerbook of a Cloud of Witnesses* (Minneapolis: Fortress Press, 1993), 100–102. See also the discussion of this scroll and its impact on the understanding of canonization in James A. Sanders, "What's Up Now? Renewal of an Important Investigation," in *Jewish and Christian Scriptures: The Function of 'Canonical' and 'Non-Canonical' Religious Texts*, ed. James H. Charlesworth and Lee M. McDonald (London: T&T Clark, 2010), 1–7.
3. See, for example, Konrad Schmid, "The Canon and the Cult: The Emergence of Book Religion in Ancient Israel and the Gradual Sublimation of the Temple Cult," *Journal of Biblical Literature* 131 (2012): 289–305.
4. For a clear explanation of the problematic assumptions with which biblical scholarship has operated, see Brennan W. Breed, *A Theory of Biblical Reception History* (Bloomington, IN: Indiana University Press, 2014), 1–4.
5. For a more thorough accounting of how scholarship came to erase this supposed gap, see James C. VanderKam, "Mapping Second Temple Judaism," in *The Early Enoch Literature*, ed. Gabriele Boccaccini and John J. Collins (Leiden: Brill, 2007), 1–20.

The discussion above argues for a greater sense of continuity between the literature of the Tanak and the works that ended up outside of it, in terms of the historical setting in which their final forms were produced and their authority evaluated. Emerging evidence about the context of Second Temple Judaism in the last two or three centuries before the Common Era, however, is beginning to indicate that these "noncanonical" works may have participated in major theological, political, and ideological conflicts of that period, and may represent the side(s) that lost. This means that even when we retrieve them and begin to give them greater attention, the possibility that we are only reading them through the lens of the traditions that became canonical is a grave danger to our understanding. Michael Stone identifies the "vicious circle" in which dominant or orthodox forms of Judaism and Christianity have formed the cultural context in which the nondominant or nonorthodox literature is now perceived. This is a conundrum from which we may not be able to escape fully, but constant awareness and questioning of it is essential.[6] Some of the most important examples of this literature were preserved only in Jewish and Christian communities like the collectors of the Dead Sea Scrolls and the Ethiopian and Armenian churches. They seem to have become the literature of the periphery, but they may not always have been so.

This book will be an attempt to join two streams of scholarship together. One is the growing interest in and increased understanding of the literature of Judaism that lies just outside the boundaries of the Tanak and, therefore, the Protestant Old Testament. The other is the long line of development that is the field of Old Testament theology, particularly as it leads up to the kind of approach I have developed that examines the narrative development of the divine character.[7]

---

6. Michael E. Stone, *Ancient Judaism: New Visions and Views* (Grand Rapids, MI: Eerdmans, 2011), 4–12.

The central question the book will seek to answer is whether it is possible to trace a continued development of this divine character beyond the boundaries of the Tanak/Protestant Old Testament and, if so, what that character looks like. The answer will follow multiple paths because Judaism developed in diverging contexts, and understandings of God evolved to address different questions in each of them.

Defining the Literature

The past few decades have witnessed growing interest in, and attention to, the literature that sits on the edges of the various canonical traditions within Judaism and Christianity. The primary impetus among scholars has been to examine the literature in order to reconstruct a history of Judaism during the late Persian, Greek, and early Roman periods. This effort has produced a large quantity of work, some of which will intersect with and be helpful to this study, but I wish to ask a quite different question, one that has received far less attention: When taken collectively, what kind of divine character does the Jewish literature of the last two to three centuries before the Common Era portray? This subject receives brief treatment from a different angle in Jacob Neusner's book, *Judaism when Christianity Began*. Neusner's primary texts in this exploration are those among rabbinic literature that, in written form, lie outside the time frame of this study, though it is natural to assume they reflect earlier traditions. In his discussion of "The Characterization of God," Neusner contends that, "however we know God, in whatever form or aspect, it is always one and the same God." Further, in his discussion of talmudic texts he states, "That God may show diverse

---

7. See my description of the development of this approach in light of those which came before it in *Portraits of a Mature God: Choices in Old Testament Theology* (Minneapolis: Fortress Press, 2013), 1–22.

faces to various people is now established. The reason for God's variety is made explicit. People differ, and God, in the image of whom all mortals are made, must therefore sustain diverse images."[8] The need for this discussion among the ancient rabbis, and in Neusner's contemporary interpretation of them, was created by the changing characterizations of the divine being that stretch the claims of monotheism near to their breaking point. If Neusner is correct that the characterization of God varies in order to accommodate human variation, then the ways the human race—particularly those people within the traditions of Judaism that produced the texts examined in this study—changes collectively through time ought to bring about a changing characterization of God that can be traced along the trajectory of the stories of those people. What makes this a great challenge for this collection of literature is that it is not as cohesive as the Tanak. The cohesive nature of the Tanak comes more from its reception than its production, however, so the challenges of tracing this divine-character development through a collective narrative is not wholly different, but the path will be more tenuous here. Closer to the point is some of the theological discussion in Shaye Cohen's *From the Maccabees to the Mishnah*. While correctly insisting that the Judaism of this period was defined more by practice than by beliefs, Cohen identifies central theological themes, such as the scope of divine kingship and systems of reward and punishment that reflect directly on divine behavior. Cohen describes Jewish thinking on these subjects as "a series of conflicting truths" that "appear to be mutually exclusive, but to the Jews of antiquity, they were simultaneously true."[9] Still, Cohen's chronological boundaries begin and end somewhat later than my own.

8. Jacob Neusner, *Judaism when Christianity Began: A Survey of Belief and Practice* (Louisville, KY: Westminster John Knox, 2002), 31–32.
9. Shaye J. D. Cohen, *From the Maccabees to the Mishnah*, 3rd ed. (Louisville, KY: Westminster John Knox, 2014), 102.

It is easy enough to decide where to begin a study like this. The wide variety of Christian canonical traditions has insured the survival of a significant collection of literature from this period, a collection most often known as the Apocrypha. That collection lies at the center of this literature but it is considerably more difficult to decide how to draw the boundaries. Two highly influential works of scholarship offer significant help in making the decisions. First, in the predigital age, the invaluable two-volume work edited by James Charlesworth, *The Old Testament Pseudepigrapha*, made available in one place a large collection of texts in contemporary English translation. This was, of course, an updating of the classic work of R. H. Charles during the early years of the twentieth century. Charles's masterpiece of 1913 had carried the title *The Apocrypha and Pseudepigrapha of the Old Testament*. The elimination of the first portion of that title by Charlesworth is ample testimony that the Apocrypha had gained such a level of both availability and status that it no longer required such publication. The inclusion of the Apocrypha in the translation project called the Revised Standard Version in the 1950's was one of the most important forces behind this change.[10] It was also significant that commentaries on the books of the Apocrypha began to appear in series like the Anchor Bible Commentary.[11] The second major development was the work of George Nickelsburg, *Jewish Literature between the Bible and the Mishnah*, first published in 1981 then revised for a second edition in 2005, which took the study of this literature a large and important step further. Rather than offering independent translations of the works with introductory articles by a large collection of specialists, as the Charlesworth volumes do,

---

10. The writings of the Apocrypha were translated as part of the King James project, but were rarely included in printed versions of the King James Bible.
11. More recently the Hermeneia commentary series has begun to produce volumes related to this literature, the most significant of which so far is Nickelsburg's two-volume work on 1 Enoch.

Nickelsburg's work draws texts together into categories with commentary by a single author, providing a move toward a more synthetic treatment.

Both Charlesworth and Nickelsburg go beyond the chronological boundary I would like to draw at the turn of the eras, though. Determining precise dates for this literature is notoriously difficult, and any text that is placed beyond the middle of the first century CE faces the prospect of having been produced or heavily edited by Christian writers, or being shaped significantly by a response to Christianity.[12] Therefore, I will use the turn of the eras as an approximate terminus. The use of the Apocrypha as a beginning point creates an important overlap with the Tanak, because the Greek versions of Esther and Daniel become important anchors near the beginning of this study, and 1 Esdras reiterates the ongoing story of the restoration of Judah, as depicted in parts of Ezra-Nehemiah. The Maccabean literature helps to provide a continuing plotline and leads out of the Apocrypha. At this point, it may be most helpful to produce a list of the texts that will play a part in the primary discussion:

---

12. The fascinating text known as the *Ascension of Isaiah* is a great example of this kind of mixed origin.

Table 1-1

The Literature Treated in This Book

Chapter 2

Jubilees	1 Enoch 1–36[13]	1 Esdras[14]		

Chapter 3

Judith	Tobit	Daniel 1-6, 13-14 (Greek)	Esther (Greek)	3 Maccabees

Chapter 4

Sirach	Baruch	Wisdom of Solomon

Chapter 5

1 Maccabees	2 Maccabees

Chapter 6

1 Enoch 72–108	Daniel 7–14 (Greek)	Jubilees 1 and 23

Chapter 7

1 Enoch 37–71	Damascus Document	Community Rule	War Scroll	Psalms of Solomon	Temple Scroll

---

13. Because it has a single name, and because there are other books with related names like 1 Enoch and 1 Enoch, 1 Enoch is often construed as a single book, but it is really more of a collection of books. Some scholars have even proposed the idea that it was an alternative to the Mosaic Torah. Therefore, different part of the 1 Enoch collection will be treated at different places in this book, where they best fit. See Gabriele Boccaccini, "Introduction: From the Enoch Literature to Enochic Judaism," in *Enoch and Qumran Origins: New Light on a Forgotten Connection*, ed. Gabriele Boccaccini (Grand Rapids, MI: Eerdmans, 2005), 1–16.
14. Most of this book is drawn from the end of Chronicles and Ezra-Nehemiah, but there are additions, particularly 1 Esdras 3–4, which, like the additions to Esther and Daniel, fit within the scope of this work. There is a growing body of scholarship on 1 Esdras, some of which raises legitimate questions about the assumed priority of the biblical Ezra-Nehemiah in relation to it. See the collection of essays in Lisbeth S. Fried, ed., *Was 1 Esdras First? An Investigation into the Priority and Nature of 1 Esdras* (Atlanta: Society of Biblical Literature, 2011).

Some readers will notice immediately the prominent pieces of literature that are omitted from the list, a few of which require some explanation. In terms of both date and genre, Philo and Josephus both fall outside the scope of this literary collection. Both of these writers will play a role in the discussion, however, because of the assistance they provide in understanding the forces that shaped and preserved the writings. The literary traditions that took on the names of Enoch, Baruch, and Ezra (Esdras) continued beyond the selections included in this list, but there is growing evidence that this extended literature was at least heavily influenced by persons and events in the Christian era. In addition to the appearance of the Christian sect within Judaism, the destruction of Jerusalem in 70 CE is also an event of massive influence that needs to be kept outside the boundaries of this discussion.[15] It is tempting to include the material known as the Testaments of the Twelve Patriarchs because it presents a large and fascinating body of literature, but it has become apparent in recent years that even if these texts had Jewish origins they have been both preserved and heavily shaped by later Christian traditions.[16] The period bounded approximately by 300 BCE and 200 CE was enormously productive.[17] I have chosen about the first half of this period and the literature is still too vast to include all of it. Some writings must be excluded because the extant manuscripts are too fragmentary, which points to the near certainty that some have been lost entirely.[18]

15. Nickelsburg, *Jewish Literature*, 270–85.
16. Ibid., 301–3.
17. For more detail on the productivity of this period and the collective nature of its literature, see Timothy Michael Law, *When God Spoke Greek: The Septuagint and the Making of the Christian Bible* (Oxford: Oxford University Press, 2013), 58–61; and James L. Kugel, *The Bible as It Was* (Cambridge, MA: Belknap Press, 1997), 36–42.
18. At the time of this writing, texts like 4QInstruction, the Testament of Levi, and the Testament of Moses are receiving increased scholarly attention, and our understanding of them may eventually reach a level of confidence that might allow a more thorough inclusion of them within this discussion.

The methodology of this study is necessarily multifaceted because of the nature of the literature it uses. The selections in the list above were chosen because they were most likely produced before the beginning of the Common Era. The earliest manuscripts of most of them come from a considerably later period, however, so there is no guarantee that they were not edited to some degree at a later point. Nevertheless, this study will seek to read these texts in their extant forms and will not depend on specific attempts to trace their compositional histories back to hypothetical earlier versions, except where evidence of such development helps elucidate the meaning of difficult texts. More significantly, because this study will seek to follow the divine character through a plot presented by these collected works, they will be treated in the order of the points in that plot to which they most clearly attach, and not their relative dates of composition. Because Jubilees is, in large part, a retelling of the book of Genesis and the first part of Exodus, it will be necessary to go back to the beginning of the story of Israel and its God. Smaller portions of Jubilees, such as chapter 23, which deal with future events, will need to be addressed at points further along in the plot. First Esdras contains within it the last two chapters of 2 Chronicles and parts of Ezra-Nehemiah, so it is another place of significant overlap between the Tanak and the literature examined in this study. The book called 1 Enoch looks back at traditions in Genesis but also moves into the future and an alternative plane of existence. The composite nature of 1 Enoch will require treating major sections in different chapters of this book. Back on earth, this literature continues the story of Israel in the traditional land of Judah but also in many locations of the diaspora. It is, therefore, a splintered plot we will have to follow. It is not the contention of this study that the collective authors of this literature deliberately produced a long plot in which God is a character. The original authors of the literature in the Tanak did not deliberately work together to do this either, though there are longer complexes woven together deliberately by editors to produce a more easily discernible macroplot. The story of Israel's God in the apocryphal and pseudepigraphical literature is the result of putting together a disparate collection of literature, some elements of which may even seem to be in conflict with each other. This is not entirely unlike the collection of literature now found in the Tanak, but the story of Israel is one of increasing fragmentation, including the formation of sectarian movements, so conflict and tension within the literature is to be expected. Moreover, the contest to describe the divine character may have been one of the major forces driving the development of sectarian Judaism in the period.

Another kind of literature from the era will require occasional attention, though it is not included in the list above. It was during the time period under consideration in this study that the Hebrew Scriptures were being translated into the Greek language. The translation process was conducted by many people over a long period of time, and the standards of translation varied significantly in different books of the Hebrew Scriptures. So, while the production of the Greek versions of the Hebrew Scriptures may have, at times, approached an act of authorship, it is difficult to characterize it consistently. There are cases when this literary work may shed additional light on the way Israel's God is portrayed in books that were initially composed during the period in which the Hebrew Bible was being translated, and these will appear from time to time in this study. It is a common habit, even within biblical scholarship, to refer to these Greek translations as the "Septuagint," which is problematic on two counts. First, this word is based on a legendary story of just the Torah being magically translated into Greek by seventy-two scholars under the sponsorship of Ptolemy II in Alexandria. Second, and more important, this term refers more precisely to a set of fourth- and fifth-century-CE manuscripts of the Christian Bible in Greek. The Greek translations initially produced by Jews, only preserved in fragments of copies, are more precisely called the "Old Greek" version.[19] Of lesser importance here are the works known as *targumim*, which are Aramaic versions of the books of the Hebrew Scriptures, and many were likely completed long after the middle of the first century CE. These works are often quite expansive to the point of being a running commentary on the Hebrew Scriptures. Potentially, the *targumim* offer significant insight into how the divine character was understood in the era during which they were produced, but the extant written forms cannot be reliably dated before the Christian era.[20] Therefore, points of comparison with the literature examined here must be made sparingly and cautiously.

Sketching the Cultural Matrix

My intent in this work is to examine literature and to do it in such a way that is not dependent upon a detailed and precise reconstruction of its historical background and development. Nevertheless, it is careless to discuss a collection of literature without a broad framework of understanding about the settings from which it arose and about which it speaks. There are some things about the last three centuries BCE that we can know with relative certainty. In addition to this, one must operate with some assumptions about the period, and these should be stated clearly. Perhaps the most helpful

---

19. See pertinent discussions of these issues in Sidney Jellicoe, *The Septuagint and Modern Study* (Oxford: Oxford University Press, 1968), 29–58; Karen H. Jobes and Moisés Silva, *Invitation to the Septuagint* (Grand Rapids, MI: Baker Academic, 2005), 30–33; and Emmanuel Tov, *Textual Criticism of the Hebrew Bible* (Minneapolis: Fortress Press, 1992), 134–48.
20. For a useful description of the *targumim*, where they came from, and how they operate, see Paul V. M. Flesher and Bruce Chilton, *The Targums: A Critical Introduction* (Waco, TX: Baylor University Press, 2011), 3–37.

statement with which to begin comes from one of the preeminent historians of the period, Lester Grabbe: "The new mixture of Greek, Persian, and local cultures created the 'Hellenistic world'—a world that was neither Hellenic (classical Greek) nor Oriental but its own particular synthesis."[21] This statement is a helpful antidote to the problematic tendency to throw the word "Hellenistic" around as if it defined an area of the world and a period in history in relatively simple and straightforward terms. The great advantage is that the term, as defined by Grabbe, provides a distinct label for the cultural experience that gave rise to the literature engaged by this study. This survey will need to begin two centuries earlier in order to understand the context of the Hellenistic world in which our literature was written.

Israel's experience with the Persian Empire began just after the middle of the sixth century BCE when the Persians conquered Babylon. The biblical perspective of this event is that it was a moment of liberation reminiscent of the exodus (Isa. 45:1, Ezra 1:2–4), though this may have been an exaggeration for theological effect. Jon Berquist identifies the central problem in studying the Persian province of Yehud as determining whether the forces that shaped the character of this entity were external, Persian imperial policies, or internal, the revived traditions of the nation of Judah. After reviewing the history of the arguments about this question Berquist concludes that the most powerful forces were the external ones, while internal forces were able to play some role because of the distance of Yehud from the center of the Persian Empire and a certain degree of autonomy granted by the latter.[22] While some have proposed that Persian policies were based on greater tolerance or religious

---

21. Lester L. Grabbe, *A History of Jews and Judaism in the Second Temple Period*, vol. 2, *The Early Hellenistic Period (335–175 BCE)* (New York: T&T Clark, 2008), 331.
22. John L. Berquist, *Judaism in Persia's Shadow: A Social and Historical Approach* (Minneapolis: Fortress Press, 1995), 6–10.

sympathies, it seems much more likely that these emperors simply considered allowing groups to live in their homeland and maintain their religious traditions to be a more efficient and profitable way to run an empire.[23] Nevertheless, the practice allowed for some Jews who had lived in captivity in Babylon to return to their homeland, if they chose, and to rebuild Jerusalem and its temple.[24]

It is not possible to determine how many citizens of Judah were actually deported to Babylon during the late seventh and early sixth centuries. The biblical documents that tell the story are written from the perspective of the group that was taken captive and returned, so those who never left Judah, or who stayed in Babylon permanently, are virtually ignored. Hans Barstad argues that the Babylonian destruction of Judah and the deportation of its citizens were far less extensive than many have assumed simply from reading the biblical texts.[25] This may well be the case, but the story of exile and return became the dominant, formative theological motif of Persian Yehud in the biblical tradition, and the canonical status of Ezra-Nehemiah is both a sign of the success of this biblical tradition and a driving force behind its continuing significance.[26] Neither of these claims addresses the reality of Jewish communities that remained, persisted, and even spread in the remains of Babylonian territory and the Persian homeland itself, but ample evidence exists of these communities. All of these diverse groups and others, such as those

---

23. Ibid., 24–29.
24. A Persian record of this policy is recorded in the inscription on the object known as the Cyrus Cylinder, which agrees in basic terms with the so-called Decree of Cyrus in Ezra 1:2–4 and 6:3–5. The 2013 tour of the Cyrus Cylinder in the United States has brought a great deal of attention to this object and the emperor for which it is named. It is sometimes being billed in the media as something like "the world's first declaration of human rights," which may be an overstatement of Cyrus's benevolence.
25. Hans Barstad, *The Myth of the Empty Land: A Study in the History and Archaeology of Judah in the "Exilic" Period* (Oslo: Scandinavian University Press, 1996).
26. For an extensive discussion of this development, see Daniel Smith-Christopher, *A Biblical Theology of Exile* (Minneapolis: Fortress Press, 2002), 30–48.

who fled to Egypt before the Babylonian invasion, leading to flourishing Jewish communities in places like Alexandria and Elephantine, compelled Jill Middlemas to coin the useful phrase, "The Templeless Age," as a way of describing the common experience of all Israelites for much of the sixth century.[27] Their religion had lost its geographical and architectural center, and they began to fill the void with written texts.

The situation in Judah during the late sixth century and much of the fifth century was complex, and sources of information are fragmentary, but the central political feature was the rise to power of the priesthood.[28] Because the hopes for a restored monarchy, beginning with the Davidic descendant, Zerubbabel, seem to have dissolved, and because the Persians were at least tolerant, perhaps even supportive, of the development of local religious institutions within the lands they controlled, there was significant space within which the priesthood could develop.[29] There is considerable dispute about the identity of the priesthood during this period, and the primary ancient source of information about them is Josephus, who frequently gives their names and reports events in which they were involved in book 11 of the *Antiquities of the Jews*. Modern historians debate the veracity of Josephus's reports and have reconstructed the history of the priesthood in a variety of ways. One of the more detailed attempts at reconstruction is that of Gabriele Boccaccini, who argues for the rise to power of a distinctly "Zadokite" priesthood that traced its familial roots to the Zadok who was appointed high priest by David in 2 Sam 8:17. This group held not only religious

---

27. Jill Middlemas, *The Templeless Age: An Introduction to the History, Literature, and Theology of the "Exile"* (Louisville: Westminster, 2007), 10–27.
28. See the discussion in Cohen, *From the Maccabees to the Mishnah*, 103–7.
29. The reformation of the Davidic monarchy is a point of disagreement within the Tanak itself, with books like Micah, Haggai, and Zechariah in favor of it, while Isaiah, Ezekiel, and Psalms were opposed, and Ezra-Nehemiah was apparently ambivalent.

authority in the Persian province of Judah, but also significant political power.³⁰ They were responsible for the production of the Bible, including Chronicles, Ezra-Nehemiah, and the Priestly source of the Pentateuch that helped to present the group's views and establish its authority.³¹ According to Boccaccini the "Zadokite worldview" was pervasive and dominant during the Persian period of Israel's history, and many of the new ideas that would arise in the Hellenistic period can best be understood in terms of their opposition to the Zadokite views.³²

Grabbe takes a more cautious view of the period and is unwilling to conclude that the "sons of Zadok" comprised a distinct group of priests in Judah during the Persian period or that the priesthood held significant political power in addition to its religious authority.³³ A further result of Grabbe's more cautious conclusions is the rejection of Boccaccini's description of a specific "Zadokite Judaism." In Grabbe's words, "The priesthood was a profession, not a sect."³⁴ Others have argued effectively that the reconstruction of communities in conflict that lie behind literary collections that are in tension with each other is simply too hypothetical an enterprise.³⁵ The rebuilt temple became an important locus for religious life in the Persian period, and the priesthood had significant power and authority, but exactly how these were apportioned among rival groups at various times cannot be determined with useful certainty,

---

30. Gabriele Boccaccini, *Roots of Rabbinic Judaism: An Intellectual History, from Ezekiel to Daniel* (Grand Rapids, MI: Eerdmans, 2002), 43–45.
31. Ibid., 49–50.
32. Ibid., 73–89. Boccaccini is particularly interested in using a dominant Zadokite Judaism as the backdrop for the development of the opposition movement he calls "Enochic Judaism," which is expressed in the book of Jubilees and 1 Enoch (89–103).
33. Lester L. Grabbe, *A History of Jews and Judaism in the Second Temple Period*, vol. 1, *Yehud: A History of the Persian Province of Judah* (New York: T&T Clark, 2004), 224–235.
34. Grabbe, *A History of Jews and Judaism in the Second Temple Period*, 2:239.
35. See, for example, Helge S. Kvanvig, "Jubilees—Read as a Narrative," in *Enoch and Qumran Origins: New Light on a Forgotten Connection*, ed. Gabriele Boccaccini (Grand Rapids, MI: Eerdmans, 2005), 81–82.

so it is best to interpret texts against a general background of social and religious conflict. An emphasis on religious power and authority points toward what was missing in this era of Israel's story—political autonomy, and the situation continued into the Hellenistic period as the political and military hegemony of the Greek empire replaced that of the Persians. The economics of the period typically remain hidden behind more overt religious and political concerns, but emphasis on divine intrusion into the world, divine judgment of dominating empires, and rewards in an afterlife makes sense as responses to a system of oppression in which taxation and other economic burdens must have also played a role.[36]

An important place where the cultural matrix described above intersects the body of literature the period produced is the notion of authorship, which says something about how ancient people viewed their literature and also shapes the way we perceive it today. The arguments in this study will be crafted in ways that are not dependent upon who actually wrote the texts it examines, but a general sense of authorship is important in at least two respects. First, knowing something about the kind of person who wrote a text can help readers understand it better, perhaps even more than putting a precise name or identity on that person. Second, understanding something about how the world in which these texts were produced viewed authorship may also reveal something of the meaning and significance of the literature. The latter aspect has been the subject of an extensive study by Jed Wyrick called *The Ascension of Authorship*. Wyrick's arguments are too broad and extensive for a full presentation here, but a few of his conclusions have significant bearing on this study. There was a time in Israel's history when

---

36. For more on how these economic and social issues express themselves in the wisdom and apocalyptic literatures of the Hellenistic period, see Samuel L. Adams, *Social and Economic Life in Second Temple Judea* (Louisville, KY: Westminster John Knox, 2014), 196–205.

literary compositions did not need to be attached to an author, but this came to an end in the late Second Temple period when the practice of attributing texts became significant. Wyrick demonstrates the processes by which previously anonymous texts were attributed to authors, a process motivated by the formation of authoritative collections. Those developing such collections needed a criterion to make decisions, and connection to an authoritative figure became the primary one.[37]

The subject of authorship in relation to this literature leads to the problem of deliberate pseudonymity. The works of the Tanak are largely anonymous, providing no information about who is doing the writing. A common practice of the last three centuries BCE, however, was for writers to assume the persona of famous figures of the past. Anathea Portier-Young emphasizes important differences between anonymity and pseudonymity in certain political situations. While the purpose of anonymous authorship in dangerous contexts appears to be the safety and protection of the writer, pseudonymous authorship does a number of other things in addition.[38] Wyrick and others note that pseudonymous authorship can be a way of lending authority to a literary work, but Portier-Young extends the idea further. Attributing a document to an ancient figure like Daniel or Enoch also enables them to participate in a common discourse. More significantly, such a discourse "testifies to an alternative source of power and alternative vision of reality" over against the power and

---

37. Jed Wyrick, *The Ascension of Authorship: Attribution and Canon Formation in Jewish, Hellenistic, and Christian Traditions* (Cambridge, MA: Harvard University Press, 2004), 382–84. This time period is imprecise, but it falls within the scope of the last two centuries before the Common Era, the period with which this study is concerned.
38. Anathea E. Portier-Young, *Apocalypse against Empire: Theologies of Resistance in Early Judaism* (Grand Rapids, MI: Eerdmans, 2011), 40–41. The understanding of anonymity with which Portier-Young interacts is primarily that of James C. Scott in *Domination and the Arts of Resistance: Hidden Transcripts* (New Haven: Yale University Press, 1990). Though Scott's objects of study are dominated cultures of more recent eras, his discussion of "Voice under Domination: The Arts of Political Disguise" (136–82) seems appropriate to a broad range of such contexts.

vision of the dominating empire.[39] Finally, Portier-Young claims these pseudonymous works of resistance correspond to "the hidden power and providence of God, relocating ultimate power from earth to heaven, and asserting the conditional, finite, and partial nature of temporal rule."[40] Such a shift in location of the divine presence and work is an idea that will be tested against the presentation of a narrative development of the divine character throughout this book.

In the introduction to his monumental work, Charlesworth identifies "four significant theological concerns" that characterize the collection he labels *The Old Testament Pseudepigrapha*: the origin of sin and evil, divine transcendence, the coming of a messiah, and resurrection.[41] This set of issues overlaps significantly with the primary theological issues Cohen identifies with the Judaism of the last two centuries before and first two centuries after the turn of the eras.[42] All of these emphases point toward a sense of distance between God and the world. These themes, and some others closely related to them, have become the subjects of some of the most recent developments moving scholarship on this literature forward, and they will arise regularly throughout this study. One of the underlying assumptions about the behavior of God revealed by the very nature of much of the literature of this period is that God resided in heaven, receiving legendary human emissaries like Enoch, Baruch, Daniel, and Ezra, and sending them back to God's people with complex coded messages. Granted, one may argue that this elaborate mode of pseudepigraphy was entirely a literary construct, and that ancient readers did not believe the process was "really happening," but that is not the issue which this study seeks to illuminate. Rather, it intends

---

39. Portier-Young, *Apocalypse against Empire*, 42–43.
40. Ibid., 44.
41. James H. Charlesworth, "Introduction for the General Reader," in *The Old Testament Pseudepigrapha*, ed. James H. Charlesworth (Garden City, NY: Doubleday, 1983), 1:xxix–xxxii.
42. Cohen, *From the Maccabees to the Mishnah*, 78–100.

to ask: What sort of divine character does the literature produced in this era portray? The need for this movement of heavenly messengers was the result of an overriding emphasis on divine transcendence. This means the trend of divine withdrawal or movement toward hiddenness, which I trace in *Portraits of a Mature God*, continues in some cases and transforms further in others.

Establishing a Narrative Theological Approach

The field of Old Testament theology has conducted its work using a wide variety of approaches over the last couple of centuries. I have discussed and evaluated these elsewhere, so a full discussion is not necessary here, but a broad outline of the development may be helpful.[43] Until the last quarter of the twentieth century, Old Testament theology was dominated by approaches closely tied to reconstructions of the history of Israelite religion and its institutions.[44] The immense size and complexity of this work, based upon increasingly hypothetical evidence, caused the field to fall in upon itself, a phenomenon that led Leo Perdue to coin the phrase "the collapse of history."[45] In the midst of the collapse a rigorous new

---

43. See Mark McEntire, "The God at the End of the Story: Are Biblical Theology and Narrative Character Development Compatible," *Horizons in Biblical Theology* 33 (2011): 171–89; McEntire, *Portraits of a Mature God*, 175–210.
44. Terminology is challenging in this area. The interpretive enterprise that I am describing has taken place primarily among scholars associated with the Christian tradition, so the "Old Testament" label can be appropriate. Jon D. Levenson wrote a famous essay in the early 1990s about the lack of participation in this discussion by Jewish scholars. See Levenson, "Why Jews Are Not Interested in Biblical Theology," in *The Hebrew Bible, the Old Testament, and Historical Criticism* (Louisville, KY: Westminster John Knox, 1993), 33–61. This had much to do with the historicist framework that dominated the subdiscipline, a factor that has changed significantly. In recent years Jewish scholars have both joined in the conversation and sought to emphasize past work that indicates a greater involvement than the title of Levenson's essay might indicate. See, for example, Benjamin D. Sommer, "Dialogical Biblical Theology: A Jewish Approach to Reading Scripture Theologically," in *Biblical Theology: Introducing the Conversation*, ed. Leo G. Perdue et al. (Nashville: Abingdon, 2009), 1–54; and Marvin A. Sweeney, *Reading the Hebrew Bible after the Shoah: Engaging Holocaust Theology* (Minneapolis: Fortress Press, 2008), 1–22. This welcome change has made the challenge of terminology even more complex.

approach to Old Testament theology was proposed and developed by Walter Brueggemann, a method I have described as "dialogical." The great strength of Brueggemann's work is its recognition that the task of Old Testament theology is to describe the actions of God presented in the text of the Old Testament that lead to a sense of God's identity and character. His approach also leads to the realization that the God of Israel is a complex character whose ways of being are often in significant tension with each other. The tension is the result of competing religious traditions in ancient Israel, but the goal of an Old Testament theology is not to reconstruct the situation that produced the text. Instead, in the process of articulating the tension, Old Testament theology becomes, like much of the Old Testament itself, a dialogue or debate about the character of God. Brueggemann eventually develops a courtroom context in which to hear "testimony" and "counter-testimony" about the actions of this character, a process with enormous heuristic value, but which handicaps some texts that are not well equipped to participate in the format.[46]

My approach adopts many of the same assumptions and observations about the Old Testament as Brueggemann's (particularly the recognition that it does not present a clear, consistent, coherent portrait of Israel's deity), but rejects the courtroom-debate, or dialogical, model in favor of examining the development of God as a narrative character through the plot of the Old Testament from beginning to end. This approach has led to the conclusion that much greater emphasis needs to be placed on the end of that narrative trajectory and the way the divine character is portrayed in books like Ezra-Nehemiah, Daniel, and Esther, which

---

45. Leo G. Perdue, *The Collapse of History: Reconstructing Old Testament Theology* (Minneapolis: Fortress Press, 1994), 3–7.
46. Walter Brueggemann, *Theology of the Old Testament: Testimony, Dispute, Advocacy* (Minneapolis: Fortress Press, 1996), 117–44.

have seldom received significant attention in Old Testament theology.[47] An additional goal of *Portraits of a Mature God* was to bring an emerging strand of literary study focused on the development of the divine character in the Bible into the discussion of Old Testament theology. The notion of a hidden deity has been present in theological discussions, but has typically been cast as part of the tension between immanence and transcendence.[48] These categories, borrowed from systematic theology and the history of religion, may have worked well in dialogical approaches to Old Testament theology, but can easily miss the linear movement of a character within an ongoing plot. While there may be fluctuation in the Old Testament literature between divine transcendence and divine immanence, there is an unmistakable, larger movement toward hiddenness, which fits in the category of transcendence more easily.

Earlier sections of this chapter traced some of the development of scholarship on the Jewish literature of the Hellenistic period over the past century, but did not highlight some of the most recent advances that help to make a study like this one possible. Beyond a survey of the literature and reconstructions of the historical matrix from which it emerged, some important work has been done over the past two decades to begin to develop a theology of this literature. One important work of this type is John Collins's *Jewish Wisdom in the Hellenistic Age*. The wisdom literature of the Tanak has been notoriously difficult for Old Testament theology to fit into its various methodological schemes, and this will continue to be a methodological challenge for the present study. In *Portraits of a Mature God*, I sought to attach portions of the wisdom literature to

---

47. McEntire, *Portraits of a Mature God*, 175–210.
48. See the discussion in Richard Elliott Friedman, *The Disappearance of God: A Divine Mystery* (New York: Little, Brown, and Co., 1995), 78–80.

particular places along the narrative trajectory presented within the Tanak. This was easy to do with the pieces of the literature like Proverbs 8 and Job 38–39 that deal with the creation of the world.[49] It is more challenging to do this with elements like the large collections of proverbial sayings in Proverbs 10–29. I attempted to resolve this problem by observing that the book of Proverbs begins in the court of Solomon, and ends in a foreign court, that of King Lemuel. Thus the whole of the book of Proverbs moves into the diaspora, along with much of the Judaism of the Persian period.[50] Daniel Smith-Christopher draws important connections between Proverbs and Daniel, particularly in the way that they seem to address persons living under the dominion of a foreign power.[51] Collins similarly notes the conservative, pragmatic tendencies of Proverbs and uses that observation as a beginning point to illustrate the degree to which the wisdom books of the Hellenistic period, Sirach and the Wisdom of Solomon, would have to change.[52] Thus the broader wisdom literature also attaches itself to an aspect of the narrative of Israel, its movement into the Hellenistic world. These wisdom books are still about divine behavior because they counsel specific human behaviors within the context of assumed divine responses, but the mechanisms of that response become subtler and more complex in a foreign world.

Another crucial example of this kind of work is Anathea Portier-Young's *Apocalypse against Empire: Theologies of Resistance in Early Judaism*, a work concerned primarily with apocalyptic writings in the book of Daniel and portions of 1 Enoch. One important aspect of the study of divine behavior in such literature will be the apparent change

---

49. McEntire, *Portraits of a Mature God*, 1–26.
50. Ibid., 199–201.
51. Smith-Christopher, *A Biblical Theology of Exile*, 173–75.
52. John J. Collins, *Jewish Wisdom in the Hellenistic Age* (Louisville: Westminster John Knox, 1997), 9–10.

in location of divine action from the physical, observable world, in which its writers and readers lived, to an unseen world of conflict between good and evil. Portier-Young argues against a frequent understanding of such a move as denial of the physical world. Instead she contends that it is a denial of the "ultimacy" of the forces that control this world.[53] This is an issue that will require considerable discussion in this study. A change in the sphere in which the divine character acts represents a significant change in the nature of that character.

The most thorough effort to develop a theology of Judaism in this period is probably Mark Adam Elliott's *The Survivors of Israel: A Reconsideration of the Theology of Pre-Christian Judaism*, but the scope, method, and purpose of Elliot's work are all significantly different from mine. First, he bases his analysis on the literature of the Dead Sea Scrolls and the apocalyptic literature of the Pseudepigrapha, but not the Apocrypha or narrative works of the Pseudepigrapha, so that his study has less continuity with the Tanak.[54] In addition, his study includes works that were still in development until the end of the first century CE, somewhat beyond the boundary I have drawn. A major reason for this particular selection of texts is found in Elliott's explicit statement of the purpose of his book, "to offer vital *prolegomena* to the study of Christian origins."[55] Second, his examination is primarily systematic in nature, organizing the material around particular subjects or questions. Elliott mounts a significant defense for such an approach: Treating the pieces of literature with which his study and this one are concerned in an isolated manner fails to develop a fuller context in which they were written, thus limiting

---

53. Portier-Young, *Apocalypse against Empire*, 384.
54. Mark Adam Elliott, *The Survivors of Israel: A Reconsideration of the Theology of Pre-Christian Judaism* (Grand Rapids, MI: Eerdmans, 2000), 2–3.
55. Ibid., 12.

the understanding of each individual piece.[56] It bears repeating that my approach attempts to look at the literature collectively by asking a single theological question: How does it portray the divine character as the story of Israel progresses? The purpose of asking such a question is to determine whether a continuing narrative development of the divine character presented at the end of the Tanak can be discerned, even if it is multidirectional. Elliott's work can be useful to this task, however. One of his most important conclusions is that before the appearance of Christianity, at least certain segments within Judaism held a belief that only some groups within Judaism would be the beneficiaries of God's election and salvation, always including themselves, of course. Elliott characterizes his conclusion as one in conflict with the bulk of scholarship on this issue, which has argued instead for what he calls the "conventional nationalistic view" of God's election of Israel.[57] It remains to be seen whether a similar observation can be made by exploring the nature of divine behavior in the literature used in this study by asking questions about who can interact constructively with the divine character.

There have also been some advances in scholarship on individual works within the literature that go far beyond introduction and survey. By far the most notable example of this is the work that has been done on 1 Enoch over the past few decades. The result has been a significant advance in understanding of the Enochic literature and its place within the Judaism of the period. The most expansive achievement has been the identification of an "Enochic" Judaism reflected in this literature as an influential force in the theology of that time period. Not everyone who has argued for the existence of such a strand sees it in the same manner, but it has become clear that the traditions reflected in 1 Enoch were not obscure and esoteric in

56. Ibid., 4–11.
57. Ibid., 40–66.

the time period that produced them.[58] There may or may not have been a cohesive, identifiable group that understood itself as "Enochic" as opposed to Mosaic, but the large collection of literature contained in 1 Enoch represents a serious theological development that almost certainly had wide-ranging influence in that time.

Plan of the Book

The narrative that the literature examined in this study presents is fragmentary in nature. It overlaps with the narrative of the Tanak/Protestant Old Testament in at least two significant ways: 1) by selectively retelling part of the story of Israel in 1 Enoch 1–36, Jubilees, and 1 Esdras[59] and 2) by presenting the lives of faithful Jewish persons living in the diaspora settings of Mesopotamia in the days of the Neo-Babylonian and Persian Empires. Chapters 2, 3, and 4 will all carry the main title "God of the Defeated and Scattered." Chapter 2 will treat the divine portrayals in Jubilees, 1 Enoch 1–36, and 1 Esdras, which reach into the past and reorient the divine activity of judgment; then chapter 3 will continue by examining the stories in Judith and Tobit and in the Greek versions of the books of Daniel and Esther, then will travel to the other end of the ancient Near East by examining the stories of Jews in Egypt contained in 3 Maccabees. In all of these stories, Jewish people dispersed throughout the world are presented as faithful, resilient, and resourceful, and they receive divine assistance in various ways as they struggle to survive and succeed in these contexts. The struggle against persecution at the hands of the Greek Empire will point toward the fifth chapter of this

---

58. See the summary and evaluation of this research in Gabriele Boccaccini, "Introduction: From the Enoch Literature to Enochic Judaism," 2–13.
59. The relationship of Jubilees to Genesis and Exodus and the relationship of 1 Esdras to Chronicles and Ezra-Nehemiah are different in the extreme. Each of these relationships will be explained more fully in chapter 2.

book and the beginnings of 1 and 2 Maccabees, which carry us to the land of Israel and the descendants of the restoration community.

Chapter 4 will be an exploration of the extension of the wisdom literature in books like Sirach, the Wisdom of Solomon, and Baruch, which continue to offer guidance to the faithful as they make their way in the complex world of shifting empires. The primary emphasis in reading all of these texts will be an examination of how Israel's God is portrayed as acting toward, with, and for the people of Israel. The wisdom books will reveal significant shifts in how these issues are understood as they search for a way of understanding the world in light of those shifts. One of the most significant movements in the later wisdom books will be the effort to attach wisdom to the other prominent traditions of ancient Israelite religion.

Chapter 5 will explore a very different part of the story in the books of 1 and 2 Maccabees when the Jews living in Israel revolt against the Seleucid powers that are ruling over them. Because of the nature of these texts, the story is somewhat convoluted. First and Second Maccabees are not sequential books, but overlapping ones. Still, they offer a plotline this study can follow through most of the second century BCE. This is a story of persecution, war, and triumph. The Jewish people in Palestine gain a measure of political independence, so this part of the story has connections to the period of the monarchy narrated in the Tanak, but these books have their own view of the divine character and how that character acts to help the Jewish people in their cause.

Chapter 6 will move back to a portion of the story that is not as geographically focused on Israel. One of the responses to a deity who seemed too transcendent was the literary appearance of heavenly messengers who brought divine words to a beleaguered people and angelic beings who acted in the world on YHWH's behalf. These latter figures will have already been central to the story in works like

Enoch 1–36 and Jubilees. Often these messengers of the former type were great voices from the past, such as Enoch, Ezra, and Baruch, whose names are on some of these books. These books made use a story line divided both spatially and temporally. These dualisms are typically understood as the defining characteristics of the literary genre known as apocalyptic. Such writings explain the persistence of evil in the world by placing God in a heavenly realm, while God's agents struggle against the forces of evil in the ordinary world of human existence. They also look forward to a time beyond, when these worlds will be rejoined, and divine righteousness will reign without opposition.

The seventh chapter will look at the plot leading up to that fusion of the divine realm and the human world, and particularly at texts that explore ways to talk about divine action in the meantime. There will be two primary points of emphasis here: the various beliefs about divine presence or intervention that fall into the category of messianic belief, and the growing understanding of written texts and their use to bring divine activity into the world.

The final chapter of this book will begin by exploring the ways that different answers to the many questions raised in this study contributed to a diversity of belief within Judaism at the turn of the eras. There have been many studies that have examined this context in various ways, but this one will attempt to keep its focus on the different understandings of the divine character. The wide variety of literature that will be explored to get to this point cannot be easily divided among different sectarian groups, but it does offer a divine plot that can be read and understood in various ways. At later points both Judaism and Christianity relegated this literature to a secondary status, or to no status at all, but it seems increasingly unlikely that persons at that time thought and read in our canonical categories. This study will stop short of trying to explain how various groups of

Jews and Christians chose and continued to develop these theological traditions after the first century CE, but will attempt to paint a picture of what kinds of choices were available to them.[60]

---

60. All quotations for books in the Tanak and the Apocrypha are from the New Revised Standard Version, unless otherwise noted. The translations I have used for the other books are noted as they arise. I have attempted to balance the desires to have both the most current, well-informed translations and ones that are accessible to most readers.

2

God of the Defeated and Scattered, Part I

There is a significant overlap between the body of literature contained within the Tanak/Protestant Old Testament and the literature in the Apocrypha and Pseudepigrapha. This is made most obvious by the presence of the expanded Greek versions of Daniel and Esther in the Apocrypha and expanded Christian Old Testament canons. Another point of overlap, which receives less attention, is the mysterious existence of the books called Jubilees, 1 Enoch, and 1 Esdras, which are canonical only in some Orthodox Christian traditions. Jubilees falls into the category sometimes called rewritten Bible, and because it presents much of the plot of Genesis and Exodus it is a necessary starting point. The first major section of 1 Enoch is a much larger version of the Watchers story in Gen. 6:1–4, which incorporates other elements of Genesis. The appearance of the last two chapters of the book of Chronicles, along with all of Ezra, in 1 Esdras means the destruction of Jerusalem and rebuilding of the temple will be a part of the divine story examined in this chapter. First Esdras lies somewhere in the murky area between rewritten Bible and translation, because it puts together Greek translations of parts of two books from the Tanak, and an additional story set in the Persian court of Darius.[1] The discussion will continue in chapter 3 by examining a collection of stories set in the late Babylonian, Persian, and early Hellenistic periods in which Jewish people, scattered about these ancient empires, are protected or rescued by the God of Israel. The wisdom books from the Apocrypha, which appear to be instructions for Jews living in the diaspora in order to live a faithful and productive life, will await discussion in chapter 4. All three of these chapters carry the same primary title because the texts they treat function in the wake of the disruptions of the sixth and fifth centuries and attach themselves to the story of destruction and dispersion.

The discussion of divine-character development in this chapter will give attention to how Israel's God acts in relation to the Israelite people both in Judah and the diaspora, in both the distant and the relatively recent past. One of the challenges of this presentation is that books like Jubilees and 1 Enoch, which reach into the distant past, also contain significant apocalyptic elements or assumptions. Apocalyptic writings present two problems for any attempt to follow a plot. First, they portray a narrative that is operating on a different plane of existence, an unseen world, which is difficult to connect to the plot that is going on in the ordinary world of human experience. The latter world is something of a reflection of the former, but it is difficult to describe a precise connection. The second problem is that apocalyptic works often project their narratives into a distant future, in which God will act differently than in the present. Most interpreters of apocalyptic literature have recognized the use of both a cosmic dualism and a temporal dualism as this genre's defining

---

1. First Esdras differs from the relevant portions of the Greek versions of Chronicles and Ezra-Nehemiah, both in the Hebrew *Vorlage* each used and in translation technique. See Zipora Talshir, *1 Esdras: A Text Critical Commentary* (Atlanta: Society of Biblical Literature, 2001), ix–x.

characteristic.² The attempt to follow a plot in this study will mean that some books, especially ones like 1 Enoch, will have to be treated in more than one place on that plotline. Dealing with the cosmic dualism will require recognizing that the stories going on in the two different realms are reflections of each other. The connection between the two parts of the dualistic framework is the revelatory figure, like Daniel or Enoch, who can move back and forth between the worlds, or at least see into the other world in dreams and visions.³ The more overtly apocalyptic portions will be treated in later chapters, but many of the same assumptions lie behind the portions this chapter addresses.

The theological questions of this literature appear to be centered around the issues identified by this chapter and the next two, divine judgment and divine guidance. First, how does God interact with God's people to help them find a productive way of living in a world expanding in size and complexity? Second, how does God act on behalf of God's people who are scattered around the world, often living in conditions of deprivation and suffering? Both questions are aspects of the problem of the origin of evil, which preoccupies much of the literature of the period. Much of the Hebrew Bible locates the origin of evil in the inclinations of human beings, but a few other possibilities lie buried in the text. In Gen. 2:9 God plants the tree of the knowledge of "good and evil" in the garden, and God's own voice confirms in Isa. 45:7, "Forming light and creating darkness, making good and creating evil, I YHWH do all of these."⁴ Is evil

---

2. Nickelsburg's introduction to this idea is very helpful. See George W. E. Nickelsburg, *1 Enoch 1: A Commentary on the Book of 1 Enoch, Chapters 1–36; 81–108* (Minneapolis: Fortress Press, 2001), 37–41. See also the efforts to arrive at a normative definition for apocalyptic in John J. Collins, "Introduction: Towards the Morphology of a Genre," *Semeia* 14 (1979): 1–20.
3. See the discussion of this "spatial axis" of apocalyptic in Todd R. Hanneken, *The Subversion of the Apocalypses in the Book of Jubilees* (Atlanta: Society of Biblical Literature, 2012), 1–3. In addition, Hanneken provides a useful summary of the academic debate over definitions of apocalyptic over the last three decades (16–24).

inherent in God's creation? A second possibility is the mysterious appearance of the "sons of God" in Gen. 6:1–4. Much of the literature of the Hellenistic period would develop this tradition in its attempt to understand the origin of evil.

A Judging God

The narrative created by the assembling of this literature begins in the book called Jubilees, which is often understood, perhaps too simplistically, as a Hellenistic revision of Genesis. It continues in the first major section of the book called 1 Enoch, which also focuses on traditions in the book of Genesis, specifically the characters called "the sons of God" in Gen. 6:1–4. Finally, it will require examination of the book called 1 Esdras, which overlaps significantly with the biblical books of Chronicles and Ezra-Nehemiah, so it takes readers almost to the end of the story told by the Tanak.

Jubilees

Biblical scholarship was virtually unaware of Jubilees until the middle of the nineteenth century because it had only been preserved in the Ethiopic tradition of Christianity. Whether this piece of literature had a significant place in Second Temple Judaism was a matter of dispute until a century later when fragments of numerous copies were discovered among the Dead Sea Scrolls. With its place within Judaism thus assured and additional manuscripts available, scholarship on Jubilees has accelerated over the past half century, and it is now an essential component of a study like this one.[5]

---

4. The translation here is my own, and I have stayed close to the word order of the Hebrew. There is a text-critical problem here. The Masoretic Text has "making peace and creating evil," but the Qumran Isaiah scroll has "good" instead of "peace."

5. For a more thorough discussion of the textual evidence related to Jubilees and its history, see James VanderKam, "The Manuscript Tradition of Jubilees," in *Enoch and the Mosaic Torah: The*

There has not yet been an extensive and careful debate about the composition of Jubilees. In the most comprehensive study of the subject to date, Michael Segal contends that most interpreters "share the assumption that Jubilees is a unified, homogeneous composition."[6] This is a somewhat confusing statement, since it is obvious that the books of Genesis and Exodus served as sources for Jubilees and were combined with other materials. Segal seems to mean that most interpreters assume that a single author both revised the biblical material and wrote all of the additions, but he argues, seemingly to the contrary, that the writer of the book of Jubilees took an already revised version of Genesis and Exodus and added the additional elements, which he characterizes under four headings: laws, chronological notes, angelology, and priestly elements.[7] Segal bases his argument primarily on observations of contradictions and tensions in Jubilees that can best be explained by constraints placed on a final author by a preexisting source. James Kugel argues, on the other hand, that Jubilees is the product of two distinct authors, whom he calls the "original author" and the "Interpolator." As the name of the latter suggests, his work consisted primarily of insertions. The primary concern of the Interpolator was to assert a purely divine origin for the law. Texts concerned with the "heavenly tablets," like 1:29 and 6:17, resist the sense in some other texts that parts of the law are the product of human initiative (e.g., 7:20).[8] This study is not concerned with the compositional history of Jubilees or the delineation of sources as subjects in and of themselves, but the observations in Segal's and Kugel's work reveal a great deal about

Evidence of Jubilees, ed. Gabriele Boccaccini and Giovanni Ibba (Grand Rapids, MI: Eerdmans, 2009), 3–21.
6. Michael Segal, *The Book of Jubilees: Rewritten Bible, Redaction, Ideology and Theology* (Leiden: Brill, 2007), 14.
7. Ibid., 5–11.
8. See James L. Kugel, *A Walk through Jubilees: Studies in the Book of Jubilees and the World of Its Creation* (Leiden: Brill, 2012), 213–20.

the final form of Jubilees, and these may point toward some of the purposes of the writers.

Jubilees recalls so much of Genesis that it has sometimes been called the "Lesser Genesis." It is important, however, not to let such a description disguise the way Jubilees does its work of recollection. An account of the creation of the world very similar to Genesis 1 appears in Jub. 2:2–17, followed by an extensive elaboration of Sabbath law in 2:18–33. This observation may immediately generate curiosity about what comprises the first chapter of Jubilees. The book does not begin with creation, but with the meeting of YHWH and Moses on Mount Sinai. The framing divine activity on this occasion is the "teaching" of Moses. In 1:5–17 God summarizes the full story of the people of Israel, including the promise of the land to the ancestors, the disobedience of the people in the land, and the resulting destruction and captivity. As early as 1:13, Jubilees contains a divine declaration of the intent to "hide my face from them."[9] The act of divine concealment, which becomes so prominent by the end of the plot in the Tanak, is now placed at the beginning, as an element of divine intent before the plot even begins. Perhaps the cue to make this expression of intent part of the conversation between YHWH and Moses comes from a similar conversation, near the end of the Torah in Deut. 31:14–22, in which God makes a similar comment about the intent to "hide my face" (v. 18), but the Deuteronomy comment seems more of a threat than the foregone conclusion with which Jubilees opens.[10] Jubilees 1 ends, however, with a divine promise of restoration, an event for which Moses himself prays to YHWH in 1:18–20.[11] Jubilees balances the divine

---

9. All translations of Jubilees are from O. S. Wintermute, "Jubilees," in *Old Testament Pseudepigrapha*, ed. James H. Charlesworth (Garden City, NY: Doubleday, 1985), 2:81.
10. See the discussion of this text and the role it plays in the process of divine disappearance in the Tanak in Richard Elliott Friedman, *The Disappearance of God: A Divine Mystery* (New York: Little, Brown, and Co., 1995), 82–87.

intent to "hide my face" with a divine promise that "I will not forsake them" in 1:17. The opening of Jubilees insures that the stories of the ancestors and the exodus event reside within a framework that already acknowledges the exile and restoration of Judah.

The final verses in the first chapter of Jubilees (1:26–28) introduce the figure called "the Angel of the Presence," who writes the story of Israel from creation to the building of an eternal sanctuary. YHWH also commands Moses to write down all of the words. So when Jubilees 2 opens the angel is providing Moses with the story of creation, and the text invites the audience to see both of them writing the story; the communication framework of Jubilees is thus layered and complex. Divine speech to Moses in Jubilees 1 transforms into angelic speech to Moses in Jubilees 2, and this mode of speech continues to the end of the book, which, having recounted the Israelite story all the way to the events of Exodus 12, elaborates the Passover legislation in Jubilees 49 and expounds on Sabbath law once again in Jubilees 50. This is the opposite direction of movement from the pattern typical in the Tanak, where the initial encounters of human characters are with the "angel of YHWH," but transform into more direct divine interactions.[12] The divine meeting with Moses in Exodus 3 is the classic example of the pattern. The different pattern of divine representation means Jubilees presents itself as Moses's copy of the words the Angel of Presence writes, at the command of YHWH. Helge Kvanvig describes the important distinction at this point between "narrative" and "story." The outer narrative in Jubilees is a conversation on Mount Sinai, with YHWH, Moses, and the

---

11. Perhaps it is important to recall here that Psalm 90 is also characterized as a "prayer of Moses" by its title. This psalm stands at the beginning of book 4 of the book of Psalms in its final form, the point in the book that is often understood to correspond to the restoration of Israel after the Babylonian captivity. See Mark McEntire, *Portraits of a Mature God: Choices in Old Testament Theology* (Minneapolis: Fortress Press, 2013), 187–88.
12. Ibid., 103–8.

angel as its characters, while the inner story the conversation tells is primarily a retelling of Genesis 1– Exodus 12.[13] This keeps the reader several steps away from the story and keeps the presence of the divine character at a distance from the world and the religious experience of the reader.

It is remarkable how many difficulties presented by the book of Genesis are resolved in Jubilees. A good, early example is the identification in Jub. 4:1–11 of two daughters of Adam and Eve, Awan and Azura, who become the wives of Cain and Seth, respectively, removing one of the most puzzling aspects of this part of the story in Genesis. More important for this study, however, are the many problematic aspects of the divine character in the biblical book of Genesis resolved within the story told to Moses in Jubilees. The first is the removal of the divine naïveté of Genesis 1 by the elimination of all the divine declarations of goodness.[14] Even the statements of divine blessing from Genesis 1 are absent from the creation of humans in Jub. 2:14 and the Sabbath in 2:17. The divine character in Jubilees demonstrates greater awareness of the inherent flaws in the creation. Jubilees mitigates the futility of the divine decision to flood the earth and kill all of the animals and humans, except those on the ark, when God chooses to put a new nature (5:12) into creation after the flood, which would supposedly prevent it from descending back into the corruption that made the flood necessary. The flood story in Genesis is filled with divine tension and regret, and accomplishes nothing, but the writer of Jubilees seems aware of the problem and seeks to resolve it. Of course, the revision creates massive tension in the text, since it is obvious that humans after the flood are not sinless.[15] It also means the divine character

---

13. Helge S. Kvanvig, "Jubilees—Read as a Narrative," in *Enoch and Qumran Origins: New Light on a Forgotten Connection*, ed. Gabriele Boccaccini (Grand Rapids, MI: Eerdmans, 2005), 75–83.
14. See the discussion of this aspect of divine behavior in McEntire, *Portraits of a Mature God*, 30–31.
15. See the discussion of the many difficulties this insertion raises in Segal, *Book of Jubilees*, 132–35.

deliberately created the world before the flood with a more sinful nature than necessary, but this is consistent with the absence of the declarations of goodness in the adaption of Genesis 1 in Jubilees 2 as noted above. The possibility of such accusations is softened, however, by subtle shifts in Jubilees that transform the disobedience of humans and fallen angels from evil to the results of weakness and bad judgment.[16] The primary theological difficulty such changes generate is the implication of some divine responsibility for the fate of the earth and the humans living in it.

The tension between the divine intent and the reality of human existence created by Jub. 5:11–12 may be resolved, to some degree, by the appearance in Jub. 10:8 of the mysterious Mastema character. After the flood, demons begin leading humans astray and God commands the angels to bind them, but Mastema, the leader of the demons, steps forward and convinces God to leave one-tenth of them free to roam the earth. In Jub. 10:9–13 the angels bind the other nine-tenths and teach Moses the magical secrets to cure the diseases that the remaining demons will cause. Mastema appears prominently in Jub. 17:16 where, much like the adversary figure in Job 1–2, he challenges the loyalty of Abraham and suggests to YHWH the command to sacrifice Isaac.[17] Jubilees 18 repeats many of the details from the Akedah story of Genesis 22, but in Jubilees the event also becomes a contest between the Angel of the Presence, who is telling Moses the story, and Mastema. The conflict is resolved in 18:9–12 when the Angel of the Presence wins the argument before YHWH, puts Mastema to shame, and halts the hand of Abraham.[18] The revised

---

16. For more on this idea, see Annette Yoshiko Reed, *Fallen Angels and the History of Judaism and Christianity: The Reception of Enochic Literature* (Cambridge: Cambridge University Press, 2005), 90.
17. On this connection, see James L. Kugel, *Traditions of the Bible: A Guide to the Bible as It Was at the Start of the Common Era* (Cambridge, MA: Harvard University Press, 1998), 301–2.
18. See the discussion of this text and the development of the Mastema character in Jubilees in Segal, *Book of Jubilees*, 266–67.

Akedah story is a good example of the problem raised early in this chapter about texts that operate in more than one space. The idea begins to emerge in Jubilees that even famous events of the past were reflections of events going on in a different realm where God acted more directly. Meanwhile, in the ordinary world of human beings, YHWH is a much more diminished character in Jubilees compared to Genesis, an aspect of Jubilees that has received relatively little attention. James VanderKam, for example, places significant emphasis on the ways Jubilees alters the human characters of Genesis, typically representing "the biblical heroes in a more favourable light and the villainous as even more heinous."[19] His examination of the divine character, however, is almost exclusively focused on continuity with Genesis, despite significant differences.[20]

Mastema makes another appearance in Jub. 48:1–3, again as a substitute for God in a biblical story that presents a troubling divine character. The episode in 48:1–3 is a revision of the biblical account of YHWH attacking Moses in the wilderness in Exod. 4:24–26, one of the most perplexing episodes in all of the Tanak.[21] In Jubilees the Angel of the Presence reminds Moses of the event and explains that Mastema had discovered the divine plan to free the Israelites by sending plagues on the Egyptians and sought to save the Egyptians by killing Moses. Like the revision of the Akedah, the revised "bridegroom of blood" story puts Mastema in a role the Tanak gives to YHWH. The revision not only keeps God out of earthly affairs and direct contact with humans, but also stabilizes the volatile divine personality in parts of the Tanak.[22]

---

19. James C. VanderKam, *The Book of Jubilees* (New York: T&T Clark, 2001), 109. VanderKam illustrates the positive side of this statement most extensively with Abraham and Jacob.
20. Ibid., 121–23.
21. See the discussion of this event and its impact on the development of the divine character in the Tanak in McEntire, *Portraits of a Mature God*, 64–65.
22. The move is reminiscent of the way the writer of Chronicles substitutes "an adversary" for YHWH in the 1 Chronicles 21 revision of the census story in 2 Samuel 24.

Jubilees makes important revisions in the story of Abraham that shape its portrayal of the divine character. Jubilees 12 is one of the places where later Jewish tradition presents an expanded story of Abraham's rejection of polytheism and idolatry. After burning the house of the idols and moving to Haran with his father, Abram stays awake all night and utters a lengthy prayer, which includes the line, "Save me from the hands of evil spirits which rule over the thought of the heart of man, and do not let them lead me astray from following you, O my God" (12:19). The wording of the prayer reflects the general view in Jubilees of a world inhabited by demons. The report to Moses in 12:22 illustrates the divine withdrawal, when the Angel of the Presence says that God sent a reply to Abram "by my hand," a reply that matches Gen. 12:3 very closely. In canonical Genesis the initial journey of Abram and Sarai through Canaan is followed by the baffling story of their sojourn in Egypt.[23] The alterations in Jubilees are not surprising. The story receives a sense of timing in 13:10–12, which reports that Abraham lives in Hebron two years before a famine drives him to Egypt where he lives for five years before Pharaoh steals Sarai from him, resulting in plagues sent by God. Gone is Abram's deliberate deception of the Egyptians and God's punishment of innocent Egyptians in Genesis, so both God and Abram are more stable and trustworthy characters.

In the midst of the Abraham story in Jubilees, the angel explains the future fate of Israel, in the context of a law concerning circumcision. The text in Jub. 15:23–34 is parallel to Gen. 17:11–14 in many ways, but explains the selection of Israel differently. Jubilees 15:31–32 describes how God placed spirits to rule over the other nations, but rules personally over Israel through all of the angels and spirits. The selection of Israel from among the nations in this text is similar to

---

23. For more on the impact of this story on the development of the divine character in Genesis and the Tanak, see McEntire, *Portraits of a Mature God*, 52–53.

the description in the Song of Moses in Deut. 32:8. Tension arises, however, in Jub. 15:33–34 when the angel narrates Israel's failure to follow the circumcision ordinance and the subsequent wrath of God resulting in their loss of the land. The tension between 15:31–32 and 15:33–34 leaves the destiny of Israel uncertain. Mark Elliott argues that according to Jubilees the dualism reflects "two camps" in Israel, those who follow the circumcision ordinance and those who do not, with the latter abandoned to demons like the gentiles.[24] Whether the divide is this sharp or not, it moves the divine action that determined it back to Israel's very beginning, and portrays a more consistent divine choice than in Genesis. The idea of a dualistic division within Israel will be explored in chapters 6 and 7.

Two of the most remarkable stories of divine behavior in Genesis are the encounters in which YHWH appears to have an ordinary human body. The stories in Gen. 18:1–15 and Gen. 32:22–32 are identified by Esther Hamori as the only two occasions in the Hebrew Scriptures of an "*'sh* theophany," a text where the deity appears in the form of an ordinary human.[25] It is not difficult to imagine that these texts would pose some difficulty for the writer of Jubilees and not surprising that they are sufficiently altered. The parallel to the divine visitation to Abraham and Sarah in Gen. 18:1–15 is in Jubilees 16. In 16:1 the Angel of the Presence refers to the visitors simply as "we," providing no indication that YHWH is included in the party. The references to the shared meal are gone along with most of the other details, leaving no trace of direct divine presence, embodied or otherwise.[26] Readers familiar with Genesis cannot help but be

---

24. Mark Adam Elliott, *The Survivors of Israel: A Reconsideration of the Theology of Pre-Christian Judaism* (Grand Rapids, MI: Eerdmans, 2000), 393–99.
25. Esther Hamori, *"When Gods Were Men": The Embodied God in Biblical and Near Eastern Literature* (Berlin: de Gruyter, 2008), 1–25. This phenomenon is rare in the Tanak but more common in other ancient Near Eastern literature.
26. See the discussion of this passage in Genesis and its significance in McEntire, *Portraits of a Mature God*, ch. 3.

stunned by Jub. 29:13. In this single verse, Jacob crosses over the Jabbok, reconciles with Esau, and the two depart on their separate ways. The writer is so eager to be rid of the wrestling match between YHWH and Jacob in Gen. 32:22–32 that he is willing to jettison the story of how Israel got its name. Such a choice would seem to reveal a strong desire on the part of the writer of Jubilees to present a different portrayal of Israel's deity, even in the distant past.

In biblical Genesis, the divine visit to announce Isaac's birth in 18:1–15 also serves to introduce the narrative of the destruction of Sodom, because the angels go on to visit the city, without God, after eating with Abraham and Sarah. Their departure provides the occasion for YHWH to share the intent to destroy Sodom with Abraham and for Abraham to question the divine plan in Gen. 18:16–33. In Jub. 16:5–6 God destroys Sodom, Gomorrah, and Zeboim[27] with fire because of the wicked actions of those dwelling in the cities, but the dramatic scene from Genesis in which Abraham challenges God's decision and negotiates for Lot is absent from Jubilees. The Angel of the Presence saves Lot simply because God "remembers" Abraham.

One of the surprising inclusions of Jubilees is the banishing of Hagar and Ismael after the birth of Isaac in 16:4–14. Having omitted the initial story of the pregnant Hagar running away and being rescued by a divine visitation (Genesis 16), the second Hagar story (Genesis 21) might seem to have presented similar problems for the writer of Jubilees, but God and Abraham have a direct conversation about Hagar and Ishmael in Jub. 16:6–7, and the entire episode looks very similar to biblical Genesis.[28] The portrayal of Abraham in Jub. 19:15–22:30 is significantly different from biblical Genesis, but the

---

27. Most English Bibles, in places like Genesis 10:19, transliterate the Hebrew of this place name as "Zeboyim."
28. Jubilees does alter the wording so that it does not appear Hagar carries the teenaged Ishmael, as in Genesis.

difference this might create for the portrayal of the divine character is difficult to determine. Abraham interacts significantly with Jacob in this section, showing favoritism for him while Isaac favors Esau. Abraham pronounces long blessings on Jacob in 19:15–29 and 22:10–24, and a brief one in 22:28–30. Abraham's death forms a much more significant boundary in Jubilees. In Jubilees 20–21 he recites long collections of teachings to all of his offspring, through Hagar, Sarah, and Keturah. After his burial in 23:1–7, the angel describes the decline in life spans since the days of "the ancients," but is clear that Abraham was not guilty of the evil that led to the shortening of life spans (23:9–10). The remainder of Jubilees 23 tells of a future evil generation that will lead to God's judgment of Israel and ultimate salvation in an even more distant future. Thus Abraham is a different kind of person in Jubilees, and Jacob enjoys some direct contact with him before his death. The difference in Abraham is consistent with the claim in Jub. 5:12 that God put a different spirit in humans after the flood to keep the destruction from being an exercise in divine futility. Jubilees 24 proceeds, however, to tell the story of Jacob and Esau in a way similar to biblical Genesis.

The character of God in the biblical Genesis is challenged by God's association with Jacob, a character many readers find unsavory. Jubilees retains the episodes in which Jacob gains the birthright and blessing of Esau by trickery and manipulation, and the discussion above has already dealt with the removal of the wrestling scene. Jacob's return to Canaan is thus reduced to a single verse in Jub. 29:13 that includes an abbreviated account of the reconciliation with Esau. Jubilees adds a significant text immediately following in 29:14–20 that is unparalleled in Genesis, much of which describes Jacob's care for his parents in their old age, in contrast to Esau's greed.[29] Jubilees

---

29. The blessing of Levi and Judah in 31:11–20 does seem to borrow some elements from Jacob's blessing of Esau and Manasseh in Gen. 48:1–22.

29:18 makes a minor alteration to Gen. 36:6 so that Esau steals Isaac's livestock and moves to Seir, rather than just taking his own. Jacob further demonstrates his care for Isaac and Rebekah with a visit in Jub. 31:5–30 that has no Genesis parallel. The bulk of the scene consists of Isaac's blessing of Levi and Judah. Jubilees struggles much more than Genesis with the choosing of Jacob and rejection of Esau, as further interactions of the family fill Jubilees 35–36, none of which is contained in biblical Genesis. As her death nears, Rebekah fears future conflict between her twin sons, but Isaac reassures her of God's protection of Jacob in 35:17. Nevertheless, she still seeks assurances from her sons in 35:18–27 that they will not attack each other. When Isaac begins dividing the inheritance in 36:1–20 Esau acknowledges the exchange of the birthright with Jacob, and the sons bury Isaac together as in Gen. 35:29, but Jubilees 37–38 reports the displeasure of Esau's sons and a war that results between the families of Jacob and Esau. In sum, the behavior of Jacob and Esau, exacerbated in Jubilees by Esau's sons, confirms the divine choice of Jacob as the inheritor of the covenant and the progenitor of God's chosen people, as opposed to the seemingly arbitrary divine choice in Genesis.

Given the pattern of divine-character development in Jubilees so far, it should come as no surprise that the divine portrayal in the Joseph story of Genesis fits well in Jubilees, which reproduces much of the story with relatively little change. Statements of divine favor in Jub. 39:12–14 and 40:5 match Gen. 39:21–23, and Joseph progresses from slave to prisoner to dream interpreter to ruler in Egypt. Joseph's statement of the divine plan that brought him to Egypt in order to provide care for his family in Jub. 43:18–19 matches Gen. 45:7–8 closely. Jacob receives divine sanction for the sojourn in Egypt in Jub. 44:5–6 just as in Gen. 46:2–4. Many interpreters have recognized the change in the divine character in the book of Genesis from the directly present, speaking character in the early parts of the book to the "agent" who sends symbolic dreams and wields subtle influence over humans at the end.[30] In Jubilees the divine character is much like this from the beginning, as it flattens the divine-character development and produces a God throughout the book who is safe and carefully mediated, both by the Angel of the Presence and Mastema.

The condensed version of Exodus 1–12 in Jub. 47:11–48:19 requires some explanation. Jubilees recounts very little of the content in Exodus 5–11, offering little more than a list of the plagues. YHWH sends the plagues in Jub. 48:12, but the dramatic confrontation is between the angels and Mastema in 48:8–19. God's repeated hardening of Pharaoh's heart in Exodus in order to extend the plot would certainly have produced difficulties for the divine characterization in Jubilees. The one place the hardening theme appears is in the pursuit of the Israelites to the sea in Jub. 48:15–17, another event involving Mastema, who seems to be the one who hardens the hearts of the Egyptians. The text credits the idea of the pursuit to Israel's God who uses it as an occasion to avenge the drowning of the Hebrew baby boys in the Nile. Jubilees ends with legislation concerning Passover and the Sabbath, without the dramatic story of the Israelites at Mount Sinai.

Perhaps the central element of divine behavior in the biblical book of Genesis is the making of covenants with human beings. This is an activity highlighted in Jubilees to such an extent that William Gilders declares that "Jubilees is fundamentally a covenant document," and that "the purpose of the book as a whole is to stand as a witness to the Israelites that God has remained faithful to the covenant despite their failures."[31] The word "covenant" is even more prominent in Jubilees

---

30. On this point, see W. Lee Humphreys, *The Character of God in the Book of Genesis: A Narrative Appraisal* (Louisville, KY: Westminster John Knox, 2001), 241; and McEntire, *Portraits of a Mature God*, 51–62.

than in biblical Genesis, and at least two important differences are present in the idea.³² First, in Jubilees a covenant does not initiate but "enacts" the relationship with Israel, which already existed before the covenant.³³ This is a change that fits the portrayal of the story of Israel that begins in a meeting between YHWH and Moses. Second, in Jubilees sacrificial ritual always precedes divine speech about covenant, which requires some alterations of the Genesis narrative.³⁴

Aside from the retelling of Genesis and Exodus, Jubilees includes three other significant kinds of materials. The first is a constant pattern of insertions that align past events with a solar calendar.³⁵ The calendrical material has only a little impact on the portrayal of the divine character in the book. I have noted in other places that the book of Genesis is not consistent in its approach to time,³⁶ an aspect of the book that did not suit the purposes of the writer of Jubilees, who sought to fit the stories of the primeval world and the ancestors into a chronological framework suitable to a Hellenistic audience. This change in chronological framework helps create the sense of a deity more concerned with the precise timing of events.

The contents of Jubilees raise an additional question for which there can be no definitive answer. Does the end at the departure from Egypt presume a particular telling of the remainder of the Israelite

---

31. William K. Gilders, "The Concept of Covenant in Jubilees," in *Enoch and the Mosaic Torah: The Evidence of Jubilees*, ed. Gabriele Boccaccini and Giovanni Ibba (Grand Rapids, MI: Eerdmans, 2009), 178–79.
32. Gilders counts thirty-two occurrences of the primary Ethiopic word for covenant in Jubilees, and several more occurrences of other words that seem roughly equivalent to Hebrew *berit* (ibid., 189).
33. Ibid., 187.
34. Two of the most significant of these involve language in the Jubilees equivalent of Genesis 15 to make the ritual more explicitly sacrificial and the addition of a sacrifice in Jubilees 15 to correct for the lack of a sacrificial act in Genesis 17 (ibid., 188).
35. Segal, *Book of Jubilees*, 1–4.
36. See Mark McEntire, *Struggling with God: An Introduction to the Pentateuch* (Macon, GA: Mercer University Press, 2008), 45–49.

story? The wilderness episodes in Exodus and Numbers present a particularly challenging view of Israel's God, a deity that is unaware, unstable, and threatening. An idea as simple as providing food and water for the Israelites in the wilderness does not occur to God until the Israelites are on the verge of death and start complaining. The wilderness complaint tradition in Exodus and Numbers results in numerous episodes when God decides to kill the Israelites and Moses has to calm God down and negotiate a solution to the problem.[37] A divine portrayal like this would be a difficult fit for Jubilees, so bringing the story to an end with the departure from Egypt seems advantageous, but ending the story at that point forces Jubilees to deal with some issues Genesis does not, and a significant one is the status of Jacob's fourth son, Levi. At the end of biblical Genesis, Levi is most remembered for his participation in the slaughter of Shechem, and the single line about Simeon and Levi in Jacob's song (49:5) is not promising. Specific elements later in the Torah serve the rehabilitation of Levi's tribe, beginning with the tribal identity of Moses and Aaron and their act of divine vengeance at Mount Sinai in Exod. 32:25–29. The book of Leviticus elevates the family of Aaron to priestly status and the zeal of Phinehas at Peor in Numbers 25 confirms the validity of the choice. Jubilees, however, must go back into the Genesis story to accomplish the divine identification of Levi's family with the priesthood. The process begins with the surprising statement in Jub. 30:6 that God assisted Simeon and Levi in the defeat of Shechem. The story becomes an occasion for the angel to provide Moses with a strict law against marriage to foreigners in 30:7–17. Following this law, the angel appoints Levi to the priesthood. The description of the slaughter of Shechem as an exemplary act of zeal in Jub. 30:18 reflects the description of Phinehas in Num. 25:6–13 and

---

37. For a more complete discussion of the development of the divine character in the wilderness traditions, see McEntire, *Portraits of a Mature God*, 79–85.

the divine response to his display of zeal. The Angel of the Presence describes the role of the Levites as a reflection of the work of the angels who minister before God. In Jub. 31:11–17 Isaac blesses Levi before he blesses Judah. The result of such changes in Jubilees results in a more consistent picture of Israel's God and an earlier expression of divine intent to choose Levi for the priesthood that is not as reactionary as in the plot of the Tanak.

From the very beginning, Jubilees places the stories of Genesis within the framework of mediation, not developed in the Tanak until the middle of the book of Exodus. The development of divine mediation within the biblical tradition has received major attention from Walter Brueggemann. It is precisely at the point in Exodus 19–20 when the Israelites arrive at Mount Sinai and Moses makes his first journey up that mountain that Brueggemann identifies "a prompt move to mediation."[38] The writer of Exodus has the Israelites say out loud that they do not want any part of direct divine contact. The book of Jubilees seeks out such mediation from a different direction, though. It is not humans who need it in order to be protected from a frightening and dangerous deity, but a deity who needs it in order to be buffered from the messiness of the human world. The God of Jubilees is both more vulnerable and more responsible for the course of human history.

1 Enoch

The book called 1 Enoch presents enormous possibilities and challenges for this study. Scholarship on this book has exploded in the last two decades, including a journal dedicated to it, a large, international seminar that meets every other year and publishes its proceedings in large volumes of articles, and the recent publication of

---

38. Walter Brueggemann, *Theology of the Old Testament: Testimony, Dispute, Advocacy* (Minneapolis: Fortress Press, 1995), 569–70.

the second volume of the commentary on 1 Enoch in the Hermeneia series, completing this massive project. A proposed "Enochic Judaism," as an alternative to the "Zadokite Judaism" that accentuated the role of Mosaic torah and the temple and ended up controlling the canonization of the Hebrew Scriptures, dominates current scholarly discussion of 1 Enoch. Aside from the apparent division of 1 Enoch into five sections, like the Torah, much has been made of the absence in 1 Enoch of the central institutions of Judaism, such as temple and torah. Critics have responded that this is primarily an argument from silence, and the lack of such elements in the literature does not necessarily indicate the presence of a group that rejected them.[39] The section in chapter 1 entitled "Understanding the Cultural Matrix" summarized the current debate. Perhaps the central point in the debate is whether the written documents we possess and the differing perspectives they express represent separate groups within Second Temple Judaism, which split from each other over their differences. Matthias Henze urges appropriate caution concerning such an approach, observing the tendency to exaggerate differences and arguing that "we are first of all comparing texts, not sociological groups, and second, there is no reason why such different positions on theological issues could not have existed in a single group."[40] The appeal of forgotten groups and their buried literature is nearly boundless, as the attraction to the Qumran sectarians and their Dead Sea Scrolls and Gnostic Christianity and its Nag Hammadi library indicates. The attempt to capture popular imagination with ideas of suppressed or censored literature and mysterious groups that secretly preserved them has become a common temptation.

---

39. See, for example, the discussion in Andreas Bedenbender, "The Place of the Torah in the Early Enoch Literature," in *The Early Enoch Literature*, ed. Gabriele Boccaccini and John J. Collins (Leiden: Brill, 2007), 69–72.
40. Matthias Henze, "Enoch's Dream Visions and the Visions of Daniel Reexamined," in Boccaccini, *Enoch and Qumran Origins*, 18.

The portion of the Enoch literature relevant to this chapter is the so-called Book of the Watchers in 1 Enoch 1–36.[41] Most interpreters agree on the isolation of a core story within this section in chapters 6–11, which follows a brief account of creation and human disobedience to the divine commands.[42] The story of the Watchers has obvious connections to the strange, fragmentary text in Gen. 6:1–4 about the *bene-elohim*, and in Enoch this tradition becomes a highly developed story of a heavenly revolt. First Enoch 6 begins in a fashion very similar to Genesis 6, but departs from it quickly in 1 En. 6:3 by identifying a figure named Shemihazah as the leader of the Watchers who make a pact of loyalty to each other before they descend to earth to beget children with the human women. First Enoch 7 continues the Genesis 6 story line but soon departs again to compound the wickedness of the Watchers, who begin to eat human men and animals and drink their blood. According to David Jackson, Shemihazah represents a deviation from the created order of God, so carefully developed in 1 Enoch 1–5. The result of the deviation is the presence of supernatural evil beings on the earth, a reality the Tanak rarely acknowledges and never explains.[43] Like Jubilees, 1 Enoch starts explaining the origins of evil near the beginning of its narrative. The most important narrative role God continues to play in 1 Enoch is supreme judge. The portrayal of God as judge from an early point in the human story has an important impact on scenes in the book that will take place in the future[44] because it establishes God's role as cosmic judge and serves as a context for the failure and

---

41. "Watchers" is the term 1 Enoch uses for the heavenly beings who look down and see human women in 6:2 and take them as wives and have children with them. The prominence of these characters in the first major portion of 1 Enoch appears to have led to its common designation a the "Book of the Watchers."
42. Nickelsburg, *1 Enoch 1*, 165.
43. David R. Jackson, *Enochic Judaism: Three Defining Paradigm Exemplars* (New York: T&T Clark, 2004), 32–37.
44. Ibid.

destruction of Israel, which is forecast immediately in Jubilees 1. This role, however, lifts Israel's God up and out of the world of human existence.

In Jubilees the Angel of the Presence acts for God in the world of human existence, and acknowledges the assistance of other angels as well. Angels also play a necessary role in 1 Enoch, making their first explicit appearance in 9:1. Michael, Sariel, Raphael, and Gabriel[45] observe the chaos and violence on the earth resulting from the work of Azazel[46] and Shemihazah. God is dependent on the angels for the observation of events on earth, and they also urge God toward action on behalf of suffering humans. The angels report that humans who have died are making complaints to heaven, and they lament their own lack of instructions from God concerning the situation. God's response to the plea of the angels is long and puzzling. The initial element in 10:1–2 involves sending Sariel to warn Noah about the coming deluge, an odd response to a complaint centered on the suffering of humanity. Further instructions to the angels in the remainder of 1 Enoch 10 include binding Azazel, attacking the children of the Watchers, causing war between the Watchers and their children, and binding the Watchers for seventy generations. The end of the seventy generations will bring the final judgment of the Watchers and their eternal imprisonment. Meanwhile, Sariel's instructions to Noah include how he should save himself from the coming destruction. The righteous will survive the destruction, according to 10:17–19, in order to repopulate the earth. The text does not explicitly name Noah here, but the planting of vines and

---

45. The number of angels and the forms of their names vary somewhat in the manuscripts of 1 Enoch. See Nickelsburg, *1 Enoch 1*, 202. Later texts in 1 Enoch expand the cohort of angels to seven members by including Uriel, Remiel, and Reuel (207).
46. Azazel appears prominently in 1 Enoch 8–9 as one who helps to corrupt human beings by teaching them how to work with metal and other substances. The skills he teaches them become a means of oppression. The sharing of his name with the mysterious desert figure in Leviticus 16 is intriguing, but there is no clear, discernable connection between the two.

making wine in 1 En. 10:19 looks like a reference to Noah's activity in Gen. 9:20. The purpose of the flood is to cleanse the earth and 1 En. 10:20–11:2 portrays the blessings that result from the cleansing. All the people of the earth will become righteous and will worship God, and God will not send punishment upon them again. God will then send abundant blessings from heaven to earth and unite "peace and truth" forever (11:2). The final promise points toward an end to the present spatial dualism that restricts God to the heavens while the angels act on earth as God's reflection or mediation.

First Enoch 12–16 performs two important functions, providing further explanation for the events in chapters 6–11 and introducing the Enoch character and his role in the drama.[47] By 12:3 Enoch is speaking or writing and 14:1 states explicitly that God commanded him to write down the words of the present book. God is speaking to humanity through Enoch, like God had worked through the angels in chapters 6–10. Enoch states in 14:3 that God created and taught him to reprimand the Watchers, a task one would think should fall to God, since they are angels. Enoch is a divine agent, and after this introduction to his character the text proceeds to explore his visions and heavenly journeys that serve to qualify him for the role. In the initial vision Enoch sees the Glory of God siting on a throne (14:21) and remarks that even the angels are unable to look at the divine face.[48] Such a claim goes even further than texts in the Tanak in separating God from the world of human experience. On his heavenly journeys Enoch sees things that surprise and puzzle him, and the angels carry him and respond to his questions. In 1 Enoch 22 he sees the separate places the angels are preparing for the righteous

---

47. Ibid., 229.
48. On the complexities of divine embodiment and the human ability to observe it, see McEntire, *Portraits of a Mature God*, 51–52; and Howard Schwartz, "Does God Have a Body?," in *Bodies, Embodiment, and Theology of the Hebrew Bible*, ed. S. Tamar Kamionkowski and Wonil Kim (New York: T&T Clark, 2010), 217–23.

and the wicked. In 1 Enoch 25 Michael explains to Enoch that God will eventually come down to the earth for the final judgment and has prepared punishment for the wicked and rewards for the righteous. The Book of the Watchers ends in 36:4 with a grand doxological statement from Enoch. He has witnessed all the works of God in creation and the preparations for the future, and he praises God for these great works and for making them visible to the angels and to humans like himself.[49]

The next section of 1 Enoch, which interpreters call either the Parables or Similitudes of Enoch (37–71), contains a lot of material similar to the Book of the Watchers, but they also feature a new figure. The role of the "Anointed One" or "Son of Man" at the final judgment means the discussion of the Similitudes of Enoch will fit better in chapter 6 of this book, which gathers material presenting a messiah figure. Other portions of 1 Enoch will appear in other chapters, including chapter 6, which will explore apocalyptic visions of the future more fully and will reach back to places where this element appears in 1 Enoch 1–36.

Jubilees and 1 Enoch accomplish two significant tasks related to the development of the divine character. First, the behavior of this character is reshaped so that his behavior in the distant past more closely resembles the divine character present at the end of the plot presented in the Tanak. This reshaping is performed in the act of rewriting Scripture by the removal of many elements of divine behavior in the books of Genesis and Exodus in which God is presented as an active character in the world of human affairs. An important innovation that makes this removal possible is the magnification of the role of angelic beings. The Tanak makes

---

49. There is some dispute about the original ending of the Book of the Watchers. Nickelsburg argues that a section now in 81:1–4 in the Book of the Luminaries may have ended an earlier version of the Book of the Watchers. See *1 Enoch 1*, 332.

significant use of the character called the angel of the LORD, but this character is typically a precursor to direct divine presence, rather than a replacement.[50] In Jubilees and 1 Enoch angels become true mediating figures for YHWH's presence and act in the world of human affairs on YHWH's behalf. The second task is the creation of a parallel plot in the heavenly realm, in which God can continue to have an ongoing role as a character. Todd Hanneken argues that judgment works differently in 1 Enoch and Jubilees, beginning with the role the great flood plays in the process. In Jubilees 5 the flood is a great act of divine judgment, particularly upon the Watchers. In 1 Enoch 10 the flood accompanies the binding of the Watchers so that they may be held over for a future judgment.[51] Jubilees functions with a spatial separation like that of apocalyptic literature, and with some temporal separation, by placing Moses back at the beginning of the creation of the world, but it does not have a forward-oriented temporal separation that delays judgment until a distant future event.

The persistent activity of God is justice, but divine justice is separated from the world of present experience both spatially and temporally. Jubilees 1 begins by establishing divine justice as the context of Israel's entire story from the beginning. First Enoch explains the causes of injustice in the world by pointing to the presence of evil spirits, but also establishes a future pattern for the enactment of divine justice by assuring its readers that "the mechanisms that will facilitate the judgment already exist and are operative in the heavenly realm."[52] The spatial and temporal travels of Enoch allow him to witness to those mechanisms. The heavenly messenger sees that "[i]n places uninhabited by live mortals, God's will is done and the apparatus that will execute God's will stands

---

50. See the discussion of this figure and how it typically transforms into YHWH in McEntire, *Portraits of a Mature God*, 103–8.
51. Hanneken, *Subversion of the Apocalypses*, 158.
52. Nickelsburg, *1 Enoch 1*, 40.

at the ready."⁵³ The collapse of both the spatial and the temporal dualisms, which will allow that justice to rule the world humans inhabit awaits discussion in later chapters that deal with the distant future, the end of the plot presented by these works.

Excursus: The Genesis Apocryphon

The text most often called the Genesis Apocryphon exists in one fragmentary Aramaic manuscript from the Dead Sea Scrolls, 1QapGen.⁵⁴ The scarcity of this work and the poor condition of the only manuscript make its inclusion in the primary discussion of this chapter problematic. Nevertheless, the way the Genesis Apocryphon interacts with the two most important books in the discussion so far, Jubilees and 1 Enoch, makes a separate discussion informative.⁵⁵

The Genesis Apocryphon opens with Lamech speaking in first-person language about his concern that his pregnant wife, Batenosh, might be carrying a child of one of the Watchers. His quest to discover if the child is his own leads to his father, Methusaleh, and his grandfather, Enoch. The early appearance of both Enoch and the Watchers invites immediate comparison to 1 Enoch, and Nickelsburg documents the parallels between the Noah birth story that opens the Genesis Apocryphon and 1 Enoch 106–7.⁵⁶ Noah narrates the next portion of the work in first-person language, including his survival of the flood and apportioning the land among his sons after the flood.

---

53. Ibid.
54. A helpful English translation of the Genesis Apocryphon by John C. Reeves is at http://clas-pages.uncc.edu/john-reeves/course-materials/rels-2104-hebrew-scripturesold-testament/translation-of-1q-genesis-apocryphon/.
55. For a detailed exploration of the possible literary connections between the Genesis Apocryphon and Jubilees and 1 Enoch, see Daniel A. Machiela, "The Genesis Apocryphon (1Q20): A Reevaluation of Its Text, Interpretive Character, and Relationship to the Book of Jubilees" (PhD diss., University of Notre Dame, 2007), 19–41.
56. Nickelsburg, *Jewish Literature between the Bible and the Mishnah*, 2nd ed. (Minneapolis: Fortress Press, 2005), 173–74.

The text moves on to provide a first-person account from Abram of some of the events in his life.

The nature of the Genesis Apocryphon may lead to its classification as rewritten Bible like Jubilees.[57] The readable portions of the scroll demonstrate no apocalyptic concerns or tendencies. The most important element for understanding divine behavior are the dreams that Noah and Abram experience, which reduce the differences depicted in Genesis between the divine experience of early characters like these and the later ones like Jacob and Joseph, the latter of whom has divine contact only through symbolic dreams. The leveling of divine behavior through time, present in Jubilees, also appears in the Genesis Apocryphon.

1 Esdras

The mere existence of the book called 1 Esdras is a mystery, as noted in the introduction above. This piece of Greek literature contains material from 2 Chronicles 35–36, almost all of the book of Ezra, and part of Nehemiah 9. While some have argued that it is the product of a series of accidents,[58] this seems highly unlikely.[59] Furthermore, the apparent use of this work by Josephus and its appearance in the canons of some Christian traditions argue for an early understanding of the book as something other than an incidental fragment. Assuming that it is a deliberately crafted piece of literature offers

---

57. Joseph A. Fitzmyer highlights the connections between Jubilees and the Genesis Apocryphon. See *The Genesis Apocryphon of Qumran Cave 1 (1Q20): A Commentary* (Rome: Biblical Institute Press, 2004), 20–21.
58. Most famously, this was the position of Charles. C. Torrey, the most influential scholar on this part of the biblical tradition in the early twentieth century. See *Ezra Studies* (Chicago: University of Chicago Press, 1910), 11–30.
59. See the arguments for deliberate literary production of 1 Esdras in Lester Grabbe, "Chicken or Egg? Which Came First, 1 Esdras or Ezra-Nehemiah?," in *Was 1 Esdras First? An Investigation into the Priority and Nature of 1 Esdras*, ed. Lisbeth S. Fried (Atlanta: Society of Biblical Literature, 2011), 31–44. Grabbe does not argue that 1 Esdras was the source of Ezra-Nehemiah, but that the two works are independent developments of an original Ezra source.

opportunities to look at how its writer(s) wished to present this story and the divine behavior within it. Because of its connection to the canonical books of Chronicles and Ezra-Nehemiah, 1 Esdras offers an important transition from the Tanak into the literature with which this study is concerned.

The element of 1 Esdras not present in the Tanak is the curious story of the three young men who serve as bodyguards to King Darius of Persia in 1 Esdras 3–4. The Story of the Youths requires initial treatment because the writer of 1 Esdras may have produced the book in order to present this story and to provide the return of the exiles to Judah as a context for it.[60] The primary character in the story is Zerubbabel, who appears prominently in Ezra without any initial explanation for his status.[61] The story describes a contest Zerubbabel wins in order to get the attention and admiration of King Darius, which provides Zerubbabel an opportunity to remind the king of his promise to sponsor the rebuilding of the temple in Jerusalem (1 Esd. 4:42–46), so the event also explains why Zerubbabel is among the leaders of the returning group. God plays no apparent role in the story until the end approaches, and even then the divine participation is oblique. As the final part of his answer in the contest in 4:36–40, Zerubbabel argues that truth is the strongest force in the world and attributes truth to his God. The event concludes in 4:58–63 when Zerubbabel thanks God for giving him the wisdom to win the contest, and his companions in Babylon praise God for providing them the opportunity to return to Jerusalem to rebuild the temple. Such a portrayal of God fits the general pattern of Ezra-Nehemiah, where divine action operates within human beings, even influencing foreign kings and using their power to accomplish the

---

60. A review of the pertinent issues and a convincing case for this position is in Zipora Talshir, *1 Esdras—From Origin to Translation* (Atlanta: Society of Biblical Literature, 1999), 58–105.
61. Haggai 1:1 identifies Zerubbabel as the governor, but does not explain how he reached this position.

divine purpose.⁶² Zerubbabel not only looks like Ezra and Nehemiah, who gain the favor of Persian kings in order to further their work for Israel, but also like Daniel and Esther, who gain favor in foreign courts because of their courage, intelligence, and attractiveness. The Story of the Youths in 1 Esdras 3–4 is much like the diaspora tales the next chapter will present, but it needs the setting of the exile and restoration from Chronicles and Ezra-Nehemiah in order to explain why Zerubbabel is a significant character about whom to tell such a story.

First Esdras begins with a massive sacrificial ritual, the Passover celebration conducted by Josiah, the king of Judah. The number of animals reported in 1 Esd. 1:7–9 is 41,600, precisely the same number as reported in 2 Chron. 35:7–9.⁶³ This beginning is reminiscent of Jubilees 1, two very different pieces of literature that both focus on YHWH's judgment and destruction of the nation of Israel while giving almost no attention to the long story of the nation leading up to that point. The divine character performs six direct actions in 1 Esdras 1–2, and two or three others can be attributed to God indirectly. Table 2-1 lists these actions.

---

62. On the divine cooperation with foreign kings in Ezra-Nehemiah, see McEntire, *Portraits of a Mature God*, 178–80.
63. There is not a parallel passage in 2 Kings, which does not report this Passover or the earlier one celebrated by King Hezekiah of Judah. On the significance of these additions in Chronicles, see Mark McEntire, *The Function of Sacrifice in Chronicles, Ezra, and Nehemiah* (Lewiston, NY: Mellen Biblical Press, 1993), 37–43.

Table 2-1

The Actions of God in 1 Esdras 1–2

<u>Direct Actions</u>

1:50	"sent his messenger to call them back"
1:51	"whenever the Lord spoke, they scoffed"
1:52	"he gave command to bring against them the kings of the Chaldeans"
2:2	"the Lord stirred up the spirit of King Cyrus"
2:3	"The Lord of Israel . . . has made me [Cyrus] king of the world"
2:8	"whose spirit the Lord had stirred to go up to build"

<u>Indirect Actions</u>

1:6	"according to the commandment of the Lord that was given to Moses"
1:24	"the words of the Lord fell upon Israel"
1:27	"The Lord is with me, urging me on!" (a claim made by the Egyptian pharaoh, Neco)

It is striking that despite all the praise heaped upon Josiah in 1 Esd. 1:32–33, he is unable to halt the divine judgment. Josiah dies a tragic death and his nation is destroyed at the hands of empires from the east and the west. Depending on the veracity of Pharaoh Neco's claim in 1:27, it seems that Israel's God is operating through the brutal power of foreign empires, and it would seem that the writer of 1 Esdras supported the claim of the pharaoh. In the parallel verse in 2 Chron. 35:21, Neco uses *elohim* to refer to "god," so it is possible to understand that he is speaking of his own god, but in 1 Esd. 1:27 he uses *kyrios*. This word choice indicates that the Egyptian king's claim concerns Israel's God.[64] Moreover, the next verse speaks of a warning from the prophet Jeremiah.[65] No content of the warning is present in

1:28, but it is most reasonable to associate it with the warning that comes from the king in 1:27. Still, it is a claim made by a foreign king, and its truthfulness is open to question. This issue will arise later in the discussion of 1 Esdras, and evidence will accumulate that the narrator intends the reader to take the claims of foreign kings about the intent of Israel's God at face value.[66]

The most striking divine act is described in 1:52, and the nature of the description cannot be understood without careful comparison with other textual traditions. There is no parallel to this verse in 2 Kings, so the necessary comparisons are with the Masoretic Text of 2 Chron. 36:17 and the Greek translation of 2 Chron. 36:17 in manuscripts known collectively as the Septuagint.[67] In necessarily different grammatical constructions, the Hebrew and Greek texts of this verse make God the subject of the opening verb. God "brings up" or "causes to go up" the king of the Chaldeans against Judah as punishment for the failure to heed the warnings described in the previous verses. Though it is often disguised in English translations, God is also best understood as the subject of the verb "killed" in the second clause of 36:17, in both its Greek and Hebrew versions.[68] First Esdras 1:52 presents this part of the story differently. As the translation in table 2-1 indicates, there is an additional layer of causation or mediation. Israel's God is still the ultimate cause, but he commands someone else to "bring" the enemy king against Judah.[69]

---

64. See the discussion of this text in Talshir, *1 Esdras: A Text Critical Commentary*, 47.
65. Ibid., 50.
66. See the discussion of this issue in McEntire, *Portraits of a Mature God*, ch. 6.
67. There are numerous problems associated with the naming of these text traditions and the simplistic manner in which they are understood. The readings here are based on the Christian Bible written in Greek from the fourth and fifth centuries CE. It is assumed that these texts are relatively close to the Greek translations of the Tanak produced by Jewish scribes in the last two centuries BCE. This latter tradition is more properly called the Old Greek and is preserved only in indirect fragments. See the discussion of this problem in McEntire, *Portraits of a Mature God*, ch. 5.
68. See the discussion of this in McEntire, *Function of Sacrifice*, 44–46.

While 1 Esdras does not contain direct references, like Jubilees and 1 Enoch, to the kinds of angelic beings that populate the world of human existence and do the work of God, who resides in heaven, this text looks consistent with that view. In one of the texts of 1 Esdras that has no parallel anywhere in the Tanak, the narrator refers to God as "the King of heaven" (4:58), a title consistent with the more removed understanding of God.

Another important aspect of the divine involvement in the invasion of Jerusalem in 1 Esdras 1–2 and its results calls for attention, and that is its location. Both the Hebrew and Greek of 2 Chron. 36:17 place the killing of the Israelite young people "in" the temple. This is a highly charged description because of the unavoidable connection between killing inside the temple and the act of sacrificial ritual for which it was designed and built. The description of killing young people in the temple looks like a sacrificial purifying of the temple for future use after the exile. Whether this was the intent of the writer of Chronicles is impossible to say, but 1 Esdras removes the possibility by changing the pronoun to "around" the temple, removing the killing of the young people from inside the holy place.[70]

Once the attention shifts to Cyrus and the end of the exile in 1 Esdras 2, the divine actions become positive, but 1 Esdras follows Ezra in keeping the actions of God invisible and interior. God works subtly within human beings, most notably a foreign king, to influence their behavior. In the portion of 1 Esdras that parallels parts of Ezra-Nehemiah, God is seldom active, serving most often as a means to identify religious traditions or institutions. The phrase "temple (or house) of (or for) God/the Lord" appears dozens of times along with "law of God/the Lord," which appears in varying

---

69. See the discussion of this text in Talshir, *1 Esdras: A Text-Critical Commentary*, 83–84. Talshir recognizes the shift but attributes it only to "an attempt to express the causative aspect," without recognizing the additional layer of agency created by this expression.
70. Ibid., 81-84. Also see the discussion of the issue in McEntire, *Function of Sacrifice*, 44–45.

formulations many times. The law was "given by" God, but the giving happened long ago "to Moses." There may be exceptions to this lack of activity, such as 1 Esd. 6:5 where "the providence of the Lord was over the captives" while they were in Babylon, but this is a divine role that lacks specificity. King Darius prays that Israel's God will destroy anyone who opposes the building of the temple in Jerusalem (6:33), but no corresponding divine action is portrayed. When the Judahites complete the temple, the narrator of 1 Esdras reports that they finished the work "by the command of the Lord God of Israel" (7:4), in a line very close to the one in Ezra 6:14. First Esdras continues to reflect the divine behavior in the book of Ezra when God changes the will of the Assyrian king in 7:15 (= Ezra 6:22 which says "turned the heart").[71] When the character named Ezra praises God in 1 Esd. 8:25 (= Ezra 7:27) he says that God put the idea of rebuilding the temple into the heart of the king. First Esdras continues to follow Ezra-Nehemiah in its subtle portrayal of Israel's God, who brings foreign kings into participation in the task of restoring Judah.

Conclusion

Whether deliberately or not, the assembling of the Tanak created a story in which the God of the past acted differently from the God of the present. The clearest juxtaposition of the two patterns of behavior is seen in the creedal statement in Neh. 9:6–37. The deity in the narrative present of the story being told in Ezra-Nehemiah acts in an entirely different way than the one portrayed in the creed.[72] Those who assembled this collection of literature and those who,

---

71. It is a peculiarity of both Ezra and 1 Esdras that Darius is described as "king of Assyria." On the possible explanations, see H. G. M. Williamson, *Ezra-Nehemiah* (Waco, TX: Word, 1986), 85–86.
72. McEntire, *Portraits of a Mature God*, 176–87.

throughout time ever since, have chosen to place the collection at the center of their religion have been willing to tolerate the tension created by this story of the divine character. Our exploration of the literature of the Apocrypha and Pseudepigrapha thus far has demonstrated that some may have been unwilling to make that choice. They chose instead to do three things that would remove the cognitive dissonance created by that story. The first was to rewrite the Bible in such a way that the divine character of old was not so strikingly different. The deity in Jubilees and 1 Enoch is invisible and detached from the workings of the ordinary world of humanity, as is the God of Ezra-Nehemiah or Esther. Every solution to such a problem, however, creates a new problem. These writers were not willing to write Israel's God entirely out of existence, so their second task was to develop a new realm in which God could be active. This created the spatial dualism so characteristic of apocalyptic literature. The third task was to develop connections between these two worlds. The first part of this task was populating the human world with supernatural beings, both good and evil, who could support or oppose YHWH's agenda in the human world. The struggle between angels and evil spirits depicted in Jubilees and 1 Enoch provides background for specific conflicts like the one we will see in Tobit. The second aspect was the introduction of human figures who could move between the two worlds, such as Enoch and Daniel.

The incorporation of the Story of the Youths into the restoration story in 1 Esdras provides a portrait of a young Jewish person, Zerubbabel, who is successful in a foreign court because of the wisdom Israel's God gives him and who returns to Jerusalem to apply his leadership talents to the rebuilding. The next section will focus on the stories of heroic young Jews in the diaspora, but the Zerubbabel of 1 Esdras 3–4, a Davidic heir, will provide a connection between these kinds of figures and the homeland.

3

God of the Defeated and Scattered, Part II

The books within the Apocrypha that have the earliest narrative setting may be Tobit and Judith. The reason it is difficult to make a definitive statement is that Judith has what seems to be a deliberately confused historical context. The first verse of the book establishes the setting of the story during the reign of the Babylonian king Nebuchadnezzar in the early sixth century BCE, but it identifies Nebuchadnezzar incorrectly as the ruler of the Assyrian Empire, centered in Nineveh, which had been destroyed by his father a few decades earlier. The situation is further complicated when Jth. 4:3 places the events after the return from the exile, in the late sixth century.[1] Biblical interpreters have explained these historical incongruities in a variety of ways. It is quite possible that these writers were sometimes in possession of faulty information, or a lack of information that led to the invention of inaccurate historical

---

1. On the various scholarly attempts to explain the many historical anomalies, see Carey A. Moore, *Judith: A New Translation with Introduction and Commentary*, Anchor Bible 40 (New York: Doubleday, 1985), 46–49.

details. This seems an unlikely explanation, however, for many of the seeming discrepancies in these books. In some cases writers may have changed details deliberately to disguise the intent of their writing. Some have argued, for example, that the Nebuchadnezzar of Judith is really Antiochus IV.[2] Readers need to remain aware of the distinction between the settings of the narratives and the likely settings of their intended audiences.

A Protecting God

The tensions highlighted above, concerning the chronological settings of stories and the contexts in which they appear to have been written, might be resolved if we recognize that a narrative like Judith is a historical amalgam, told at a later point to encourage Israelites in the midst of struggle. It then becomes important to ask how the divine character is portrayed in these stories, set in Israel's past, especially when it is apparent the stories are addressed to a much later context. All of the texts addressed in this section share this similarity. Daniel, Judith, Tobit, and Esther all contain stories in which the settings have connections to the fifth to seventh centuries BCE, yet all of these books have features that reveal the time of their writing and their intended audiences to be Jewish people in Israel and in the diaspora three or four centuries later.[3] Third Maccabees has a later setting than the other books, but its similarity as a rescue story set in the diaspora connects it to most of the other books this chapter examines. The writers of the stories may not have known the precise

---

2. George W. E. Nicklesburg, *Jewish Literature between the Bible and the Mishnah*, 2nd ed. (Minneapolis: Fortress Press, 2005), 101. Others have attempted to establish a larger scheme of pseudonymity in the book of Judith. See Moore, *Judith*, 53–54.
3. On the commonality of the parts of this collection that are "court tales" set in foreign empires, and the parallel literature from other cultures besides these Jewish expressions, see Carol A. Newsom with Brennan W. Breed, *Daniel: A Commentary* (Louisville, KY: Westminster John Knox, 2014), 12–14.

details of their settings, but even if they did, such precision was not their goal. Rather, they likely wanted to tell stories of particular kinds for their audiences and they shaped their setting for this purpose. The primary issue for this study will be the assumptions about the divine character present in their stories and what the resulting portrayal might have meant for their audiences.

Judith

Perhaps the most remarkable element of divine characterization in Judith comes in 5:5–21. Having been offended by the refusal of the nations to his west to join him in a military campaign, Nebuchadnezzar has declared war on all of them and sent his general, Holofernes, to destroy them. Holofernes reaches the borders of Judea, having defeated every nation in his path and, while the Israelites prepare for invasion, he receives counsel about them from an Ammonite named Achior. Achior recites the story of the Israelite people, including their Mesopotamian origins, their movement into Canaan, their bondage in Egypt, the exodus, and the settlement of the land of Canaan. This includes acts of YHWH on behalf of Israel like sending plagues against Egypt (5:12) and parting the Red Sea (5:13). In this foreigner's words,

> As long as they did not sin against their God they prospered, for the God who hates iniquity is with them. But when they departed from the way he had prescribed for them, they were utterly defeated in many battles and were led away captive to a foreign land. The temple of their God was razed to the ground, and their towns were occupied by their enemies.[4] But now they have returned to their God, and have come back from the places where they were scattered, and have occupied Jerusalem, where their sanctuary is, and have settled in the hill country,

---

4. Perhaps this is the point of greatest irony created by the mixing of historical details. The recipient of this speech, Holofernes, is portrayed as the lead general of Nebuchadnezzar, the Babylonian king who led this very invasion of Israel and destruction of Israel, so Achior would seem to be telling Holofernes of his own actions.

because it was uninhabited. So now, my master and lord, if there is any oversight in this people and they sin against their God and we find out their offense, then we can go up and defeat them. But if they are not a guilty nation, then let my lord pass them by; for their Lord and God will defend them, and we shall become the laughingstock of the whole world.[5] (Jth. 5:17–21)

What is provided to a general as a bizarre military strategy is a heavily ideological statement to the people of Israel regarding the earning of God's protection through obedience. Holofernes refuses this advice and has Achior handed over to the Israelites as a prisoner, but the Israelites reward him for his proclamation of their faith. The resulting invasion by Holfernes and the distress it causes in Israel is the occasion to introduce Judith into the story at 8:1.

The speeches and prayers of Judith in 8:9–9:14 make numerous claims, past, present, and future, about the actions of Israel's God. In the previous chapter, the Israelite leader, Uzziah, had made an agreement with the desperate people who were dying of thirst to wait five more days for divine deliverance before surrendering to the "Assyrian" army. Judith clearly sees such bargains with God as inappropriate and unfaithful, but her own description of Israel's God is conflicted: "Do not try to bind the purposes of the Lord our God; for God is not like a human being, to be threatened, or like a mere mortal, to be won over by pleading. Therefore, while we wait for his deliverance, let us call upon him to help us, and he will hear our voice, if it pleases him" (8:16–17). Like the three young men in Dan. 3:16–18, Judith believes God is able to help and prayer is the only proper human response to the situation, but she assumes no causal relationship between prayer and divine salvation. This is hardly the only element of conflict in Judith's portrayal of Israel's God. In 8:18 she refuses to accept the possibility that the people of her own time

---

5. Quotations of Judith come from the New Revised Standard Version.

have committed any act of idolatry similar to the behavior of past Israelites:

> For never in our generation, nor in these present days, has there been any tribe or family or people or town of ours that worships gods made with hands, as was done in days gone by That was why our ancestors were handed over to the sword and to pillage, and so they suffered a great catastrophe before our enemies. But we know no other god but him, so we hope that he will not disdain us or any of our nation. (8:18–20)

"The God of Judith is a deliverer of God's people, yet remains sovereign and not obligated to act in their behalf (8:15–17)."[6] While such thinking about God is not unprecedented, this is a fundamental shift away from the predominant theology of the Tanak. Margarita Stocker contends that the ways of God in the book of Judith may not just be simply too mysterious for human comprehension, but God acts in ways that "shock or outrage human beings."[7] In this case, God works through a woman, uses the woman's beauty to seduce a man, and uses the seduction as occasion for a brutal assassination. The story also functions to link the feminine and the divine, both of which are characterized by qualities like irrationality, passivity, and emotion, as opposed to male qualities like rationality, intellect, and activism.[8] The connections between Judith and some of the heroic women in the Tanak are many, but Deborah and Jael in Judges 4–5 probably offer the most significant connections. Sidnie Ann White observes "the absence of miracles in the prose narrative of both stories."[9] Judith relies on the guidance of God more explicitly than Deborah or Jael,

---

6. Nicklesburg, *Jewish Literature between the Bible and the Mishnah*, 100. On this theological tension, see also Benedikt Otzen, *Tobit and Judith* (London: Sheffield Academic Press, 2002), 100–101.
7. Margarita Stocker, *Judith: Sexual Warrior; Women and Power in Western Culture* (New Haven: Yale University Press, 1998), 205.
8. Ibid., 10–11.
9. Sidnie Ann White, "In the Steps of Jael and Deborah: Judith as Heroine," in *"No One Spoke Ill of Her": Essays on Judith*, ed. James VanderKam (Atlanta: Scholars Press, 1992), 12.

but God neither tells Judith exactly what to do nor helps her do it in any supernatural way.[10]

Judith also presents some interesting interpretations of the stories of the ancestors in Genesis. In Jth. 8:25–26 she refers to divine testing of Abraham, Isaac, and Jacob.[11] These references are not detailed enough to tie them to specific events in Genesis, but it is difficult to identify any event Genesis presents as a test of Isaac, nor any part of Jacob's sojourn in Haran that is described this way. Judith uses such recollections of the past to claim that suffering may be God's testing of the faithful rather than punishment of the disobedient. As Nickelsburg claims, "In moments of evident defeat this God tests the faith of God's people (8:25–27)."[12] Perhaps it is not surprising that the human characters are at an utter loss to understand the behavior of Israel's God. Judith chastises Uzziah and the other leaders in 8:11–17 for presuming that they can, but then she goes on to speak and act as if she herself understands and can affect divine behavior in the next few chapters.

When Judith begins to pray directly to God in 9:2, she continues to interpret the ancestral narratives in an original way. In her recollection, her own ancestor Simeon was given a sword by God in order to take vengeance on the inhabitants of Shechem for the rape of Dinah in Genesis 34. In the Song of Jacob in Genesis 49, Simeon and Levi are condemned for this act, and this seems to be one reason why Simeon has vanished from the list of tribes in the Blessing of Moses (Deuteronomy 33), while the tribe of Levi has redeemed itself through its actions at Mount Sinai and subsequent achievement of the priesthood. Judith also uses a fascinating description of God in Jth. 9:7 when asking for divine defeat of the Assyrian army. The

---

10. Ibid., 12–13.
11. On the many traditions in the Tanak to which the book of Judith has some connection, see Otzen, *Tobit and Judith*, 74–79.
12. Nickelsburg, *Jewish Literature*, 100.

phrase she uses to describe God as one "who crushes wars" is the same phrase used to describe God in the Greek version of Exod. 15:3. This description is also repeated at Jth. 16:2 in the song performed by Judith at the end of the book. This Greek phrase mysteriously replaces the Hebrew "man of war" in Exodus 15 and has been taken by some interpreters to be a move away from the divine warrior imagery so prominent in the Tanak.[13] This is not the sense in Jth. 9:7, where it seems to describe God's potential defensive action against the attacking Assyrian army.

Judith brings her prayer to a conclusion by reminding Israel's God of his identity as "God of the lowly, helper of the oppressed, upholder of the weak, protector of the forsaken, savior of those without hope" (9:11). She acknowledges that she plans to use deception against the enemies of Israel (9:13) and she appeals to concern for the divine reputation (9:14). By the time Judith begins to put her plan in motion in chapter 10, she has made attempts to utilize almost every understanding of divine behavior that can be found in Israel's traditions. Like other heroic individuals in this tradition who faced long odds against powerful foreign empires, Judith makes use of her superior intelligence, physical beauty, and virtue to get herself in a position to help her people. She is able to make use of the theology of retribution that Achior had explained to Holofernes earlier in order to gain some freedom of movement within the enemy camp. In 11:17 Judith convinces Holofernes that she must go out to pray every night so that God can inform her when the Israelites have sinned and forfeited God's protection. The closing chapters of Judith contain several declarations of God's powerful action on behalf of Israel in 13:11, 14, 15; 14:10; 15:8, 10; 16:2, 17. It is unclear how to interpret such claims because of the ways in which the acts are actually accomplished. Many interpreters have noticed a surprising

---

13. Ibid., 99.

lack of the miraculous in Judith. Carey Moore, for example, observes that "[t]he destruction of Holofernes and his army was accomplished through human efforts rather than by divine or miraculous intervention."[14] Some of the language of the book of Judith fits with the stories of Israel's warfare in the distant past, such as in the books of Joshua and Judges, while the actual description of events sounds more like later stories in Ezra-Nehemiah.[15]

Moore identifies fifteen different designations for Israel's God in the book of Judith, and a list of attributes nearly as long.[16] The immediate response to such quantity might be that the writer and his implied audience believe a lot of things about their God, but it seems equally likely, and more fitting with the story presented in Judith, that they were not quite sure what to believe, and the book compensates for uncertainty with sheer volume. Within the story the Israelites are threatened by the army of Nebuchadnezzar. The book of Jeremiah, with which the book of Judith has some significant connections,[17] presents the pending invasion of Nebuchadnezzar and his army as divine punishment, which should not be resisted or avoided, while Judith understands such hardships as divine testing of the faithful.[18] But what is the proper response to such testing? Should the Israelites accept the invasions as part of God's purpose, wait patiently while fasting and praying for divine deliverance, or take decisive action, confident God will grant success? The book of Judith struggles to hold together four significant ideas about the God of Israel and this deity's relationship to the people. First, God is in conflict with the other nations of the world, some of which threaten Israel. Second, attacks and threats against Israel at this time are not the

---

14. Moore, *Judith*, 45.
15. On this distinction, see McEntire, *Portraits of a Mature God*, 178–83.
16. Moore, *Judith*, 60.
17. Otzen, *Tobit and Judith*, 101.
18. See Moore, *Judith*, 63.

result of disobedience for which God is punishing them. Third, God possesses the power to overcome these enemies, but, finally, God may or may not choose to exercise that power. This sense of theological ambiguity may fit well with the general elusiveness of the story of Judith, which continues to resist precise placement within the plot of the people of Israel and their God.

Tobit

The book of Tobit is extant in many of the languages used in early Christianity, including Greek, Latin, Syriac, Coptic, and Ethiopic, and it appears in the larger Old Testament canons of Christianity. Until 1952 the most logical assumption was that Tobit was originally written in Greek, but Joseph Fitzmyer has identified fragments of five copies of Tobit from Qumran Cave 4, four in Aramaic and one in Hebrew, and from this evidence he argues that Aramaic was its original language of composition.[19] The geographical setting of its composition is impossible to determine with any certainty, but there is widespread agreement that Tobit was written in the late third or early second century BCE.[20] The date of composition and the presence of multiple copies at Qumran indicate Tobit had significant influence in the period that concerns this study.

Unlike Judith, the book of Tobit is set in the diaspora. The book opens with the introduction of a faithful family, Tobit and Anna and their son, Tobias, who live in Nineveh because they were deported by the Assyrian Empire. After a brief genealogical superscription the story begins at 1:3 in the voice of Tobit himself. One of the

---

19. Joseph A. Fitzmyer, *Tobit* (Berlin: Walter de Gruyter, 2003), 10–28. Carey A. Moore argues that the Maccabean revolt formed the late boundary for the composition of Tobit and leaned toward a date early in the third century BCE and a setting for composition in the eastern diaspora. See Moore, *Tobit: A New Translation with Introduction and Commentary*, Anchor Bible 40A (New York: Doubleday, 1996), 41.
20. Ibid., 50–54.

distinct features of the story is the family's devotion to the torah of Moses. Tobit's descriptions of his temple worship and offerings in 1:3–9 introduce the idea of torah observance. Even after being deported, he keeps the dietary laws and claims God granted him favor with the Assyrian king Shalmaneser (1:13). It is when this king dies that Tobit's good fortune comes to an end and the story becomes complicated. The implication is that, like in canonical books such as Ezra-Nehemiah, the fortune of an Israelite depends upon divine influence on a foreign king. Tobit's charitable and faithful habit of burying Israelites killed in and around Nineveh becomes the source of his trouble. At one point he is forced to flee the city and eventually becomes blind from the droppings of birds falling in his eyes when he must sleep outside after burying a body. The prayer of Tobit after his misfortune is reminiscent of Judith's prayer. Like Judith, Tobit acknowledges that the judgments of God upon his ancestors for their sins were just (3:3–4), but unlike her he sees his own suffering as punishment for current sins, and he asks God for death (3:6).

Tobit's prayer for death provides occasion to move the story to a new location hundreds of miles away in Ecbatana in Media. There a young woman named Sarah, who will turn out to be a relative of Tobit's, is also praying for death. Sarah has lost seven consecutive husbands, each on their respective wedding nights, to the power of the demon Asmodeus, and when her story opens in 3:7–9 a female servant of her father is accusing her of killing them herself. She considers taking her own life, but decides against it and asks God to take her life instead. God responds to the prayers of the two distant characters by sending the angel Raphael to help them.[21]

The hero of the story is Tobit's son, Tobias, whom his father sends to Media to recover some money he had left there. Before sending

---

21. Fitzmyer contends that "the efficacy of heartfelt prayer," to which God responds by sending help through an angelic mediator, is a major emphasis of the book (*Tobit*, 159).

Tobias on the journey, Tobit instructs him to fear God and live in a way consistent with the law. A young man whom Tobias recruits to make the journey with him and whom he calls Azariah (meaning "the Lord helps") turns out to be Raphael, and Tobit pronounces God's blessing on his son and the angel and sends them on their way. The decisive event on the course of the journey occurs on the bank of the Tigris River, when a fish tries to bite Tobias's foot, and he catches the fish and cuts it up according to Raphael's instructions. Along the way, Raphael explains to Tobias how he can use the heart and liver to chase away a demon and the gall to cure blindness. The story moves along quickly in Tobit 7, as Raphael guides Tobias to the house of Raguel (Sarah's father), they discover their family relationship, and Tobias marries Sarah. When the wedding night arrives in Tobit 8 and Tobias and Sarah are alone, he burns the fish heart and liver, expelling the demon, whom Raphael pursues and binds.[22] Then Tobias and Sarah pray, asking God that they might grow old together. Meanwhile, Raguel digs a grave for Tobias and sends a servant to find out whether he survived the night. When Raguel and his wife discover Tobias is still alive, he also utters a prayer.[23]

Throughout the entire narrative in the book of Tobit there is a great deal of divine language. The words "God" and "Lord" appear about ninety times combined in the fourteen chapters of the book. The majority of divine designations are in the speech of the human characters, when they pray and when they pronounce blessings on each other. The most decisive action God takes is sending Raphael, an action the narrator describes in 3:17 and Raphael confirms to Tobit and Tobias in 12:14–15, when he discloses his angelic identity. Titles

---

22. There is also a text in 1 En. 10:4 in which Raphael binds the demonic figure Azazel. On the connections between these two passages, see ibid., 243.
23. For more on the significance of prayers in Tobit, see Patrick J. Griffin, *The Theology and Function of Prayer in the Book of Tobit* (Washington, DC: Catholic University of America, 1984).

for God in Tobit, such as Most High (1:13 and 4:11), King of heaven (13:7, 11), King of the ages (13:6, 10), and Lord of heaven (6:18; 7:16; 10:11; etc.), demonstrate a transcendent view of God, who must use angels to work on earth; but the constant prayers of the main characters and the reference to God as "our Father" in 13:4 offer some qualification of the theology of transcendence.[24] At the same time, Moore argues that Tobit provides "a major step in the evolution of biblical understanding of demons and, especially angels."[25] The conflict between Raphael and Asmodeus portrayed in Tobit became significant in the development of Jewish tradition about supernatural beings operating in the human world.

Tobit helps to reveal some important connections among the disparate pieces of literature this study examines and between these pieces and the Tanak. The latter concern is fulfilled by the many reflections of older traditions in the Tobit story. The two older men in the narrative, Tobit and Raguel, resemble the patriarchs of Genesis in numerous ways, most significantly in the ways they pray to God and bless their children. The two older women, Anna and Edna, each have only one child and, though their families struggle with difficulties threatening the perpetuation of their heritage, they join faithfully with their husbands in the practice of hospitality; so they look like Sarah, Rebekah, Rachel, and Hannah.[26] Young Tobias resembles many biblical characters, such as Jacob and Moses, who must leave home and family but benefit from divine presence and care along the way; and one of those benefits is finding a wife in their temporary home. Sarah is reminiscent of Tamar and Ruth. All three

---

24. For a more thorough discussion of transcendence and references to God, see Moore, *Tobit*, 27–28.
25. Ibid., 28.
26. On the many parallel attributes between the Tobit characters and the Israelite ancestors, see Irene Nowell, O.S.B., "The Book of Tobit: An Ancestral Story," in *Intertextual Studies in Ben Sira and Tobit*, ed. Jeremy Corley and Vincent Skemp (Washington, DC: Catholic Biblical Association of America, 2005), 4–7.

suffer the deaths of husbands and, having no children yet, depend upon the custom of levirate marriage for redemption and progeny. Tobias and Sarah become engaged and married in scenes similar to the betrothals of Isaac and Rebekah in Genesis 24, Jacob, Rachel, and Leah in Genesis 29, and Moses and Zipporah in Exodus 2.[27] The story of Tobias reminds readers of Israelites in the past who endured trials outside the promised land with God's assistance. Tobias is a faithful and heroic young Israelite living in foreign contexts like Daniel, Esther, and Susanna, but the book of Tobit also demonstrates God's continuing concern for the Israelite homeland. The dying speech of Tobit in 14:1–11 acknowledges the destruction of Israel and the scattering of its people by the Assyrians and Babylonians, but looks ahead to the restoration of Israel and rebuilding of the temple, thus joining the stories of diaspora heroes to the land of Israel and its future.[28]

A final aspect of Tobit points forward toward the advancement of Israelite wisdom literature in the Hellenistic period, the primary subject of the next chapter. Several interpreters have attempted to demonstrate parallel patterns in Tobit and Job, a connection the Latin version of Tobit in the Vulgate mentions specifically.[29] Tobit and Job suffer from physical affliction, pray for death, and receive a divine restoration in the end. Both books make heavy use of themes of light and darkness.[30] Perhaps more important than the structural

---

27. For more on the parallel betrothal scenes in Tobit and Genesis, see ibid., 9–10. On the connections between Tobias/Sarah and Moses/Zipporah, see Irene Nowell, "The Book of Tobit: Introduction, Commentary, and Reflections," in *The New Interpreter's Bible*, ed. Leander E. Keck (Nashville: Abingdon, 1999), 3:981–82.
28. Carey A. Moore demonstrates the connections between Tobit 14 and Deuteronomy. There has been some debate concerning the status of Tobit 13–14 in the history of composition of the book. Moore summarizes these positions and argues effectively that whether or not the final two chapters and the tale of Tobias have the same origin, chs. 13–14 are integral to the book of Tobit and its purpose. See Moore, *Tobit*, 294–96.
29. On this element in the Vulgate, see Anathea E. Portier-Young, "'Eyes to the Blind': A Dialogue between Tobit and Job," in Corley and Skemp, *Intertextual Studies in Ben Sira and Tobit*, 14.
30. Nowell, "Book of Tobit," 982.

similarities of the narratives, Portier-Young emphasizes how both stories tend to the subject of exile: "Yet just as the author of Tobit develops the theme of chaos common to Job and Tobit to symbolize the condition of exile, so the author expands this theme of restoration to include the rest of Israel."[31] The portrayal of God's interaction with humans in Tobit thus acts as an important point of connection among many traditions, both older than and contemporary with its own composition, in the diaspora and in a restored Israel.

Greek Daniel 1–6, 13–14

The Apocrypha inherits a Greek translation of the Hebrew and Aramaic book of Daniel and adds three significant texts to it. One of these is an insertion into Daniel 3, which contains the story of the three young men, friends of Daniel, thrown into a furnace by Nebuchadnezzar. The insertion is most commonly known by a title that is a description of its two primary components, "The Prayer of Azariah and the Song of the Three Jews." The other two additions, commonly referred to as Susanna and Bel and the Dragon, are typically placed at the end of the book as Daniel 13–14.[32] All three additions fit with the tales that make up Daniel 1–6, so they will be treated here, while the apocalyptic visions in Daniel 7–12 will be discussed in chapter 6. The Greek text of Daniel presents significant difficulties because it exists in two different forms, most often labeled the Old Greek and the Theodotion texts. According to the writings of St. Jerome in the late fourth to early fifth century, the Theodotion text replaced the Old Greek in Christian usage by the fourth century,

---

31. Portier-Young, "'Eyes to the Blind,'" 26–27.
32. There is one Greek tradition, that of Theodotion, that places the story of Susanna at the beginning of the book of Daniel, a placement that seems logical because the story introduces Daniel as if this is his first appearance to the audience (v. 45). For more detail, see Louis F. Hartman and Alexander A. Di Lella, *The Book of Daniel: A New Translation with Introduction and Commentary*, Anchor Bible 23 (Garden City, NY: Doubleday, 1978), 24.

so the Theodotion text is found in the early Greek manuscripts of the Christian Bible that are more properly called the Septuagint.[33] The discussion below will distinguish between the two when textual differences create different portrayals of the divine character, and will attempt to give preference to the Old Greek version, the one that would have been in existence before the turn of the eras.[34]

The portrayal of God as a narrative character in Daniel 1–6 in the Hebrew and Aramaic version of the book is relatively minimal in scope but significant in its direction. Table 3-1 lists the explicit divine actions in this part of the book.

Table 3-1

Divine Actions in Daniel 1–6[35]

1:2 "The Lord gave King Jehoiakim of Judah into [Nebuchadnezzar's] hand"

(NRSV) "The Lord let King Jehoiakim of Judah fall into [Nebuchadnezzar's] power"

1:9 "God gave Daniel to kindness and compassion"

(NRSV) "Now God allowed Daniel to receive favor and compassion"

1:17 "and God gave these four boys knowledge and skill"

2:23 "You have given me wisdom and power"

"You have revealed to me"

"You have revealed to us"

---

33. The most important representative of the Old Greek, Papyrus 967, was rediscovered in 1931. On the significance of this manuscript and its relation to the Theodotion text, see Tim McLay, *The OG and TH Versions of Daniel* (Atlanta: Scholars Press, 1996), 1–7.
34. On the differences between the two texts and how they operate as translations, see R. Timothy McLay, "Daniel," in *A New English Translation of the Septuagint*, ed. Albert Pietersma and Benjamin G. Wright (New York: Oxford University Press, 2007), 991–92. There is now general agreement that the Theodotian text is an independent translation of a Hebrew text, but whether the two Greek versions used the same Hebrew and Aramaic text is uncertain. See John J. Collins, *Daniel: A Commentary on the Book of Daniel* (Minneapolis: Fortress Press, 1993), 220.
35. The contents of this table are taken from McEntire, *Portraits of a Mature God*, 194–95. Each of these phrases is my own, somewhat literal, translation. I have also provided the NRSV rendering in cases where this smoother translation contributes significantly to the discussion.

3:17 "Our God whom we serve is able to deliver us"

3:28 "who has sent his angel and delivered his servants"

4:34 "the Most High …who lives forever"

4:34 "his dominion is an everlasting dominion and his kingdom endures"

4:35 "He does according to his will"

5:18 "The Most High God gave Nebuchadnezzar your father kingship"

5:21 "Until he knew that the Most High God rules the kingdom of men"

6:17 "May your God whom you serve continually deliver you"

6:23 "My God sent his angel, who shut the mouths of the lions"

It is important to recognize that the divine character here is one who acts in only vague and indirect ways. When God delivers Daniel and the three friends in these stories it is through the action of angels, through attributes given to the young men, or by exercising internal influence over foreign kings. The prayer of Azariah makes one general statement about God's character, that he is just (v. 4), and it describes several of God's actions in the past in verses 5–9, focusing specifically on God's appropriate judgment against Israel for its disobedience to God's commands. The poem proceeds to request actions of God in the future in verses 11–22, all in relation to the deliverance of Azariah and his companions in the furnace. Such requests must be heard within the context of the qualified claim, also included in the Hebrew/Aramaic version of the book of Daniel at 3:17–18, that the God of Israel is able to deliver the young men, but they are uncertain if he will. It is important to note that the qualification of divine deliverance is not present in the Old Greek text. A close comparison of the three texts may be helpful here:

Daniel 3:17–18 in the Different Versions of the Book

Masoretic Text (NRSV) – "If our God whom we serve is able to deliver us from the furnace of blazing fire and out of your hand, O king, let him deliver us. But if not, be it known to you, O king, that we will not serve your gods and we will not worship the golden statue that you have set up."

Masoretic Text (trans. Louis F. Hartman) – "If there is a God able to save us, such as our God whom we serve, he will save us from the white-hot furnace and from your hand, O king. But even if there were not, you can be sure, O king, that we would not serve your gods or worship the golden image you have set up."[36]

Old Greek Text (NETS) – ". . . for there is God who is in heaven, our one Lord, whom we fear, who is able to deliver us from the furnace of fire, and out of your hands, O king, he will deliver us. And then it will be clear to you, that we will neither serve your idol nor will we do obeisance to your gold image, which you have set up."

Theodotion Text (NETS) – ". . . for there is a god whom we serve, able to deliver us from the furnace blazing with fire, and out of your hands, O king, he will rescue us. And if not, let it be known to you, O king, that we will not serve your gods, and we will not do obeisance to the image, which you have set up."

Hartman's more literal translation of the Aramaic at the beginning of v. 17 makes the first theological problem more evident.[37] The NRSV renders the phrase so that it is about God's ability rather than existence. There is not enough information about the transmission of the text of Daniel to make certain evaluations, but it looks like the Theodotion text was translated from a version closer to the Masoretic Text than was the Old Greek. Peter Coxon argues that both Greek translators made theological adjustments, particularly in the removal

---

36. Louis F. Hartman and Alexander A. Di Lella, *The Book of Daniel: A New Translation with Introduction and Commentary*, Anchor Bible 23 (Garden City, NY: Doubleday, 1978), 155.
37. On the difficulties of the Aramaic grammar and syntax, see Peter W. Coxon, "Daniel III 17: A Linguistic and Theological Problem," *Vetus Testamentum* 26 (1976): 400–402.

of the conditional element at the beginning of verse 17.[38] The other theological challenge lies at the beginning of verse 18, the phrase missing entirely from the Old Greek. Hartman's translation shifts the meaning here by use of the subjunctive, a move that, by his own admission, makes it "a hyperbolic statement that we have rendered as a condition contrary to fact, to preserve the martyrs' orthodoxy."[39] The transmission of the story, including translations both ancient and modern, shows signs of some negotiation about God's ability or willingness to intervene in order to save faithful servants. Carol Newsom emphasizes the potential scandal of a conditional statement and the apparent efforts by ancient and modern translators to remove the conditional sense.[40] None of the texts is willing for the three young men to be executed as martyrs, but the Masoretic Text and the Theodotion Greek text seem willing to raise the possibility that they could be.

The poem called the Song of the Three Jews has a narrative introduction in which an angel descends to protect the young men, a type of mediated divine action consistent with the whole of Daniel 1–6. The angel cools the temperature inside the furnace, thus rescuing the young men, who then sing a song that contains no less than thirty-eight statements of blessing about the God of Israel. The God about whom they sing is one who is highly exalted and enthroned in the heavens (vv. 30–34). The prayer for deliverance in the first poem is answered in the second, and the predicted restoration of the divine reputation is celebrated in song. As Nickelsburg observes, "The poems convert the story from mere narrative to quasi-liturgical drama, eliciting the involvement of an audience attuned to such liturgical tradition."[41] The song ends with a crescendo of

---

38. Ibid., 401.
39. Hartman and Di Lella, *Daniel*, 162.
40. Newsom, *Daniel*, 110–11.
41. Nickelsburg, *Jewish Literature*, 27.

blessing and thanksgiving for the God who has saved the three young men. This is a salvation, however, that does not include any of the traditional elements of covenant, such as land, offspring, and prosperity. It is specifically being rescued from death by persecution at the hands of a foreign power.

The story of Susanna appears in Daniel 13, after the apocalyptic visions, and follows a surprising plot, much different from the earlier stories. Like Daniel, Susanna is a Jew living in Babylon, but the forces that threaten her are not foreign. Instead, it is the lust and deceit of two Jewish elders that creates the predicament that threatens her life. The occasion allows for the introduction of Daniel, who is able to act on behalf of the deity. As in the shorter version of Daniel, divine behavior is restricted to internal influence on humans. In verses 44–45 God hears the cry of distress from the condemned Susanna and "stirs up" the spirit of Daniel, whose wit allows him to expose the deceit of the elders and rescue her from death. The cleverness of Daniel, befitting that of a modern detective, is also on display in the story called Bel and the Dragon. For most of the story, Israel's God is only present as the object of Daniel's worship and devotion. Daniel exposes the trickery of the priests of Bel and poisons the dragon, exposing both as false deities and justifying his own faith in God to his patron, King Cyrus of Persia.

Daniel's heroics and the subsequent conversion of Cyrus lead to an alternative version of the famous story of Daniel in the lions' den and an occasion to connect Daniel to the land of Israel in a startling manner.[42] The angel of the Lord visits a prophet named Habakkuk in Judah and, after a brief conversation, carries him by the hair, along with food he had been preparing, to the entrance of the lions' den in Babylon. After giving Daniel the food, Habakkuk

---

42. On the literary relationships between the two stories, see Collins, *Daniel*, 410–12.

is immediately returned to Judah. The story does not state explicitly that God prevented the lions from eating Daniel, but they do not. He remains in the den seven days, and God's provision of food through the angel and Habakkuk becomes a significant element of his survival. The story also connects Cyrus, the royal sponsor of Judah's restoration, with a prophet of the exilic period.

Chapter 6 of this book will return briefly to Daniel 13–14 in the Greek version as part of the discussion of the apocalyptic visions in Daniel 7–12. Daniel 13–14 has so much in common with Daniel 1–6 that it is necessary to ask why they are placed at the end of the Greek version. The result of the placement is that in the Greek version the apocalyptic visions do not close the book, but are fully surrounded by diaspora tales.

Greek Esther

The famous absence of any mention of God in the book of Esther has often eliminated the book from theological discussions. There have been two kinds of responses to this exclusion. One is that the presence of God is assumed in the story, while the other is that divine absence or invisibility is a theological assertion. The textual history of Esther is too complex and uncertain to attempt any kind of reconstruction here.[43] The primary focus will be on the effects of the major additions in what is most commonly called the Greek version of Esther on the presentation of the divine character.[44] There is general agreement that the additions came late in the process of the development of the

---

43. See the attempt to reconstruct that history and explain the existence of the various extant texts in David J. A. Clines, *The Esther Scroll: The Story of the Story* (Sheffield: JSOT Press, 1984), 139–40.
44. This is a simplified view of the Greek tradition of Esther because it exists in two distinct forms, though the form called the Alpha-Text is present in only a small number of manuscripts. For more on this textual situation, see Karen H. Jobes, "Esther," in *A New English Translation of the Septuagint*, ed. Albert Pietersma and Benjamin G. Wright (New York: Oxford University Press, 2007), 424.

story and, among other things, they make God an overt character within it. The labels given to the six major additions, A through F, can be confusing when juxtaposed with the chapter numbers they were eventually assigned in St. Jerome's presentation of Esther. The lettered designations place the additions in their more original positions in the Septuagint version of the story, and this study will follow that convention.[45]

Addition A is the dream of Mordecai that opens the Greek version of the book, and the dream is portrayed as divine communication that informs Mordecai of the divine plan (11:12). As Nickelsburg observes, the dreams also function to connect Mordecai, who is a rather undefined figure in the Hebrew version of the story, with characters like Joseph and Daniel.[46] The final addition (F) is Mordecai's recollection and interpretation of the dream at the end of the story, so the dream serves to frame the entire book and provide it with an overt religious context and a deity who is a character in the story, even if only one that acts indirectly by sending dreams to human characters. Addition C contains prayers uttered by Mordecai and Esther. Both prayers refer to God as "king," downplaying the power of the human king to whom the two characters are close. Both prayers also remind God, and the reader, of great work in Israel's past, using the ancient phrase "God of Abraham." Like the story into which the prayers are inserted, they assert that Israelites can operate in a foreign court while still acknowledging God as king and remembering God's faithfulness. The prayers are not misfits in the story, but they display openly the private piety that readers can only assume in the Hebrew version of Esther.

In addition D, during Esther's meeting with the king, the narrator reports that God "changed the spirit" of Artaxerxes. David Clines

---

45. See the explanation in Nickelsburg, *Jewish Literature*, 202–3.
46. Ibid., 202.

observes that the language here is reminiscent of the divine work on foreign kings in Ezra-Nehemiah. Clines argues further that one of the primary effects of the Esther additions is to bring the story into line with the portrayals of the deity in Ezra-Nehemiah and Daniel.[47] Clines points to a smaller change in the Greek text that is not part of an addition, when in 6:1 the Greek text attributes Artaxerxes's lack of sleep directly to God.[48] Addition E contains a decree of Artaxerxes that opens much like the letter in Addition B, but the Persian king speaks in more overtly religious tones, declaring the Jewish people to be "children of the living God" (v. 16). In giving instructions for the posting of the decree Artaxerxes expresses his belief that Israel's God "rules over all things" and managed the events of that time to assure the joy of the chosen people (v. 21). Clines contends that the overall effect of the additions is to magnify the nature of the threat and God's action to avert it.[49] If this is true then the portrayal of the divine has moved somewhat beyond that found in Ezra-Nehemiah.

One element that sets the story of Esther apart from Daniel and Tobit is that, like in the plot of Judith, the threat is against the entire Jewish community. Unlike Judith, however, the story of Esther takes place in a foreign land. Otzen calls such tales "rescue-stories" and links them most closely to the stories of Moses, Joshua, and the judges in the Tanak, but this association masks important differences.[50] In the end, the Greek text of Esther does not change the most important aspect of the divine behavior in the Hebrew text. The salvation of the Jewish people still depends upon the foreign king's permission to defend themselves (8:11), and there is no description of direct divine intervention on their behalf. The ending of the story of Esther varies somewhat in the Greek versions. In the Old Greek the Jews receive

---

47. Clines, *Esther Story*, 168–70.
48. Ibid., 170.
49. Ibid., 172–73.
50. Otzen, *Tobit and Judith*, 69–70.

permission to defend themselves (8:13), and they do so by defeating their enemies and killing fifteen thousand of them (9:16), a smaller number than reported in the Masoretic Text and the Alpha-Text (9:16). No text reports any details of the battles or claims any specific divine assistance, so the role of the divine character in struggles of the Jewish people remains invisible.

3 Maccabees

Despite its deceptive name, the little book called 3 Maccabees probably fits best with these texts that tell stories of faithful Israelites living in the diaspora whom God protects in moments of persecution. Unlike the examples above, the narrative setting for most of the book is Alexandria, Egypt, rather than Mesopotamia.[51] Third Maccabees is in the canon of some Orthodox Christian traditions and is preserved in Codex Alexandrinus and several other Greek manuscripts. It appears to have been written in Greek and dates for its production vary from late in the second century BCE to almost any point in the first century BCE.[52] A portion of the book (1:8–2:24) is set in Jerusalem, but the time of the story is several decades prior to the Maccabean revolt, to which the book has no connection, so the source of the book's name is a mystery.

---

51. Interpreters have made significant efforts to connect 3 Maccabees and Esther because of the structural and thematic parallels between the two. Noah Hacham successfully demonstrates that these parallels are inadequate to demonstrate any kind of literary dependence. Rather, a series of linguistic features demonstrates a dependence of the royal letters added to the Greek version of Esther on 3 Maccabees. The effect of this borrowing is to align the view of Jewish-gentile relations in Esther more closely with the view in 3 Maccabees, creating a greater sense of hostility between the two. See Noah Hacham, "3 Maccabees and Esther: Parallels, Intertextuality, and Diaspora Identity," *Journal of Biblical Literature* 4 (2007): 765–85. The effect of this issue on divine behavior involves the way in which God acts toward gentile rulers. In 3 Maccabees, Philopater is a hostile enemy whom God must assault in order to protect the Jews. In Hebrew Esther, Ahasuerus does not demonstrate this kind of enmity toward the Jews, but the letter of Artaxerxes in Addition B does.
52. For a more thorough discussion of manuscripts, language, and authorship, see N. Clayton Croy, *3 Maccabees* (Leiden: Brill, 2006), x–xiv.

The brief opening story of the battle between the Ptolemaic King Philopater and the Seleucid Antiochus III in 1:1–7 seems present only to serve as the occasion for Philopater's visit to Jerusalem in 1:8–2:24 as part of his victory tour. The initial story also introduces the idea of Jewish apostasy by describing Dositheus, who saves Philopater from assassination, as a Jew who has abandoned his traditions.[53] Philopater's visit to Jerusalem begins well when he offers a sacrifice to Israel's God in 1:9, but trouble quickly arises when he insists upon entering the holy of holies, and Philopater's inappropriate request rouses the entire community into prayer and lamentation for the sanctity of the temple. The narrator refers to Israel's God here as "the supreme God."[54] The wailing of the people leads to a great prayer by the high priest Simon II in 2:1–20. The prayer recalls great acts of God in the past, particularly those aimed at the arrogant and the powerful, such as the citizens of Sodom and the pharaoh of the exodus. At verse 9 attention turns to Jerusalem and the temple and God's role as Israel's king, and Simon reminds God in verse 10 that "because you love the house of Israel, you promised that if we should have reverses and tribulation should overtake us, you would listen to our petition when we come to this place and pray."[55] The priest acknowledges that Israel's suffering is the result of its sins (v. 13), but does not identify those sins, because the central point is that the great sin is the one about to happen if Philopater does what he wishes. Lest the idea of God being in any danger arise, Simon emphasizes in verse 15 that "your dwelling is the heaven of heavens, unapproachable by human beings." Rather, God's glory resides in the sanctified temple, and if

---

53. For more on the role of Jewish-gentile tensions and the role of apostasy in the story, see Nickelsburg, *Jewish Literature*, 201.
54. Quotations of 3 Maccabees are from the NRSV, unless otherwise noted.
55. The promise recalled by Simon resembles the request made by Solomon concerning the original temple in 1 Kgs. 8:33 and confirmed by YHWH in 9:3. For more detail on this point, see Croy, *3 Maccabees*, 54–55.

the foreigners profane it, Israel's sins will be multiplied. So preventing an unlawful entry of the temple will not only protect the honor of God but also will be an act of mercy toward Israel.

The supplication of Simon is successful, and, in shockingly direct language, God attacks Philopater and beats him senseless in 2:22. Afraid that he will die, Philopater's friends drag him away, but he returns to Egypt and increases his persecution of the Jewish community there. The movement of Philopater returns the story to Egypt for its third and longest episode. The persecution divides the Jewish community between those who save themselves by participating in the cult of Dionysus and those who remain faithful. The latter group angers the king who orders the Jews in the Alexandria area to be arrested. The arrest order is introduced in 3:11 as an act of defiance against "the supreme God." When the king's people gather all the Jews of Egypt they register and imprison them in the hippodrome at Schedia. Philopater plans to have a herd of intoxicated elephants brought in to attack the Jews in the hippodrome, but God intervenes to thwart the first two attempts by putting the king into a deep sleep (5:11) and causing him to forget his orders and become confused (5:28). Only on the third attempt do the elephants finally enter the hippodrome, and when the Jewish community appears at the brink of death a priest named Eleazar utters a prayer recalling great acts of protection performed by Israel's God in the past, including the defeat of Pharaoh and the Egyptians at the sea, the destruction of Sennacherib's army, and the rescues of Daniel and his friends in Babylon. The request for rescue by Eleazar in 6:10–12 appeals to God's reputation, for though the Jews may deserve divine punishment, its execution by the hand of gentiles would place God's power in doubt.[56]

---

56. For more on this point, see Croy, *3 Maccabees*, 101–2.

The end of Eleazar's prayer brings decisive divine action in 6:18: "Then the most glorious, almighty, and true God revealed his holy face and opened the heavenly gates, from which two glorious angels of fearful aspect descended, visible to all but the Jews."[57] The result of this event is a reversal of the king's attitude. Both his immediate command to release the Jews in 6:24–28 and his letter supporting them in 7:2–9 express faith in Israel's God and in that God's care and concern for the Jewish people. The divine intervention in 3 Maccabees is much more dramatic than in the rescue stories set in Mesopotamia, but the conversion of the foreign king is a decisive common element.

Conclusion

The protecting God moves in many directions in the stories of heroic Jewish young people examined above. The stories are international in scope, and most of them occur outside the Jewish homeland. Most involve interaction with foreign persons of great political and military power. The interactions among the foreigners, the Israelite characters, and the divine character vary tremendously. In Judith the foreigners, Holofernes and Nebuchadnezzar, are military enemies of the Israelites, and Judith is able to dupe the former, in part because of his knowledge of Israelite traditions. In Daniel the foreign kings are oppressors of the Jewish people, but in some cases only because they are duped by their own officials. The foreign kings demonstrate great admiration for Daniel, and they eventually express faith in Israel's God because of Daniel's loyal service and God's actions to protect Daniel and his friends.

Perhaps the most important theological move these stories make collectively is their acknowledgment that suffering may come to the

---

57. On the significance of angelic participation and possible explanations for why the Jews were prevented from seeing them, see ibid., 103–4.

faithful not because of sin, but precisely because of their faithfulness. In all of these cases the faithful Jewish characters ultimately receive some kind of vindication, so their suffering is a temporary condition, but such an acknowledgment raises difficult questions about the divine character. To what extent is God willing and able to help God's faithful servants? Is there some other purpose to suffering if it is no longer a corrective discipline for disobedience to God's law? Can the readers or hearers of these stories always expect the same kind of divine vindication at the end of their own suffering? Elements like the statement of the three young men in Dan. 3:17 and its complicated history of transmission and reception renegotiate the central theological questions of the diaspora stories. Even a story like Esther, with all of the added piety of the Greek additions, only gives the Jewish people permission to fight to protect themselves. Third Maccabees offers more direct divine actions on behalf of the Jewish people, though all of these are strange in character. The result, however, is a similar one. The Jewish people win the favor of the foreign king along with the status and protection that come with that favor.

4
―――

God of the Defeated and Scattered, Part III

Chapter 2 examined works of literature from the Hellenistic period that reached into Israel's past to reformulate it and develop new points of emphasis. In many cases this involved a reformulating of the stories of the past so they could address the needs of new contexts. The wisdom literature in the Tanak is famously unattached to Israel's story, and the situation was apparently already a recognized problem in the Hellenistic period because later wisdom writers sought to fix it. The two major representatives of the literature, Sirach and the Wisdom of Solomon, both connect wisdom explicitly to the story of Israel and its institutions. The primary purpose of the later wisdom literature still seems to be guidance, so that is where this chapter will begin, but it will also need to address directly the implications of attaching the task of guidance in an international context to some of Israel's narrative traditions.

A Guiding God

The wisdom literature is an element of uncertain significance in the Tanak, but the Apocrypha has augmented it with the addition of two large books, Sirach and the Wisdom of Solomon, and the smaller book called Baruch. There is a significant amount of disagreement about the purpose and audience of Proverbs, Ecclesiastes, and Job, and I have argued that the lack of specific connections to the covenant with the ancestors, the exodus story, and the religious institutions of Jerusalem connect these books most logically to diaspora Judaism.[1] The international character of Proverbs, for example, makes it a set of instructions that can travel with Israelites into foreign lands and guide them in a place with no temple or priesthood. Jewish young people like Daniel, Esther, and Tobias seem ideal recipients of such instruction. If this is true, then it would not be surprising that the Hellenistic period witnessed the continued development and expansion of wisdom material, with necessary adjustments to new cultures and perhaps even some responses to theological problems posed by the earlier literature. What might be surprising is the degree to which the book called Sirach moves back toward the peculiar traditions of Israel and its religious institutions. The books of Job, Proverbs, and Ecclesiastes do not have the same lack of overt religiosity that characterizes the Hebrew version of the

---

1. See the discussion of this in McEntire, *Portraits of a Mature God: Choices in Old Testament Theology* (Minneapolis: Fortress Press, 2013), 199–201. Two developments in twentieth-century scholarship helped reveal the difficulties surrounding this part of the canon. First, the grand "Old Testament theologies" of the middle of the century struggled to fit the wisdom material into their schemes. The struggle resulted most famously in the separate volume on wisdom by Gerhard von Rad, which explains the difficulty at the outset. See Gerhard von Rad, *Wisdom in Israel*, trans. James D. Martin (Nashville: Abingdon, 1972), 3–15. The second development was a growing tendency in the early part of the second half of the twentieth century to place more and more of the material in the Tanak into the wisdom literature category because of its imprecise definitions, a practice that came to an end primarily with the publication of James Crenshaw's article, "Method in Determining Wisdom Influence upon Historical Literature," *Journal of Biblical Literature* 88 (1969): 129–42.

book of Esther, but their presentation of the divine character is not specifically Israelite, and that may be a difficulty some later wisdom writers sought to resolve. The book of Proverbs moves from the context of Solomon's court in 1:1 to the court of Lemuel, a foreign king, in 31:1. Gregory Mobley argues that the "backstory" of the wisdom literature is a divine design of the cosmos that humans can only occasionally glimpse.[2] The broad spectrum of such an element of faith allows it to operate in an international milieu. The imposition of a Solomonic framework onto Proverbs and Ecclesiastes may indicate attempts to draw the wisdom tradition into a more particularly Israelite mold, but these were not very successful. Ecclesiastes and Job seem especially resistant to such theological control. In Mobley's words, "the questions raised in these books in particular serve as antidotes to the poisonously parochial pieties of many other parts of Scripture."[3] Later wisdom writers appear to have been making a more concerted effort to bring the wisdom tradition back home and to attach it more rigidly to other Israelite traditions.

Sirach

The book most commonly called Sirach often sounds so much like Proverbs that it seems a natural fit for the Old Testament, but this quality also means it bears many of the same interpretive difficulties as the preeminent wisdom book in the Tanak. There are no difficulties establishing a date for Sirach with adequate precision in the pre-Maccabean, Hellenistic period. Perhaps more important in understanding the purpose of the book and its portrayal of Israel's God, however, is its implied geographical setting. There is a tendency among interpreters to place it in Seleucid Palestine, based

---

2. Gregory Mobley, *The Return of the Chaos Monsters—and Other Backstories of the Bible* (Grand Rapids, MI: Eerdmans, 2012), 110–14.
3. Ibid., 111.

primarily on two texts near the end of the book. One of these is the designation of the author in 50:27 as "Jesus son of Eleazar son of Sirach of Jerusalem."[4] The other is the emphasis placed on the temple and the high priest, Simon son of Onias, in 50:1–21.[5] The degree of certainty about time and place, however, may not produce a clear picture of the audience, or a sense of how collections of proverbial sayings fit into the understanding of the world the book is constructing. Proverbs exudes a confidence and certainty about life that does not connect with the experience of many readers, while Job and Ecclesiastes seem to challenge that certainty. In this regard, Sirach matches Proverbs more closely, and its assumptions about the dependability of the world, like those of Proverbs, seem to be aimed at a privileged class of persons. An important aspect of this privilege is maleness, and many readers find Sirach notoriously misogynistic. While such teachings are not frequently stated directly in terms of divine behavior, the opening verse of Sirach, after the prologue, frames everything that follows with a divine origin:

> All wisdom is from the Lord,
> and with him it remains forever. (1:1)[6]

So questions about whether Sirach's divine character is a God for an elite, male class will persist.

Sirach contains a wide variety of literary units, including two prayers in 22:27–23:6 and 36:1–22, an element not present in Proverbs. Prayers create divine behavior by casting God in the role of listener, and in their affirmations and requests they at least imply

---

4. There are textual problems involving the geographical phrase. On this and other issues surrounding this verse, see Leo G. Perdue, *The Sword and the Stylus: An Introduction to Wisdom in the Age of Empires* (Grand Rapids, MI: Eerdmans, 2008), 259.
5. See the discussion of this in John J. Collins, *Jewish Wisdom in the Hellenistic Age* (Louisville: Westminster John Knox, 1997), 23–24.
6. Unless otherwise noted, quotations of Sirach are from the New Revised Standard Version.

the kind of divine behavior assumed by the one who is praying. In the first prayer, the speaker is asking God, whom he calls "O Lord, Father and Master of my Life" (23:1, 4), for help controlling his speech and desires. He wants help against "enemies," but these appear to be gluttony and lust (23:6) rather than other people who are opposing or hurting him. In the second prayer the speaker wants God to "have mercy" (36:1), to "lift up your hand" (36:3) against foreign nations, and to act on Israel's behalf to gather the people (36:13) and protect Jerusalem (36:18). James Crenshaw argues that the speaker of the second prayer "gives vent to frustration over God's apparent inactivity," asking for "new signs" (36:6).[7] The speaker seems to long for the God of long ago, who is now hard to see in the midst of world affairs. So the first prayer aligns better with the type of concerns common in the wisdom literature of the Tanak, in its emphasis on careful human behavior and the struggle against destructive desires, but Sirach seems to be trying to bring together these sorts of individual, internal matters with concerns for the communal and national welfare of the Jewish people, expressed in the second prayer.

Another poem in 24:1–34 is reminiscent of Proverbs 8 as Wisdom, portrayed as a female figure, sings of her own beginnings and her part in God's creation of the world. The poem in Sirach takes a different turn, however, when it connects the wisdom/creation tradition specifically to Israel and its national religious traditions. In 24:3 Wisdom is like a mist covering the earth, much like the stream in Gen. 2:6; and Sir. 24:23–29 uses the images of the four rivers from Gen. 2:10–14, but it adds a fifth, Israel's river, the Jordan. Most significantly, the poem places Wisdom in Israel, in the tabernacle and "established in Zion" (24:8–12), and, finally, connects her to the

---

7. James Crenshaw, "Sirach: Introduction, Commentary, and Reflections," in *The New Interpreter's Bible*, ed. Leander E. Keck (Nashville: Abingdon, 1994), 5:617.

"law that Moses commanded us" in 24:23. The part of Israel's story to which the book of Sirach most closely corresponds includes the resurgence of a national Israel in the Maccabean period, so bringing Wisdom home from its international, wandering journey in this way is fitting. At the same time, the connection of Wisdom to torah in an age in which textuality would have made the torah increasingly portable would not have limited Wisdom geographically the way connecting divine presence to the temple before the exile would have. The Hellenistic period may have allowed the attachment of divine Wisdom to two sets of traditions, one tied to the Jewish homeland and the other available in the diaspora.

The depiction of the divine character in the book of Sirach is difficult to describe for many of the same reasons it is difficult in the wisdom literature of the Tanak. Wisdom often seems to operate as an invisible force built into the world by God in the work of creation, which functions as a vague mediation of divine presence. A good place to see this is in the poem in Sir. 42:15–43:33. Because this text makes extensive use of creation traditions from Genesis 1, Job 38–41, and several creation psalms, points of agreement and disagreement with those traditions are relatively easy to identify.[8] More significant for this study may be the tension between Sirach and 1 Enoch on these issues. Sirach 42:18–20 defines God as the one who knows everything, both in the depths of the earth and the human heart:

> He searches out the abyss and the human heart;
>   he understands their innermost secrets.
> For the Most High knows all that may be known;
>   he sees from of old the things that are to come. (v. 18)

---

8. See Nuria Calduch-Benages, "The Hymn to Creation (Sir 42:15–43:33): A Polemic Text?," in *The Wisdom of Ben Sira: Studies on Tradition, Redaction, and Theology*, ed. Angelo Pessario and Giuseppe Bellia (Berlin: Walter de Gruyter, 2008), 121–23.

In Sirach 15, the writer appears to address directly some who might deny human free will:

> Do not say, "It was he who led me astray";
>   for he has no need of the sinful.
> The Lord hates all abominations;
>   such things are not loved by those who fear him.
> It was he who created humankind in the beginning,
>   and he left them in the power of their own free choice. (vv. 12–14)

The book of Sirach has moved to a clear position that human choices and behavior are not overridden by God. God is available to guide and deliver, but bad choices and their effects are the responsibility of humans.[9] The question of human free will versus divine determinism is a major issue in Sirach and became a significant component of the divisions within sectarian Judaism. John Collins argues that there is still significant tension on this point in Sirach because of the book's retention of an emphasis on divine omnipotence.[10] Shaye Cohen includes these opposing ideas among several "conflicting truths" or "antinomies" that Jewish thinkers of the time period seemed to be able to hold simultaneously.[11]

The creation poem in 42:15–43:33 punctuates a long collection consisting mostly of proverbial sayings. The poem opens with this declaration:

> I will now call to mind the works of the Lord,
> and will declare what I have seen. (42:15)

As the introduction indicates, the poem is less a record of what God did long ago to create the world and more a set of observations about

---

9. On this text and its significance, see Friedrich V. Reiterer, *"All Weisheit stammt vom Herrn…": Gesammelte Studien zu Ben Sira* (Berlin: Walter de Gruyter, 2007), 206–13.
10. Collins, *Jewish Wisdom in the Hellenistic Age*, 80–84.
11. Shaye J. D. Cohen, *From the Maccabees to the Mishnah*, 3rd ed. (Louisville, KY: Westminster John Knox, 2014), 102.

the world's current operation.[12] The first section in 42:15–25 focuses its attention on the extent of God's knowledge and understanding, and how the operation of the world reflects divine qualities. The second stanza, 43:1–12, treats the sun, moon, and stars in turn, with an emphasis on orderliness and reliability of movement. The third stanza in 43:13–26 describes divine control of the weather and the sea, and the final, brief section in 43:27–33 urges the reader to glorify God because of all the qualities of creation, concluding with:

> For the Lord has made all things,
> and to the godly he has given wisdom. (43:33)

The implication is that the godly understand the orderliness with which the world operates under divine control and, therefore, they know how to act appropriately within it. While there is some dispute about the origins of the individual parts of Sirach, the flow of the final form of the book is smooth and clear at this point. The expansive text that follows, the Hymn in Honor of Our Ancestors in 44:1–50:24, exemplifies the godly, who possess wisdom from God.[13]

While the great hymn is primarily about human heroes of Israel, God also emerges as a significant character in their descriptions. Much of this poem, like some texts examined in chapter 2 of this book and others still to be presented in this chapter, may be described as either rewritten Scripture or an interpretation of Scripture. This part of the book of Sirach retells much of the narrative portion of the Tanak in brief poetic form. While there are poems in the book of

---

12. In this way, the poem is perhaps most similar to Job 38–41 and Proverbs 30. On these similarities, see Patrick W. Skehan and Alexander A. Di Lella, O.F.M., *The Wisdom of Ben Sira: A New Translation with Introduction and Commentary*, Anchor Bible 39 (New York: Doubleday, 1987), 491–96.
13. There are two major questions concerning the boundaries of the hymn. The first concerns the relationship with the preceding poem about creation in 42:15–43:33. The second is the place of 50:1–29 in relation to the rest of the poem. This is the section about the high priest, Simon son of Onias, which has no parallel in the Tanak. For the various positions on both of these issues, see Thomas R. Lee, *Studies in the Form of Sirach 44–50* (Atlanta: Scholars Press, 1986), 3–21.

Psalms that do this, such as Psalm 106, the striking difference is that Sirach 44–50 praises men directly, and if it praises God such divine praise is only indirect. Because of this feature and others, Thomas Lee classifies Sirach 44–50 as an *encomium*, a type of literature within classical Greek rhetoric that is intended to praise a great person. Moreover, the person that the poem wishes to praise in the end is the high priest, Simon son of Onias.[14] Perhaps most significant for this study is the recognition that the goal of the book of Sirach here to praise Simon means that the preliminary presentations of the great figures in Israel's past focus on their priest-like actions as divine intermediaries.[15] This observation provides an important lens through which to view the divine actions in this part of the book of Sirach. Table 4-1 contains a list of the divine actions presented in Sirach 44–45. What is apparent from looking at the list is that the primary focus is on God's interaction with these men—Abraham, Isaac, Jacob, Moses, Aaron, and Phinehas—in order to select and elevate them and to provide them with what they needed to perform their roles.

---

14. Ibid., 81–103.
15. Ibid., 15–21.

AN APOCRYPHAL GOD

Table 4-1

Divine Actions in Sirach 44–45

44:2	"The Lord apportioned to them great glory"
44:17	"Noah was found perfect and righteous"
44:18	"Everlasting covenants were made with him"
44:21	"Therefore the Lord assured him with an oath"
44:21	"that he would make him as numerous as the dust"
44:21	"and exalt his offspring"
44:21	"and give them an inheritance"
44:22	"To Isaac also he gave the same assurance"
44:23	"he made to rest [the blessing and the covenant] on the head of Jacob"
44:23	"he acknowledged him with his blessings"
44:23	"and gave him his inheritance"
44:23	"he divided his portions"
44:23	"and distributed them among twelve tribes"
44:23	"the Lord brought forth a godly man"
45:1	"and [he] was beloved by God"
45:2	"He made him equal in glory to the holy ones"
45:2	"and made him great, to the terror of his enemies"
45:3	"the Lord glorified him"
45:3	"He gave him commandments"
45:3	"and revealed to him his glory"
45:4	"he consecrated him"
45:4	"choosing him out of all"

The overall effect of such a presentation is to make the divine character primarily one who appoints those who lead Israel. Given this understanding, it is also helpful to ask about divine action in Sir. 50:1–24, the poem about Simon son of Onias, which produces interesting results because there are very few. The poem mentions God approximately ten times, most often as "the Most High." In most cases, God is the recipient or object of human actions. The first implied divine action comes in verse 21 where those who worship him "receive the blessing from the Most High." Following this verse is a prayer acknowledging a few actions of God and requesting a few more:

> And now bless the God of all,
>   who everywhere works great wonders,
> who fosters our growth from birth,
>   and deals with us according to his mercy.
> May he give us gladness of heart,
>   and may there be peace in our days
>   in Israel, as in the days of old.
> May he entrust to us his mercy
>   and may he deliver us in our days! (50:22–24)

The actions of the divine character here are in response to proper worship, which again emphasizes the significance of the priestly role.

With so much invested in the high priest Simon, including the orderly creative power of God flowing through the wisdom given to humans, such as those listed in Sirach 44–49, and coming to rest on this one figure, it may be important to look more carefully at Simon. Why is Ben Sira himself and/or the book of Sirach so intent on providing support for one particular priest? Benjamin Wright argues that Sirach 50 is a polemic against those who have been critical of the Jerusalem priesthood. He finds such views reflected primarily in contemporaneous writings like 1 Enoch and Aramaic Levi, where groups of marginalized priests may have been expressing their dissatisfaction with the priests who were in power in Jerusalem.[16] Such disputes had theological import because they determined who acted as the mediator of divine behavior. In

Wright's view, "Ben Sira's social world was one in which differing and competing notions of scribal wisdom and priestly legitimacy were hotly contested."[17] In the midst of the contest, the book of Sirach displays the priestly work of Simon as a reflection of God's creation and of the work of the great heroes of Israel's past. The degree to which Sirach describes Simon as a reflection of the divine character is surprising in 50:11:

> When he put on his glorious robe
>   and clothed himself in perfect splendor,
> when he went up to the holy altar,
>   he made the court of the sanctuary glorious.

In other contexts, it might seem more natural for such words to be spoken of YHWH. Specifically, it is the "glory of YHWH" that dwells in the temple in Ezekiel and the cloud associated with YHWH's glory that fills the temple on occasions like its dedication in 1 Kings 8 and 2 Chronicles 7. Have Simon himself and the priesthood become the glory of YHWH? The presentation of Simon finishes with a great priestly blessing and doxology in 50:20–24, in which the mercy of YHWH flows onto the people from the mouth of Simon.[18] For Ben Sira, Simon would have represented the ideal priest during the latter part of his life, and the death of Simon gave way to conflict over the priesthood between two of his sons. Onias III was the designated successor, but Jason sought Seleucid support for

---

16. Benjamin G. Wright III, *Praise Israel for Wisdom and Instruction: Essays on Ben Sira and Wisdom, the Letter of Aristeas and the Septuagint* (Leiden: Brill, 2008), 123–25.
17. Ibid., 126.
18. For more detail on the linkage of Simon with YHWH, see Otto Mulder, "Two Approaches: Simon the High Priest and YHWH God of Israel / God of All in Sirach 50," in *Ben Sira's God: Proceedings of the International Ben Sira Conference*, ed. Renate Egger-Wenzel (Berlin: Walter de Gruyter, 2001), 224–32. Mulder particularly highlights the differences between the Greek and Hebrew manuscripts here, demonstrating the significance of the use of divine names in the Hebrew text (224) and the reference to the "covenant with Phinehas" in the Hebrew text of 50:24, making Phinehas the most significant precursor to Simon (231).

a program to hellenize Judaism and eventually assumed the office of high priest.[19]

The conclusion of the book of Sirach comes back to the person of Jesus, son of Sirach, and emphasizes his role as a teacher. Sirach 44–50 connects the wisdom tradition to the narrative of Israel's past, including the great ancestors and Moses, but it seems more significant that it connects the wisdom tradition to Israel's institutional religious present, the priesthood and the temple. The use of divine designations is abundant in the book of Sirach, about twice as frequent as in the book of Proverbs, for example. Perhaps most notable is his use of the title "Most High." This English designation translates the Hebrew *Elyon* and the Greek *hypsistos*, and the use of it in Sirach moves beyond the limits of its relatively small number of appearances in the Tanak.[20] Still, divine presence and behavior are mediated through creation, which merges wisdom, temple, and torah.[21]

Baruch

The apocryphal book of Baruch introduces itself as a work written by Baruch, son of Neriah, the famous scribe of Jeremiah, while he was in Babylon in the sixth century. Within the narrative constructed by 1:1–9 it is a book he wrote in order to read it to the exiled heir to the throne, Jeconiah, and others who were with him in captivity.[22] The actual date and audience of the book are difficult

---

19. For a more detailed discussion of these events and their impact, see Perdue, *Sword and the Stylus*, 261–62.
20. Robert C. T. Hayward, "El Elyon and the Divine Names in Ben Sira," in Egger-Wenzel, *Ben Sira's God*, 180–98.
21. Perdue, *Sword and the Stylus*, 287–88.
22. The narrative introduction to the book of Baruch presents major chronological challenges, most of which are not relevant to this discussion. Whether the presumed narrative setting is between the deportations in 597–586 or after the destruction of Jerusalem in 586–538 is a matter that might affect the understanding of some passages and how they relate to the audience outside of the book, but the question is ultimately unresolvable. For a more thorough

to determine because of its composite nature. The most common view is that the prayer of confession in 1:15–3:8 is directed toward an audience in the Jewish homeland, but other portions, like the wisdom poem in 3:9–4:4 are addressed to the diaspora.[23] Most of the first two chapters of the book are a recollection of Israel's past, leading up to the exile in Babylon. Beginning at 1:15, the recollection takes the form of a penitential prayer. The fragmentary nature of the book makes it difficult to place within Israel's story, but the strong connection between the prayer in Bar. 1:15–3:8 and Daniel 9 makes a placement near the discussion of Daniel 7–12 a possibility. Baruch is not an apocalyptic book but, like Daniel, it appears to use the Babylonian setting to talk about a later time of trial for Israel.[24] A better path probably emerges from looking at the structure of the whole book, which links the recital of Israelite tradition in the prayer with the presentation of a wisdom poem in 3:9–4:4. This wisdom poem is enclosed by the final portion of the book (4:5–5:9), which is an exhortation to the audience to continue to look to God for comfort and deliverance. An important clue appears in the midst of the wisdom poem in 4:1:

> She is the book of the commandments of God,
>   the law that endures forever.
> All who hold her fast will live,
>   and those who forsake her will die.[25]

Linking wisdom with torah and the narrative tradition of Israel is a task Baruch has in common with the book of Sirach. The structure of

---

discussion, see Anthony J. Saldarini, "The Book of Baruch," in Keck, *New Interpreter's Bible*, 6:939–40.

23. See the discussion of multiple audiences and the tension they create within the book in Carey A. Moore, *Daniel, Esther, and Jeremiah: The Additions; A New Translation with Introduction and Commentary*, Anchor Bible 44 (Garden City, NY: Doubleday, 1977), 257–59, 291.
24. This book is sometimes labeled 1 Baruch in order to distinguish it from other books that have Baruch's name on them.
25. Quotations from Baruch are from the New Revised Standard Version.

the book wraps this move in Israel's past (1:1–3:8) and its present and future (4:5–5:9).

The prayer of confession acknowledges God's judgment of Israel and accepts it as just: "The Lord our God is in the right, but there is open shame on us and our ancestors this very day. All those calamities with which the Lord threatened us have come upon us. Yet we have not entreated the favor of the Lord by turning away, each of us, from the thoughts of our wicked hearts" (2:6–8). An important issue that has already been litigated in the book of Jeremiah and the book of Ezekiel flows out of this acknowledgment as it leads to a plea in 3:5: "Do not remember the iniquities of our ancestors, but in this crisis remember your power and your name." Much of Israel's tradition, perhaps centered in Exod. 34:6–7, recognizes the authority of YHWH to punish later generations for the sins of previous ones, but the "new covenant" presented in Jer. 31:27–34 pushes back against this idea, promising that there will be no more inherited punishment. The book of Jeremiah may not proceed all the way to a doctrine of individual sin and punishment, but it at least makes each generation collectively responsible for itself. The assumption of Jer. 31:33 is that with the weight of inherited guilt removed, it will be possible for each new generation to maintain its covenant relationship with YHWH. The book of Ezekiel takes the issue a step further in 18:1–32, stating unequivocally in the divine voice in verse 4, "Know that all lives are mine; the life of the parent as well as the life of the child is mine: it is only the person who sins that shall die." This is a striking change in divine behavior, and Bar. 3:1–8 counts on at least Jeremiah's version of the new divine way, pleading for God to remove the "calamities [that] have clung to us" (3:4), hoping that if the guilt of the past is removed then new life might be possible. For those in exile, Baruch makes this claim: "we have put away from our hearts all the iniquity of our ancestors who sinned against you" (3:7). This sets up the wisdom poem that follows to be the "fear of you in our hearts" (3:7), leading to a new way of life for the Jewish people.

The presentation of the fear of God (3:7) as that from which wisdom flows brings the book of Baruch into close contact with the central core of Israelite wisdom (Prov. 1:7), and the wisdom poem can proceed to connect wisdom to other components of Israelite tradition. While the wisdom tradition tends to assume a more international scope, the wisdom poem in Baruch emphasizes the failure of the human search for wisdom, and the provision of wisdom as a divine gift specifically for Israel.[26] Like other literature from the Hellenistic period, Baruch portrays God as living in heaven, yet the assumption of the book is that God can still act in the world to help Israel. In 2:16, the prayer asks, "O Lord, look down from your holy dwelling, and consider us. Incline your ear, O Lord, and hear." The prayer goes on to remind God that the dead cannot praise him while even the weakest living person can, so this sounds like a prayer for survival in the midst of circumstances threatening death. The significance of acknowledging the just punishment of God in the past is to claim God can now remove such punishment.

The theological assumptions behind a text like Bar. 2:11–26 seem to be moving toward the spatial dualism characteristic of apocalyptic literature. Apocalyptic dualism probably developed separately from the traditional idea of divine removal that is behind the wisdom tradition, but the two sets of assumptions are compatible. In Baruch 2 God is removed from the earth and dwelling in another place, but is still capable, if convinced, of coming down to help the petitioners.[27]

---

26. The closest parallels within the wisdom literature are probably Job 28 and Sirach 24, the latter of which connects wisdom specifically to Israel's religious institutions. For more on this point, see Saldarini, "Book of Baruch," 965–69.
27. On the conflicted views of God in the wisdom poem and the surrounding materials, including the variation in the use of divine designations, see Moore, *Daniel, Esther, and Jeremiah*, 259.

The highly developed angelology of apocalyptic books is not present in a wisdom book like Baruch, but its thought represents the beginnings of the merger of these traditions that would take place in the centuries to follow.[28] Baruch also lacks the imminent eschatology and the division of the Jewish people into insider/outsider or righteous/wicked groups found in most apocalyptic literature.

Baruch ends with a lengthy lament poem in 4:5–5:9. The poem concludes with an expression of hope and trust for the restoration of Jerusalem, which includes the reunification of the Jewish people:

> Arise, O Jerusalem, stand upon the height;
>   look toward the east,
> and see your children gathered from west and east
>   at the word of the Holy One,
>   rejoicing that God has remembered them.
> For they went out from you on foot,
>   led away by their enemies;
> but God will bring them back to you,
>   carried in glory, as on a royal throne. (vv. 5–6)[29]

The issue Baruch does not address is timing. When will the restoration come about and what will cause the change in fortune of the Jewish people? Is it dependent upon the people to take action against their oppressors, or are they simply to wait for direct divine intervention? If the former, then who would be the leaders of such a movement?

The Wisdom of Solomon

The book often called simply Wisdom is almost certainly later than the book of Sirach, and most interpreters agree that Alexandria

---

28. For more on the merging of these traditions, see Perdue, *Sword and the Stylus*, 370–71.
29. Most commentators recognize a dependence upon the language and ideas of restoration in Isaiah 40–66. For example, see Saldarini, "Book of Baruch," 971–73.

around the turn of the eras is the most likely setting for its production. The book is most often divided into three sections based on shifts in tone of the speaker and subject matter, though there is some disagreement about where these divisions fall. The opening chapters have an unmistakable eschatological concern. It is apparent from the beginning that Wisdom is operating in a different world, with a different set of assumptions than the wisdom literature preceding it. The most striking of these assumptions is the possibility of human immortality, and the primary concern of the "book of eschatology" (1:1–6:21) is to delineate between the righteous who will receive such immortality and the wicked who will not.[30] Wisdom literature prior to the Wisdom of Solomon does not present the idea of immortality, so the source of the concept has been a matter of contention. Collins argues that the source is primarily Greek tradition, so the Wisdom of Solomon represents a blending of Israelite wisdom and Hellenistic thought.[31] It portrays God as the one who created humans with purity and immortality as possibilities (2:23), and who protects and guards the righteous to help them toward these goals (3:1; 4:15). The Wisdom of Solomon does not back away from the logical implication arising from these claims that the righteous have been chosen for divine favor while the wicked were not chosen, and it draws sharp distinctions between the righteous and the unrighteous, in contrast to the unified picture of Israel in Baruch.[32] The development of concerns common to apocalyptic literature in Baruch expands in the Wisdom of Solomon.

While the concept of wisdom frames the discussion of immortality in Wisdom 1–6 and is a characteristic of the righteous, it emerges

---

30. The "book of eschatology" label originates with J. M. Reese, and has been used by a number of interpreters since. See Reese, *Hellenistic Influence on the Book of Wisdom and Its Consequences* (Rome: Biblical Institute Press, 1970), 109–14.
31. Collins, *Jewish Wisdom in the Hellenistic Age*, 185–86.
32. For more on the division of people into two distinct groups in Wisdom, see ibid., 193–95.

more prominently in the middle section of the book (6:22–11:1). The royal language in 7:1–14 leads to the common recognition of the speaker as a king, and the more specific reference to the task of building the temple in 9:8 points to Solomon as the character describing and praying for wisdom here.[33] The role of the divine character is to be one who grants wisdom to the speaker:

> O God of my ancestors and Lord of mercy,
> who have made all things by your word,
> and by your wisdom have formed humankind
> to have dominion over the creatures you have made,
> and rule the world in holiness and righteousness,
> and pronounce judgment in uprightness of soul,
> give me the wisdom that sits by your throne,
> and do not reject me from among your servants. (9:1–4)[34]

The idea that the earthly king who is praying here is to be a reflection of God the heavenly king is present in many places throughout this section, so the speaker in the book becomes a manifestation of God who speaks to people on earth. The spatial dualism of apocalyptic literature is present to some extent here, as God's direct actions in the world are placed in the past at creation and in the story of the exodus, which will be reiterated in Wisdom 11–19. The primary task of the Solomonic voice in this section is to introduce the character

---

33. The question of authorship must be divided into two more precise questions here. There is a near scholarly consensus that the writer of the book is an Alexandrian Jew around the turn of the eras. At 6:22 a speaker emerges, using first-person language, and this speaker is best identified as Solomon. Because this is an assumed identity, it can be appropriate to refer to this speaker as pseudo-Solomon, but the idea that this pseudo-Solomon is a literary persona adopted by the writer of the entire book is problematic. The first-person language is restricted to 6:22–9:18, so it is more precise to identify this Solomon or pseudo-Solomon as a character in the book and the speaker of this one section, not as the narrator or implied author of the whole book. See the similar approach of Michael Kolarcik, S.J., "The Book of Wisdom: Introduction, Commentary, and Reflections," in Keck, *New Interpreter's Bible*, 5:437–43. For a view contrary to this, see Andrew T. Glicksman, *Wisdom of Solomon 10: A Jewish Hellenistic Reinterpretation of Early Israelite History through Sapiential Lenses* (Berlin: De Gruyter, 2011), 6–7. Glicksman chooses the convention of referring to the author of the book as pseudo-Solomon.
34. Quotations of the Wisdom of Solomon are from the New Revised Standard Version.

of personified Wisdom, in a way that makes use of and builds upon Proverbs 8–9 and Sirach 24. In all of these traditions, the behavior of Wisdom is an aspect of divine behavior because Wisdom acts on God's behalf. Michael Kolarcik divides the work of personified Wisdom into two categories, one of which has to do with the relationship between Wisdom and humans. Wisdom is the one who formed human beings and gave them dominion over other creatures, assuming tasks Genesis 1–2 assigns directly to God. Second, according to Ws. 8:1, Wisdom has a cosmic function, as the one who puts and keeps the universe in order.[35] This portrayal of Wisdom is similar to those found in Proverbs 8 and Sirach 24, but the book of Wisdom goes further to attach this work to the establishment of the nation of Israel.

The third section of the Wisdom of Solomon is the one that most overtly connects the wisdom tradition presented in the book with the story of Israel. Andrew Glicksman argues effectively for understanding Ws. 10:1–11:1 as the transitional element that holds together the two halves of the book. Most significantly, it combines its discussion of personified Wisdom with its presentation of Israelite history. The portrayal of personified Wisdom in 10:1–21 includes protection and assistance for the ancestors, including Adam (vv. 1–2), Noah (v. 4), Abraham (v. 5), Lot (v. 6), Jacob (vv. 10–12), and Joseph (vv. 13–14). In addition to this, the abandonment of Wisdom by others, such as Cain (v. 3) and Lot's wife and the other residents of Sodom (vv. 7–8), led to their downfall. Wisdom's care and protection extend to Moses in verse 16 and finally to the Israelites in the exodus in verses 17–21. This final section of Wisdom 10 even credits personified Wisdom with bringing the Israelites across the Red Sea and drowning the Egyptians. This is an entirely new kind of portrayal of this character, who had not previously been connected

---

35. Kolarcik, "Book of Wisdom," 493–94.

to a specific event in Israel's past, but had only been responsible for creation in general. This development leads to the expansive and fascinating presentation of the exodus story in Ws. 11:1–19:22.

The language of the exodus section is confusing because 11:1 still seems to speak of personified Wisdom: "Wisdom prospered their works by the hand of a holy prophet." This verse creates enormous difficulties and there has been a wide-ranging array of attempts to resolve them by scholars and translators of the book of Wisdom. The Greek text does not mention Wisdom, but some translators, like those of the NRSV, reach back to the previous verses to bring forward this subject for the verb in 11:1, *euodōse*.[36] A better choice seems to be to let "their works" be the subject of the verb rather than its object, and this translation has been followed by many recent interpreters.[37] Even if Wisdom is retained in 11:1, this character vanishes, however, and the voice of the text begins to address God using second-person pronouns in 11:4–5:

> When they were thirsty, they called upon you,
> and water was given them out of flinty rock,
> and from hard stone a remedy for their thirst.
> For through the very things by which their enemies were punished,
> they themselves received benefit in their need.

Table 4-2 below presents a list of divine actions from Wisdom 11, and many such paired, or mirror-image, elements are present. Moyna McGlynn identifies seven "diptychs" in Wisdom 11–19 that contrast God's treatment of the Israelites with God's treatment of the Egyptians, and the first of these is in 11:1–14.[38] While the apparent shift to direct divine activity may be confusing, the principle of

---

36. Part of the rationale for doing this seems to be that this verb needs to be transitive, but this claim has been refuted. See David Winston, *The Wisdom of Solomon: A New Translation with Introduction and Commentary*, Anchor Bible 43 (Garden City, NY: Doubleday, 1979), 226.
37. See, ibid., 225–26 and Samuel Cheon, *The Exodus Story in the Wisdom of Solomon: A Study in Biblical Interpretation* (Sheffield: Sheffield Academic Press, 1997), 26–30.

divine behavior illustrated here is clear and significant. The means used to destroy the Egyptians are the same as the means used to save the Israelites. The first case of this is in 11:4–5 (printed above), where water both kills and preserves life. These verses in the first diptych proceed with other paired divine actions, such as the judgment of God in 11:10, which is like the action of a parent to the Israelites, but like an oppressive king to the Egyptians.

Table 4-2

Divine Actions in Wisdom 11

11:4	"water was given them"
11:7	"you gave them abundant water unexpectedly"
11:8	"showing by their thirst"
11:8	"how you punished their enemies"
11:9	"the ungodly were tormented when judged in wrath."
11:10	"you tested them as a parent does in warning"
11:10	"but you examined the ungodly as a stern king does"
11:15	"you sent upon them a multitude of irrational creatures"
11:17	"your all-powerful hand, which created the world"
11:17	"did not lack the means to send upon them"
11:20	"But you have arranged all things by measure"
11:23	"But you are merciful to all"
11:23	"for you can do all things"
11:23	"you overlook people's sins"
11:24	"you love all things that exist"
11:24	"[you] detest none of the things that you have made"

---

38. Moyna McGlynn, *Divine Judgment and Divine Benevolence in the Book of Wisdom* (Tübingen: Mohr Siebeck, 2001), 170–219.

11:24 "you would not have made anything if you had hated it"

11:25 "if you had not willed it"

11:25 "anything not called forth by you"

11:26 "You spare all things"

11:26 "you who love the living"

A careful examination of divine actions in the remainder of Wisdom 11 reveals the question the writer is working to resolve: How could a God who created the world, including all human beings, treat part of that creation cruelly, as an enemy? This is a question addressed directly in 11:24:

> For you love all things that exist,
> and detest none of the things that you have made,
> for you would not have made anything if you had hated it.

This claim is possible because the writer demonstrates that God did not choose to punish or destroy anyone, but rather "arranged all things" (v. 20) in such a way that the same forces could bring both life and death, depending upon human behavior.

The second diptych, in 16:1–3, contrasts the destructive force of animals on the Egyptians, presumably plagues like frogs, flies, and gnats, with the nourishment of the quails sent to the Israelites in the wilderness. The third of these constructions, in 16:5–15, builds upon the second by acknowledging the struggle of the Israelites with poisonous snakes in the wilderness. The survival of those who turned toward "a symbol of deliverance" (v. 6)[39] is contrasted with the Egyptians who died from the bites of locusts and flies (v. 9). Perhaps the most interesting of these mirror-image portrayals is in 16:16–29,

---

39. This description of the bronze serpent on a pole from Num. 21:4–9 evades the problematic understanding of the object as an image or idol, violating the second commandment. Instead it is a symbol pointing to the law. See the discussion of this exegetical difficulty in James L. Kugel, *The Bible as It Was* (Cambridge, MA: Belknap Press, 1997), 479–82.

where the destructive forces of rain, hail, and fire, falling from heaven to punish the Egyptians, are contrasted with manna falling from heaven to nourish the Israelites. This is the fourth diptych in McGlynn's scheme, and it includes this remarkable claim;

> Instead of these things you gave your people food of angels,
> and without their toil you supplied them from heaven with bread ready to eat,
> providing every pleasure and suited to every taste. (v. 20)

The book of Wisdom seems quite willing to embellish the divine care of Israel here, not only ignoring the tradition in Num. 11:1–9 where the Israelites had to work quite hard to make the manna edible and did not find it altogether satisfying, but also going so far as to name it the "food of angels."[40] The manna in this exodus story represents far more than just physical food, for it becomes a metaphor for the devotion to the word of God and to prayer (vv. 26-28).[41] The fifth diptych in 17:1–18:4 presents a greater logical challenge. The contrast is between the plague of darkness in Egypt and the pillar of fire guiding the Israelites through the wilderness. This would seem to violate the idea that the same thing can bring both punishment and salvation, but the difficulty is seemingly resolved by the Egyptians' choice of darkness to hide their sins in 17:3, even though light was available to the whole world, according to verse 20.[42] The sixth diptych in 18:5–25 pairs the attempts by Pharaoh to kill the Hebrew baby boys with the final plague, the death of the Egyptian firstborn sons.

---

40. For more on this tradition, see Tobias Nicklas, "'Food of Angels' (Wis. 16:20)," in *Studies in the Book of Wisdom*, ed. Géza G. Xeravits and Jósef Zsengellér (Leiden: Brill, 2010), 83–100.
41. See the further discussion of this aspect in McGlynn, *Divine Judgment and Divine Benevolence in the Book of Wisdom*, 198–99. McGlynn proposes that manna, a manifestation of wisdom, might even be equated with torah here, though the latter is not specifically mentioned.
42. McGlynn notes the abundance of death imagery associated with darkness in this section. Because the move toward darkness is associated with choosing false worship, it carries a particularly ominous punishment (ibid., 204–6).

The overall effect of the recasting of the exodus story in Wisdom 11–19 is that it ceases to be a story in which YHWH chooses to liberate a specific group of people and does battle against their enemies and oppressors in order to accomplish this task. Instead, it is a story about how the world God has created, infused with wisdom, produces a different fate for those who act righteously and those who act wickedly. One of the great benefits of this view is that nobody is labeled as God's inherent enemy, but the fate of humans depends on their own actions and creation's response, and the punishing effects of this arrangement of creation can even bring about repentance.[43]

Glicksman provides a careful analysis of the similarities and differences between the portrayal of the exodus in Ws. 10:15–21 and Wisdom 11–19, the most striking of which is who performs the acts of salvation for Israel.[44] The differences may be resolvable, however, by careful attention to 10:20, where, even though personified Wisdom has performed the act of deliverance at the Red Sea, the Israelites address God in response:

> they sang hymns, O Lord, to your holy name,
> and praised with one accord your defending hand.

Wisdom 11:2–19:22 is speech to God, which may be understood as a long hymn of praise concerning the deliverance of Israel in the exodus event. While personified Wisdom may be characterized as the agent of God in the world, she is not worshiped.[45]

As the discussion above indicates, the Wisdom of Solomon moves the Israelite wisdom tradition in two different directions

---

43. My understanding of the function of the exodus story as told in Wisdom 11–19 is similar to that of Cheon, *Exodus Story in the Wisdom of Solomon*, 150–53.
44. Glicksman, *Wisdom of Solomon 10*, 174–77.
45. Glicksman also observes the connections between the portrayal of personified Wisdom in the book of Wisdom and the Egyptian goddess Isis (ibid., 175). The potential of mimicking Egyptian idolatry may have been one more factor mitigating against any sense of worshiping Wisdom.

simultaneously. Like Sirach, it attaches wisdom more specifically to other Israelite traditions, but it also demonstrates a willingness to incorporate new ideas from its Hellenistic context.

Conclusion: The Attachment of Wisdom to Israel's Narrative Traditions

One reason books like Proverbs, Job, and Ecclesiastes avoided nationalistic elements may have been that they were written for a diaspora faith. Such a faith needed to be portable, and not dependent upon stationary religious institutions and traditions. Eventually, however, the Israelite narrative tradition, including the torah, became more portable once it was fully textualized, and this made it more usable for the wisdom tradition. The discussions of the books of Sirach, the Wisdom of Solomon, and Baruch above have already identified some of the ways these books individually make use of traditions that earlier wisdom writings avoided. Additional understanding may now come from looking at how this aspect of the individual books combines with and relates to the other books of the period.

Perhaps the strongest connection between the wisdom material of the Hellenistic era and the kind of narrative literature examined in chapter 2 of this book (literature that often revised Israel's narrative past) was the need to understand the origins of evil. Sirach had a clear precedent in Proverbs 8 for attaching wisdom to creation in texts like Sir. 24:1–34 and 42:15–43:33, but his use of the garden of Eden story in 25:24–26 was novel, to say the least. It is difficult to keep the question of the origin of sin as a cosmic force and the source or cause of individual sinful acts separate. First Enoch found the origins of sin as an entity in the story of the fallen angels. Is Sirach making an equivalent kind of statement by locating the origin of sin in Eve?

> From a woman sin had its beginning,
> and because of her we all die.
> Allow no outlet to water,
> and no boldness of speech to an evil wife.
> If she does not go as you direct,
> separate her from yourself. (Sir. 25:24–26)

Saying Eve committed the first sin is not the same thing as saying she is the cause of the pervasiveness of sin in the world. As described above, Sirach contends in 15:11–20 that human beings have free will, so sin cannot be blamed on God. Collins is correct about the unfortunate nature of the statement in 25:24 because of its misogynistic possibilities, and that this seems to be an "ad hoc comment."[46] He may be correct that "Sirach addresses the origin of sin most directly in 15:11–20,"[47] but this text hardly gets at the question of the origin of sin in the world, other than saying God did not do it. The origin of sin in a metaphysical sense does not seem to concern Sirach, or at least it is a question to which he has no answer. His concern is how to act in a world in which sin exists, and his view is that humans should accept responsibility for their sinful action and seek divine forgiveness:

> For the Lord is compassionate and merciful;
> he forgives sins and saves in time of distress. (2:11)

Whether this is the intent of Sirach or not, the insistence on free will and responsibility and on the desire of God to forgive sins helps to move Sirach away from the notion of inherited or collective guilt,

---

46. See the discussion of this text in Collins, *Jewish Wisdom in the Hellenistic Age*, 80–81. The statement about sin beginning with the first woman is used here as a premise in an argument about how to deal with a disobedient wife. While it is "ad hoc" in the sense of being pulled briefly into an argument as an a priori assumption, that a priori nature is exactly the problem. If Sirach thinks his argument will be effective, then he is assuming universal agreement with this assumption, so it must express a widespread way of thinking.
47. Ibid., 81.

an idea addressed more directly in Baruch, as demonstrated in the discussion above. If those praying in Bar. 3:5 get what they are asking for, then they can no longer blame the sins of their ancestors for their own difficulties. Sirach's primary concern, to provide guidance that helps his audience avoid sin, is addressed by the attachment of wisdom to the torah of Sinai. The law of Moses is compared to the rivers that water the entire world in 24:25–27. Not only are human beings capable of making free choices, but "the Most High God" also makes an abundant means of knowing how to do so available to them (24:23). The most overt and sustained connection between wisdom and Israelite narrative tradition comes when Sirach punctuates the book with the great Hymn in Honor of Our Ancestors in chapters 44–50. The great heroes of the past were "wise in their words of instruction" (44:4), so they help to embody the teachings of those like Sirach himself.

Subtle developments in the little book of Baruch, such as a sense of spatial duality and some accommodation to Hellenistic ideas, become much more pronounced in the Wisdom of Solomon. An eschatological frame of reference and a belief in the immortality of the soul are fully present in the latter.[48] Sirach may not have presented these ideas, but demonstrated a willingness to combine wisdom with other traditions, and the writer of the Wisdom of Solomon did not view eschatology and immortality as incompatible with wisdom. The process of combining these concepts with the wisdom tradition would continue in the materials among the Dead Sea Scrolls that are often identified as sapiential in nature.[49] The

---

48. Most interpreters do not find any sense of eschatology in Sirach, and consider the few brief references (e.g., 2:9; 16:22; 19:19; and 48:11) to immortality to be additions of the Greek translator and later redactors. On this and the possibility of finding resurrection in the fragments of the Hebrew text, see Collins, *Jewish Wisdom in the Hellenistic Age*, 96.
49. On this continued development, especially in the work known as 4Q Sapiential Work A. Collins argues that this work represents a continued merging of wisdom and apocalyptic (ibid., 117–21, 226–29).

portrayal of the divine character in the wisdom tradition proved to be a particularly malleable feature in the Hellenistic period, one that helped allow the tradition to be pulled in multiple directions. Jewish writers were able to connect it to religious institutions in the Jewish homeland, obedience to torah in diaspora contexts, and an apocalyptic worldview with an eschatological focus.

5

God of Revolt

The narrative books that chapter 3 treated are primarily set in the diaspora, reporting the actions of Israel's God on behalf of Jews living outside of the homeland. The wisdom books that chapter 4 explored do not have such a definite sense of setting. Wisdom literature typically has an international sense about it, but Sirach and the Wisdom of Solomon also seek to link wisdom traditions to the religious institutions of Israel, pulling wisdom back toward geographic Israel. The movement back to Israel and its geographic identity and the Jews living there becomes more pronounced in the books called 1 and 2 Maccabees.

God Responds to Suffering with Measured Assistance

Both 1 and 2 Maccabees provide a lot of dates and disagree in some ways on the sequence of events, but precise identification of the dates of events is not essential to this study. It is more important to recognize how the evils of Antiochus and the suffering they brought upon the Jews living in Israel at the time form the stories the books of

1 and 2 Maccabees tell and the plot that the divine character enters.[1] The names given to these two books may lead some to assume that they are related to each other like 1 and 2 Samuel or 1 and 2 Kings (that is, the second follows the first chronologically), but the relationship between the two is far more complicated than this. The events reported in them overlap significantly, so following the plot they present will involve some movement back and forth between the two books.[2] The discussion of each below will attempt to follow its own narrative, but will include references to the other. The book called 1 Maccabees opens by introducing Alexander the Great, as he is most often known today. First Maccabees 1:1 calls him Alexander son of Philip, the Macedonian. This places the opening of the book in the late fourth century BCE, but it quickly moves forward through the death of Alexander, the division of his empire, and the beginning of the reign of Antiochus Epiphanes (Antiochus IV) in the early part of the second century.

Second Maccabees has a strange and confusing beginning. Two letters open the book; the first of these (1:1–9) is addressed from Jews living in Judea to their Jewish kin living in Egypt, and is dated in the year that we would call 124 BCE. It refers to another letter written nineteen years earlier, the subject of which was the hardships faced by the Jerusalem community in those days. The opening of the later letter provides a more overt religious tone for the book than 1 Maccabees expresses. Second Maccabees specifically mentions the God of Israel in its opening and recalls God as the one who made a covenant with Abraham, Isaac, and Jacob. The distance between that

---

1. For an attempt to diagram the web of dates, see John R. Bartlett, *1 Maccabees* (Sheffield: Sheffield Academic Press, 1998), 36–49.
2. Jonathan A. Goldstein even argues that the writers of the two books were "bitter opponents" who offered competing views of events in the period. See Goldstein, *2 Maccabees: A New Translation with Introduction and Commentary*, Anchor Bible 41A (Garden City, NY: Doubleday, 1983), 4.

portrait of the past and the later circumstances that made the revolt necessary is the central tension of the book. Even when these books lack overt theological statements, the story of the Maccabean revolt pushes to the front of the discussion multiple theological issues at play throughout the Jewish literature of the Hellenistic period. Does YHWH continue to act in the world and if so how? What is the role of foreign leaders in the purposes of YHWH? How should the Jewish people respond to occupying empires and to the elements of their culture? For uncertain reasons, 1 and 2 Maccabees did not become part of the Tanak, but their use by Josephus attests to a continuing influence, though their absence from the Dead Sea Scrolls may mean that such appreciation was not universal in Second Temple Judaism.[3]

1 Maccabees

Interest in 1 Maccabees has been dominated by historical concerns, in part because it provides a careful report of a period about which we have limited information elsewhere. The last two decades, however, have witnessed more careful attention to the literary development and structure of the book. David Williams uses careful delineation of literary units and observation of verbal repetition in 1 Maccabees to construct a detailed division of three sections in the book, 1:1–6:17, 6:18–14:15, and 14:16–16:24.[4] The dividing lines between these sections are the death of Antiochus IV in 6:17 and the eulogy for the great Hasmonean prince and high priest Simon in 14:4–15. The

---

3. For details on how Josephus made use of the Maccabees tradition, see Bartlett, *1 Maccabees*, 16–17. Jacob L. Wright demonstrates that 1 Maccabees parts from the biblical tradition on an important issue, the glorification of heroic death as a way to establish one's name. Rabbinic tradition also appears to have resisted such an idea, making the Maccabean literature a poor fit with the Tanak and the thinking of those who shaped the canon. See Wright, "Making a Name for Oneself: Martial Valor, Heroic Death, and Procreation in the Hebrew Bible," *Journal for the Study of the Old Testament* 36 (2011): 144–145.
4. David S. Williams, *The Structure of 1 Maccabees* (Washington, DC: Catholic Biblical Association of America, 1999), 16–71.

recent study of Francis Borchardt develops a plausible history of composition for 1 Maccabees. Because the later redactional layers Borchardt identifies added new themes to the text, they are important to recognize in a reading of the final form. The first additional layer, found in brief additions throughout the first two sections, highlights internal opposition to the Hasmoneans by a group often allied with their gentile oppressors.[5] A second layer consists of much longer texts, all within the second and third sections of the book, and includes almost all of 1 Maccabees 14–16. These additions portray the Romans and Spartans and use political documents to demonstrate the recognition of the Jerusalem high priesthood by such international groups.[6] The third layer is a smaller group of texts of medium length spread throughout the book that serve to highlight the legendary status of the Hasmoneans.[7]

The reader who enters the opening section of 1 Maccabees may begin to wonder when the God of Israel will finally make an appearance in the story, but the divine absence at the beginning helps to highlight where the first section is moving by its end at 6:17. The text implies the presence of this deity when events happen in the sanctuary in Jerusalem (1:20–23), when it mentions law and the covenant (1:56, 63), or when characters designated as priests appear (2:1). The heroic Mattathias, in the face of gentile threats, boldly declares his allegiance to "the covenant of our ancestors" and "the law and the ordinances" (2:20–21), but says nothing directly about God.[8] The initial act of Mattathias in 1:15–26 presents at least one significant interpretive problem. After he declares his allegiance to

---

5. Francis Borchardt, *The Torah in Maccabees: A Literary Critical Approach to the Text* (Berlin: Walter de Gruyter, 2014), 160–64.
6. Ibid., 164–68.
7. Ibid., 168–73.
8. Unless otherwise noted, all translations of 1 and 2 Maccabees are from the New Revised Standard Version.

the law in Modein, another man comes forward to offer a sacrifice on the altar Mattathias considers illegitimate, and Mattathias kills him. The author gives the stamp of approval to the act by attributing the zeal of Phinehas to Mattathias (2:26). The text identifies the man Mattathias kills as *Ioudaios* (2:23), but there has been significant disagreement about whether this is a geographical identification (Judean) or a religious one (Jewish). Shaye Cohen argues that 1 Maccabees precedes the use of "Jewish" as a religious and cultural designation, and that this man is a Judean who came from Judea with the Seleucid officials to enforce the commands from the king concerning sacrificial ritual.[9] Benjamin Scolnic argues, to the contrary, that a religious and cultural sense of Jewishness had developed by the time of 1 Maccabees, and that the man Mattathias kills is Jewish, and part of his own community.[10] Identifying the man as an outsider, not a member of Mattathias's community, strains the comparison to Phinehas severely, even if not to the breaking point. The text (2:26) even provides the name of the man Phinehas killed, Zimri (as given in Num. 25:14). Comparison of the two stories highlights the elusiveness of the divine character in the 1 Maccabees narrative. In Num. 25:10–13, YHWH speaks immediately to Moses, granting a reward to Phinehas for his zeal, but in the end Mattathias must declare his own zeal and his success—which is unclear until the end of 1 Maccabees 2—is the only indirect confirmation of divine approval.[11]

---

9. Shaye J. D. Cohen, *The Beginnings of Jewishness: Boundaries, Varieties, Uncertainties* (Berkeley: University of California Press, 1999), 88–89.
10. Benjamin Edidin Scolnic, "Mattathias and the Jewish Man of Modein," *Journal of Biblical Literature* 129, no. 3 (2010): 476–79. Scolnic's argument is based in part on locating Modein within Judah and in part on the other uses of *Ioudaioi* in 1 Maccabees. The real difference between the positions of Cohen and Scolnic is only about half a century in the time of a clear emergence of a religious concept of Jewishness.
11. First Maccabees 2:23–26 is a primary example of Borchardt's third redactional layer that helps to elevate the Hasmoneans to legendary status by comparing them to ancient heroes. See Borchardt, *Torah in 1 Maccabees*, 56–58.

The "zeal for the law" Mattathias urges (2:27–28) ends up being the downfall for many who refuse to obey the commands of Antiochus (because they violate the torah) and flee to the wilderness to escape persecution, because when they are pursued and attacked on the Sabbath they choose not to defend themselves and are slaughtered. It is at this point that Mattathias and his followers vow to fight back, even if attacked on the Sabbath (2:41). Throughout the purifying campaign of Mattathias and even in his dying declaration there is no mention of God, only dedication to the law.[12] The divine actions the story mentions are all in the past, the making of covenants and giving of the law, and the response of present Jews produces a paradox that causes even the zealous Mattathias to rethink and reinterpret adherence to the torah. The commitment of Mattathias and his followers produces two kinds of enemies, both the Seleucids who are their occupiers and the Jews who cooperate with the Seleucids, and 2:44–48 reports the success of Mattathias in combating both.[13] The end result is that "[t]hey rescued the law out of the hands of the Gentiles and kings" (2:48).

When the story of the son of Mattathias, Judas Maccabeus, begins in 3:1, the language becomes only slightly more overtly theological. Judas's zealous action on behalf of the law is said to "turn away wrath from Israel" (3:8). The description of Judas is another likely reference to the ancient hero of the wilderness, Phinehas, in Num. 25:10–13.[14] When questioned about the size of his army, Judas insists,

12. The claim of George Nickelsburg that Mattathias indicates that "God exacts vengeance through human agents" seems overstated. He cites 2:50, 66–68 in support of this claim, and it is difficult to find reference to the divine in these passages. See George W. E. Nickelsburg, *Jewish Literature between the Bible and the Mishnah*, 2nd ed. (Minneapolis: Fortress Press, 2005), 104.
13. There is tension in 2:44–48 concerning the identity of the opposition and the goals of the Hasmoneans and the Hasideans. Borchardt argues that the tension is the result of multiple redactional layers in this passage. In the final form of 1 Maccabees, the work of these two groups is awkwardly fused. See Borchardt, *Torah in 1 Maccabees*, 59–60.
14. For more on this connection, see Jonathan A. Goldstein, *1 Maccabees: A New Translation with Introduction and Commentary*, Anchor Bible 41 (Garden City, NY: Doubleday, 1976), 245.

"It is not on the size of the army that victory in battle depends, but strength comes from Heaven" (3:19). Finally, with the war against the forces of Antiochus going badly, 3:44 reports that "the congregation assembled to be ready for battle, and to pray and ask for mercy and compassion." As the ceremony continues with fasting, mourning, and offerings, a telling response to the divine absence appears in 3:48: "And they opened the book of the law to inquire into those matters about which the Gentiles consulted the likenesses of their gods." The analogy is stunning. The text compares the Torah to a Gentile idol. Table 5-1 compares the NRSV rendering of the verse with two other possibilities that approach it quite differently, removing the problematic analogy. Goldstein's translation assumes not only a particular way gentiles read the Torah, but also an awareness of the gentile reading by the Jewish community, all of which seems unlikely. Doran's contention that they wished to read about gentiles and their idols is not as implausible, but it does not fit the context well. The Jewish community here wants to know what to do about their difficult situation, and they inquire using not just the Torah, but also other elements of their religious tradition in 3:49.

Table 5-1

Translations of 1 Maccabees 3:48

NRSV:	And they opened the book of the law to inquire into those matters about which the Gentiles consulted the likenesses of their gods.
Doran:	They unrolled the book of the Torah concerning those things about which they were inquiring, namely the Gentiles and the likenesses of their idols.[15]
Goldstein:	They spread open the scroll of the Torah, at the passages where the Gentiles sought to find analogies to their idols.[16]

---

15. Doran proposes that Deut. 4:7 might be the Torah text to which this verse refers. See Robert Doran, "The First Book of Maccabees: Introduction, Commentary, and Reflections," in *The New Interpreter's Bible*, ed. Leander E. Keck (Nashville: Abingdon, 1996), 4:65.
16. Goldstein, *1 Maccabees*, 256.

The text does not say so directly, but the implication seems to be that the Torah fails to serve this purpose and the group finally cries out "to Heaven" in 3:50. Here the language of address in the prayer is in the second person. Though no designation for God is used, except for "Heaven," the human characters in the story are finally speaking to God, so it may be understood that God has finally become a narrative character. Law has turned out to be an incomplete mediator of divine instruction and, though 1 Maccabees uses oblique language, direct divine consultation fills the void.[17] The prayer has an effect that the previous acts, including the reading of the Torah, did not. When the congregation finishes in 3:53 with "How will we be able to withstand them, if you do not help us?" they suddenly spring into action and prepare for battle. All of the speech that fills 1 Maccabees 3 concludes with a statement from Judas himself that is reminiscent of many in the book of Judith: "It is better for us to die in battle than to see the misfortunes of our nation and of the sanctuary. But as his will in heaven may be, so shall he do" (3:59–60). Israel's God is finally at least a pronoun, and Judas believes this God has the power to help him, though it is not certain that he will choose to do so.[18]

The victory of Judas and his army at Emmaus in 1 Macc. 4:1–25 provides additional ways to talk about divine action on behalf of Israel. Confronted by a superior gentile army in 4:7, Judas encourages his soldiers in 4:9–11 by reminding them of the Israelites facing the army of Pharaoh at the Red Sea, beginning with passive language that becomes active, if vague: "Remember how our ancestors were saved at the Red Sea, when Pharaoh with his forces pursued them. And now, let us cry to Heaven, to see whether he will favor us and remember his covenant with our ancestors and crush this army before

---

17. Borchardt, *Torah in 1 Maccabees*, 205–6.
18. On the theological language in the accounts of Judas Maccabeus, see Nickelsburg, *Jewish Literature*, 104–5.

us today. Then all the Gentiles will know that there is one who redeems and saves Israel." After the victory, the soldiers sing praises to Heaven, "For he is good, for his mercy endures forever" (4:24). The report of the battle is ambiguous because there is no report of direct divine assistance, yet the Jewish army easily routs a larger, better armed enemy. The appeal to the mighty acts of God in the distant past performs two tasks. First, within the narrative, it operates in Judas's speech to encourage his troops in a frightening situation. Second, for the reader it implies by analogy a divine assistance the text seems reluctant to claim directly. The use of trumpets in a battle to defeat a superior enemy also recalls the battle of Jericho in Joshua 6 and the battle against the Midianites led by Gideon in Judges 7. Comparison with war stories of the past points precisely to what else is missing in this report. The military leader in Maccabees 4, Judas, is courageous and victorious like Joshua and Gideon, but is not the recipient of any divine discourse providing instructions for the battle. First Maccabees goes about the characterization of God in a careful and discreet manner. The characters in the story know the past and demonstrate faith in the God of Israel, but stop short of expressing expectations of divine assistance. The final line of the story of the battle at Emmaus in 4:25 epitomizes the theological speech of the book: "Thus Israel had a great deliverance that day."

The writer of 1 Maccabees develops the pattern of theological language further in the report of the battle at Lysias in 4:26–35. Once again, Judas faces a superior army, outnumbering his own sixty-five thousand to ten thousand, and he prays, addressing God as "Savior of Israel" (4:30). In his prayer, Judas speaks of the defeat of Goliath and the Philistines by David and Jonathan, so the text connects the hero of the Maccabean revolt to two more warriors and another great military victory in Israel's past. Again, the prayer uses very careful language about what God might do to assist the Jewish army.

In 4:31–33 Judas asks God to alter the enemy soldiers internally so that his army can be used by God to win the battle: "Hem in this army by the hand of your people Israel, and let them be ashamed of their troops and their cavalry. Fill them with cowardice; melt the boldness of their strength; let them tremble in their destruction. Strike them down with the sword of those who love you, and let all who know your name praise you with hymns." This text goes further in involving God in the battle, but the details come in the form of a request from a human character.

The victorious momentum of Judas leads to the central event in 1 Maccabees, the capture of the citadel in Jerusalem and cleansing of the temple on Mount Zion. The account of the event in 4:36–61 uses "Heaven" as a way of addressing the divine character. When Judas and his brothers first witness the condition of the sanctuary they mourn and cry out to Heaven (v. 40). When the cleansing of the temple and the replacement of the profaned altar are complete, so that the people can offer sacrifices, they bless Heaven (v. 55). The depiction of this moment invites comparison with two prior events, the dedication of the temple by Solomon in 1 Kings 8 and 1 Chronicles 7 and the construction and dedication of the second temple and its altar in Ezra 3 and 6. The report in 1 Maccabees is more like the latter of course because no visible cloud representing the divine glory comes down from heaven to fill the temple and demonstrate divine presence, but the divine presence is further diminished. While Ezra 6:22 declares the "the LORD had made them joyful," 1 Maccabees says only that "There was very great joy among the people" (4:58).

With Jerusalem and its temple restored, Judas and his brothers turn their attention to other parts of the land where the Jewish people are suffering at the hands of their gentile rulers. First Maccabees 5 reports the liberation of Galilee and Gilead, with very little theological language, and a strange and puzzling event occurs in 5:55–62. When Judas and his brothers had gone to Galilee and Gilead to fight, they left two men, Joseph and Azariah, in charge of Jerusalem, with specific orders not to engage in any battles. In 5:56–57 Joseph and Azariah decide to disobey Judas's orders and attack the gentile army at Jamnia, but are defeated. Thus the text puts all authority for warfare and its decisions within the sole authority of Judas and his brothers. The realization of such a position of authority highlights the absence of any overt divine selection of Mattathias and his sons as the leaders of the Jewish people. Instead, it is their own actions that bring them to positions of leadership. The defeat of Joseph and Azariah confirms the authority of Mattathias and his sons and also emphasizes their humble, selfless motives. When Joseph and Azariah decide to fight the gentiles around them in 5:57 they do so to "make a name for ourselves," in language reminiscent of the builders of Babel in Gen. 11:4.[19] Another group of priests also decides to go to battle on their own in 5:65–68 and they also fail, then Judas comes behind them and defeats the Philistines against whom the priests had failed. The penalty for not following the commands of Judas in warfare is failure and death.

First Maccabees 6:1–17 reports the death of Antiochus, the archenemy whose policies generated the revolt, and does so in a way fitting the tendencies of theological expression in 1 Maccabees. The reports of Judas's successes reach Antiochus while he is in Persia, having experienced his own military failures there. The combination of failures sends the king to his sickbed, where he does an astonishing thing. In 6:12–13 Antiochus acknowledges his own wrongdoings against Jerusalem and claims they are the cause of his illness, which will lead to his death. While he does not go so far as to repent and uses

---

19. On the making of a name through warfare in biblical tradition, see Wright, "Making a Name for Oneself," 144–53.

no direct language about God, there is in his statement an implicit acknowledgment of the power of Israel's God to punish him with death.

Meanwhile, as the story carries the reader to Persia to witness the death of Antiochus, the Jews in Jerusalem continue to suffer at the hands of their occupiers. Many interpreters acknowledge a distinct break after 6:17 and the beginning of an entirely new section at 6:18 with its own distinct structure. A series of reversals in 6:18–63 leaves the Jewish people under the control of the Seleucid rulers who follow Antiochus. The entire section lacks any mention of God, and the only distinct religious element is the report that the Jews at a city called Beth-zur had to surrender to the Seleucid army due to a lack of food stores because it was the seventh year, implying they had been faithful to the command to give the land rest every seventh year in Lev. 25:3–5. Like the events in 2:29–38, obedience to torah costs the Jewish people defeat, so 1 Maccabees does not operate with the standard assumptions of Deuteronomic theology, that obedience leads to divine favor and success, and that defeat at the hands of a foreign enemy is divine punishment for disobedience to torah.

If the theology of the first section of 1 Maccabees (1:1–6:18) is sparse and indirect, that quality is magnified in 6:19–14:15. After the reference to "Heaven" in 5:31 there is not another one until 9:46. First Maccabees reports political maneuvering within both sides of the conflict, as the death of Antiochus that ends the first section leaves divisions among the Seleucids, while a Jewish group rises up in opposition to Judas. First Maccabees portrays the leader of the opposition group, Alcimus, as treacherous and willing to make alliances with the Seleucid rulers. Alcimus's accusations against Judas and his followers lead to the arrival in Jerusalem of Nicanor, a royal emissary and harsh enemy of the Jews. One of the surprising differences between 1 and 2 Maccabees is the portrayal of Nicanor as

Judas's friend in the latter. In 1 Maccabees Nicanor is part of a plot to abduct Judas and take back control of the temple in Jerusalem. The defeat and death of Nicanor in 7:39–49 provide an occasion for the kind of theological responses that appear in the first several chapters of the book, but none appear, even when v. 48 reports, "The people rejoiced greatly and celebrated that day as a day of great gladness."

After a diversion from the main story line to report the surprising alliance between Judas and the expanding Roman Empire in 1 Maccabees 8, chapter 9 returns to report the response of the Seleucid king, Demetrius, to the death of Nicanor. The stark divine absence in the second section up to this point fits the devastating turn of events in 9:1–22. When the report appears in 9:5 that Judas and his army are outnumbered badly by the Seleucid forces, readers might expect the kind of emotional turn so characteristic of 1 Maccabees 1–6, but the opposite happens. The troops desert Judas and he becomes faint. Judas is determined to go ahead with the battle but sounds resigned to defeat in 9:10—"If our time has come, let us die bravely for our kindred, and leave no cause to question our honor." No cry to Heaven appears, so the text does not depict divine failure, but the Jewish army falls and Judas dies in battle. The culmination of the report in 9:19–22 celebrates Judas and laments his death in language reflecting the death of Saul in 2 Samuel 1, so the best encouragement readers may find is that the survival of Judas's brothers, Jonathan and Simon, puts the former in a position analogous to David when he succeeds Judas in 9:28–31.

Jonathan begins to looks somewhat like David during his bandit days in the remainder of 1 Maccabees 9 as he moves about the wilderness with a small band of fighters, occasionally conducting small attacks. A reference to God finally appears again in 9:46, characteristically as "Heaven," but the deliverance Jonathan urges his troops to cry out for is of the most limited kind, only that they survive the apparent trap in which they find themselves. The death of Alcimus brings an end to this desperate situation, though, and Jonathan is able to make peace with the Seleucid official, Bacchides, and regain some control over Israel. First Maccabees 10 depicts a time when Jonathan's influence grows as competing Seleucid rulers, Alexander and Demetrius, vie for his support. As a result, Jonathan becomes high priest and successfully supports Alexander. Jonathan's relatively long and successful career of warfare and diplomatic maneuvering among the Hellenistic kings and officials leads to the final overt theological reference in 1 Macc. 12:15. During his attempts to make alliances with the Romans and the Spartans, Jonathan sends a letter to the latter that is presented in 12:6–18. In verse 15 Jonathan explains that the Jews did not bother the Spartans for help in their many struggles against the Seleucids because they had "help that comes from Heaven," but there is no further explanation or illustration of the divine assistance.

The remainder of the second section of 1 Maccabees reports the capture and death of Jonathan at the hands of Trypho. Simon takes over leadership of the Hasmonean cause, and 1 Maccabees reports his rule as a relative success, highlighted by regaining control of the Jerusalem citadel. The second section ends with a eulogy for Simon in 14:4–15, a text oddly devoid of religious language, even though it reports all of the success and prosperity of Israel in the days of Simon. The final line in verse 15 reports Simon's work on the sanctuary and one previous line in verse 13b describes how "the kings were crushed in those days." The latter reference might be easy to overlook if the word "crush" (*suntribō*) was not a particular favorite of 1 Maccabees, appearing in various forms about twenty times. Because this is the final use, it may be instructive to compare it to the first one in 3:22. The earlier text is in one of the great speeches of Judas who, when faced by a more numerous and powerful enemy, encourages his troops by assuring them of divine assistance and that "he himself will crush them before us." Thus the death of the last of the Hasmonean brothers is marked by the same indirect language of divine assistance as the first, though in an even subtler manner.

The final section of 1 Maccabees, 14:16–16:24, is something of an appendix. Many interpreters see it as an addition to the original form of the book that appropriately ended with the eulogy of Simon. It contains a further collection of the military and diplomatic exploits of Simon, leading up to the death of Simon and his sons, other than John who succeeded him. The lack of theological language in the last section provides a final contrast with 2 Maccabees and leaves hanging a question that the other book will take up in a new way. How should the people of God understand failure and the deaths of their heroic figures?

Goldstein contends that the absence of direct words from God and observable miracles in 1 Maccabees are part of the writer's recognition that such divine acts were "hazardous to claim openly." The recent past and current situation of the Jewish people made language about divine intent and immediacy problematic. At the same time, Goldstein recognizes that the writer could still connect famous prophecies of the past to the work of the Maccabean heroes in a way that was "leading."[20] The placement of such theological claims onto events in the story of Israel in the Tanak came centuries after the eras in which the events were set, while making theological claims about the present and the very recent past presented significant risks. Many interpreters have seen the absence and presence of such theological claims about miraculous acts of God as a key difference between 1 and 2 Maccabees.[21] The difference is subtle, however,

---

20. Goldstein, *1 Maccabees*, 13. Goldstein points to the need to acknowledge such failure in Dan. 11:14 as an example.
21. See, for example, Timothy Michael Law, *When God Spoke Greek: The Septuagint and the Making of the Christian Bible* (Oxford: Oxford University Press, 2013), 66.

and may be part of what Williams calls the "double causality" of the theology in 1 Maccabees. There is divine assistance in the book, which even acts as a thread of continuity, but it is mediated. God helps the Hasmoneans, who help Israel, and the distinction is highlighted by the failure of others who presume leadership in 5:55–68.[22] The writer of 1 Maccabees resists an unequivocal claim that God fights on the side of Israel.

The apparent reluctance of 1 Maccabees even to mention God has played a significant role in interpreting the book. The absence of divine designations has invited comparisons with Esther, but the indirect references to God in 1 Maccabees give the book a far different theological profile.[23] The most distinctive replacement for divine designations is the word "Heaven," which 1 Maccabees uses about a dozen times. The Jews in the story cry out to Heaven for help, receive assistance and strength from Heaven, and praise and bless Heaven in response. Bartlett understands the use of "Heaven" as an act of "respect," but does not explain either why this is respectful or why the writer of 1 Maccabees exhibits such a strikingly different manner of demonstrating respect from any other writer in the biblical tradition.[24] Goldstein's similar, but slightly more precise, explanation is that the divine designations are "too holy" for use in writing,[25] but this is also an assumption that separates 1 Maccabees from all other written traditions of Judaism. Both Hebrew and Greek have common nouns for "god" that other writers used freely without any sense that they were considered holy. Such holiness was attached only to the divine name in Hebrew, and the practice of writing the name was well established in Jewish literature before and after 1 Maccabees. Even the eventual injunctions against pronouncing the name allowed

22. Williams, *Structure of 1 Maccabees*, 98–102.
23. For an example of the comparison to Esther, see Law, *When God Spoke Greek*, 66.
24. Bartlett, *1 Maccabees*, 30.
25. Goldstein, *1 Maccabees*, 13.

writing it. A viable explanation for this phenomenon needs to be much more specific to 1 Maccabees and its theological and literary character. Many of the texts treated above demonstrate an analogous tendency to describe divine action in an oblique manner. The clearest example is the statement highlighted in 4:25, "Thus Israel had a great deliverance that day." The choice of a divine designation such as Heaven that fit this indirect way of talking about divine behavior seems a more likely explanation than a general sense of respect or the holiness of the divine name. This pair of theological tendencies in 1 Maccabees forms one of its clearest distinctions from the book that shares its name and follows it in some Christian canons.

2 Maccabees

The beginning of this chapter has already addressed the odd relationship between 1 and 2 Maccabees, and the discussion of the former could not avoid some references to the latter. Second Maccabees covers a similar set of events, but begins in a very unusual manner. Few works in the biblical tradition exhibit so overt a sense of self-consciousness as 2 Maccabees, until the Epistles of St. Paul appear at the end of the New Testament.[26] The writer claims that he is summarizing a five-volume work on the Maccabean revolt by someone called Jason of Cyrene (2:23). The prior work is not available, and Jason is not otherwise known, but most interpreters take the claim at face value. A writer wishing to establish the authority of a new account of past events would obviously have reasons to exaggerate the quality of the sources used, and the claim also distances 2 Maccabees from 1 Maccabees by citing a different

---

26. The first-person portions of Ezra-Nehemiah are embedded within the books, and the narrative flows into and out of them without any overt recognition that such a shift is happening. The prologues to the Gospel of Luke and the Acts of the Apostles show this kind of self-consciousness, but move rapidly into covert narration.

source for the historical information. It is impossible to say whether the writer of 2 Maccabees had access to or ideas about 1 Maccabees, but it is tempting to note that the overtly religious character of the additional material that the former contains is reminiscent of what the additions to Esther in the Greek version do to the Hebrew version of the book. The literary style of 2 Maccabees leads most interpreters to conclude it was written in Greek from the beginning, unlike 1 Maccabees.[27]

Before the prologue that explains the use of Jason's work and the purpose of the book, 2 Maccabees presents two letters, the first (1:1–9) from the Jews in Judea and Jerusalem to the Jewish community in Egypt and the second (1:10–2:18) from the people of Jerusalem and Judea to Aristobulus and the Jews of Egypt.[28] Second Maccabees makes its religious character plain from the beginning of the book. It is impossible to say for certain whether the letters were written to be sent to the stated audience or were produced as literary elements for 2 Maccabees. The greeting includes a wish for divine blessing in 1:2–6 that recalls God's covenant with Abraham, Isaac, and Jacob. The letters encourage the faithful celebration of festivals, including the commemoration of the purification of the temple that became known as Hanukkah, the original story of which will be reported in 10:1–9. The second letter credits the God of Israel with saving the community and reports two curious stories about Jeremiah and the captives during the exile preserving the sacred fire from the temple along with other holy objects, which were later

---

27. Robert Doran, "The Second Book of Maccabees: Introduction, Commentary, and Reflections," in Keck, *New Interpreter's Bible*, 4:181–82.
28. While the setting of 2 Maccabees is almost entirely the Jewish homeland, its primary audience is a matter of dispute. Daniel R. Schwartz has constructed the most thorough argument for a "diasporan" author and audience. Much of Schwartz's argument is based upon what is not in the book (e.g., details about temple procedure and ritual observance), but the letters at the beginning of the book indicate a desire on the part of someone to communicate a view of events in Jerusalem to Jewish audiences living elsewhere. See Schwartz, *2 Maccabees* (Berlin: Walter de Gruyter, 2008), 45–51.

used by Nehemiah in reestablishing the temple.[29] The purpose of the stories seems to be to demonstrate the miraculous continuity of the temple throughout all the difficulties and challenges faced by the Jewish people as a motivation for the celebration of its recent purification, which the second letter comes back to in its closing in 2:16–18. Daniel Schwartz proposes that the two letters and the Hanukkah story represent a second layer of development of the book. The original version supported the celebration of "Nicanor's day," while the two letters at the beginning and the story of the temple purification in 10:1–8 were added to serve the additional purpose of promoting Hanukkah. This proposal seems likely, but those who added the letters and the additional story found a vehicle with which their purpose was fairly consistent in terms of the presentation of the divine character, so separate analysis of the two layers is not necessary in this study.[30]

The writer of 2 Maccabees opens his own story at 3:1 during the time of Onias III, who was the high priest in Jerusalem, a point slightly earlier than when the main story in 1 Maccabees begins. The significance of Onias is that the story begins with his faithful worship of God, before it is disrupted by a plot between a Seleucid official named Heliodorus and a Jewish enemy of Onias named Simon. While 3:1 extols Onias for his piety, 3:11 describes Simon as "impious," so the book sets up a religious conflict embodied by these two individuals. The plot against Onias causes great distress, but the people of Jerusalem pray to "the Almighty Lord" (3:22), at which time a fierce rider on horseback with two companions miraculously appears and assaults Heliodorus. The appearance of supernatural

---

29. The reference to Nehemiah is somewhat confusing. Perhaps the writer has combined the Nehemiah mentioned in Ezra 2:2 with the wall-building Nehemiah of the book of Nehemiah, thus attributing him with the rebuilding of the temple. See Doran, "Second Book of Maccabees," 196.
30. Schwartz, *2 Maccabees*, 8–11.

beings combined with the designation used for God signals that the nature of this story will be quite different from the one told in 1 Maccabees. The rider strikes down Heliodorus, and while he is on the ground 3:30 uses theophanic language to describe the event—"the Almighty Lord had appeared." Robert Doran proposes that the supernatural appearance, which finds parallels in 5:2–4, 10:29–30, and 11:8–11, fits a Greek literary genre called an "epiphanic collection," in which gods defend their temples.[31] There is little precedent for this kind of supernatural appearance in the Tanak or other Jewish literature, so such influence is possible and would help to explain these texts. The pious Onias prays for his enemy and he recovers, but the three angels address Heliodorus to confirm he has been struck by the power of God and Onias has helped him by interceding with God. As a result, Heliodorus worships the God of Israel and is converted. Doran again points to Greek examples of a former enemy recognizing divine power, but in this case there are ample parallels to such a conversion in the Tanak, such as the decree of Cyrus in 2 Chron. 36:22–24, Nebuchadnezzar in Dan. 4:34–37, and Darius in Dan. 6:27.[32]

Second Maccabees 5 begins with the report of Antiochus's second invasion of Egypt, and reports the second supernatural phenomenon of the book. For forty days people in Jerusalem saw troops fighting in the sky, and 5:4 adds that they hoped it was a sign Antiochus would be defeated. Based on false rumors of the death of Antiochus, Jason attacks and tries to take control of Jerusalem but ultimately fails, and the author attributes this to the fact that Jason was fighting against other Jews. The writer understands Jason's death as fair punishment

---

31. Doran, "Second Book of Maccabees," 182.
32. Ibid., 211. Goldstein implies that 2 Maccabees was well aware of the Daniel tradition and wrote, in part, to defend it (Goldstein, *2 Maccabees*, 247). Schwartz demonstrates effectively that interpreters need not choose between strict views of either Jewish or Greek antecedents to 2 Maccabees in terms of form or perspective (Schwartz, *2 Maccabees*, 57–66).

for his "conspiracy" (5:7). Meanwhile Antiochus perceives the events as a revolt in Judea and intensifies his persecution of its inhabitants. The report in 5:11–20 is a text interpreters often use to identify the "Deuteronomic" theology of the writer of 2 Maccabees.[33] The writer presents the raid on the temple by Antiochus in 5:15–17 as divine punishment, explaining that this is why God did not prevent him from entering the temple unlike how God had prevented Heliodorus. Perhaps more shocking are two reports in 6:7–11 in which two Jewish women are killed for circumcising their sons and another group slaughtered for hiding in caves in order to observe the Sabbath. The death of Jews specifically for observing the law contradicts the Deuteronomic view. The misfortunes of the Jews are so severe that the writer steps forward again in overt narration at 6:12 to try to explain: "Now I urge those who read this book not to be depressed by such calamities, but to recognize that these punishments were designed not to destroy but to discipline our people." Such a statement can only begin to make sense if this is corporate punishment for corporate sin, falling on the innocent as well as the guilty, but the logic is strained and the description of a Deuteronomic view breaks down. The idea that a writer of this period would try to take up a purely Deuteronomic theology would be surprising because such a view had been challenged so forcefully in the prophetic literature of the Tanak. The clearest example is Ezekiel 18, which rejects inherited guilt altogether, questions a sense of immediate retribution, and ends with YHWH declaring, "I have no pleasure in the death of anyone" (Ezek. 18:32). Perhaps the writer of 2 Maccabees recognizes the tension, leading to the desperate and unconvincing explanation. Even modern interpreters can seem befuddled by the incongruity. Goldstein contends that "[i]n vv. 12–17 the writer explains how God in his mercy could allow righteous Jews to be

---

33. Doran, "Second Book of Maccabees," 226.

AN APOCRYPHAL GOD

persecuted at all,"[34] but the writer never mentions the persecution of the righteous, and Goldstein does not identify what the explanation is. He does point forward to the harsh persecutions of chapter 7 and its proposal that the persecution of the righteous "earns the mercy of God for the survivors."[35]

In light of what is to come in 2 Macc. 6:18–7:42, the author may be preparing readers for what lies ahead as much as explaining what comes before 6:12–17. If he has been promoting any sense of the Deuteronomic view of God who punishes sin and rewards obedience, that view collapses completely in the stories of the persecution of Eleazar, the seven brothers, and their mother. During his trial and martyrdom, Eleazar says two things directly about God. First, in 6:26 he says, "Even if for the present I would avoid the punishment of mortals, yet whether I live or die I will not escape the hands of the Almighty." There are two sides to this statement, the more positive of which is that Eleazar believes that if he perseveres in obedience, even if it means death, he will be in the care of God. Such a view, however, is overshadowed by the more obvious claim that if he acts in a way to avoid human punishment he will receive punishment. Such a statement draws little difference between God and his persecutors, and even the choice of obedience seems more a matter of calculation than love or loyalty. Near the point of death Eleazer utters, "It is clear to the Lord in his holy knowledge that, though I might have been saved from death, I am enduring terrible sufferings in my body under this beating, but in my soul I am glad to suffer these things because I fear him" (6:30). The statement seems designed to counter two potential claims, either that God is unaware of the suffering of Eleazar and his community or that God is incapable of acting on their behalf. The statement could

---

34. Goldstein, *2 Maccabees*, 286.
35. Ibid.

be understood as a protest to a God both aware of his suffering and able to stop it, but Eleazar's speech stops well short of a clear, direct request for God to save him. The writer of 2 Maccabees makes no attempt to explain why the fearsome angel on horseback who attacked Heliodorus earlier in the book fails to appear now.

The description of the death of Eleazar is mild in comparison to the death of seven brothers and their mother in 7:1–42. Like they did with Eleazer, Seleucid officials led by Antiochus are trying to force the members of this family to eat swine flesh. As they dismember and fry the first brother in a pan, the mother and brothers declare, "The Lord God is watching over us and in truth has compassion on us" (7:6). Like Eleazar's words, the family's speech seems to point to the opposite of the appearance of reality. The speeches of the second, third, and fourth brothers raise an entirely new issue, the hope of a personal, bodily resurrection. The third brother willingly offers up his tongue and hands to be cut off stating, "I got these from Heaven, and because of his laws I disdain them, and from him I hope to get them back again" (7:11). Just when the idea of a God who raises the faithful in an afterlife seems to be taking hold as a means to explain the suffering of the innocent, however, the sixth brother returns to a stricter Deuteronomic understanding in 7:18: "For we are suffering these things on our own account, because of our sins against our own God." This brother, along with the previous one, struggles with an issue similar to one that occupied the prophetic literature, as both of them threaten their persecutors with divine vengeance for their behavior (7:17, 19). If their suffering is divine punishment, then how are they to understand the foreign rulers who are doing God's work?

The Tanak does not contain any description of martyrdom to rival that found in 2 Maccabees 6–7. When Jeremiah narrowly avoids execution in his trial in Jeremiah 26, the text reports the death of a prophet named Uriah son of Shemaiah in 26:23, and 2 Chron.

24:21–22 reports that King Joash had a prophet named Zechariah son of Jehoiada stoned to death for opposing him. Neither of the reports are elaborate, and both are focused more on the disobedience of the ones doing the killing than on the faith of the victims. In addition, the executioners in both of these cases are Israelites, not foreigners persecuting them. The famous attempts at martyrdom in the Tanak, Daniel in the lions' den and the three friends in the furnace, fail because of divine intervention. The martyrdom stories in 2 Maccabees follow the pattern in Daniel to a point, when faithful Jews refuse to comply with a foreign law requiring false worship and they are sentenced to death. Of course, the striking difference is that the scribe, Eleazar, and the unnamed mother and her seven sons are all killed in brutal, agonizing fashion. James D. Tabor even contends that these stories and others in the Apocrypha and Pseudepigrapha compete with one another in their "lurid accounts of heroism in the face of torture."[36] These stories also include an emphasis on the refusal of the martyrs to relent, even under the most extreme conditions, and they include the dying utterances of the martyrs.[37] This observation points to another significant factor distinguishing some martyrdom stories from others, that is, whether the source of the persecution is internal or external to Israel. The stories of martyrdom in 2 Maccabees take place at the hands of the Greek Empire, so the source of oppression is external.[38] A fuller discussion

---

36. James D. Tabor, "Martyr, Martyrdom," in *The Anchor Bible Dictionary*, ed. David Noel Freedman et al. (New York: Doubleday, 1992), 4:575–76.
37. See the full description of the standard elements of these martyrdom stories and others like them in Goldstein, *2 Maccabees*, 282–317. Similar themes are present in an exhortation from a Levite named Taxo to his sons in the Testament of Moses: "Let us die rather than transgress the commandments of the Lord of lords." For this translation and further comments, see Tabor, "Martyr, Martyrdom," 575–76.
38. For more on the shape of these stories and their function within 2 Maccabees, see Goldstein, *2 Maccabees*, 282–317. In addition to the concerns of this study about martyrdom, Goldstein observes that these stories also demonstrate the idea of redemptive suffering (296) and the doctrine of the resurrection (308).

of the issue of martyrdom in 2 Maccabees will appear at the end of this section, and connections between the way 1 and 2 Maccabees treat martyrdom and how it appears in other texts of the time period will be treated in the conclusion to the chapter. The issue that all of 2 Maccabees 6–7 presents and illustrates so vividly is Antiochus's self-deification. The king's requirement for the Jews to participate in foreign worship, including worship of himself in 6:1–11, is an attempt to replace Israel's God.[39]

When the martyr reports are over, 2 Maccabees begins to tell the story of Judas Maccabeus and his revolt. The martyr stories may even serve as a framework or rationale for the revolt story. Like the martyrs, Judas and his companions are described in 8:1 as "those who had continued in the Jewish faith." The introductory text extends into a theological rationale for the revolt and its early success. Before fighting, Judas and the others pray to God to have pity and mercy on those suffering at the hands of the Seleucid enemies. They particularly highlight "the lawless destruction of the innocent babies" (8:4). The events in 2 Maccabees 8 are parallel to those in 1 Maccabees 3–4. Goldstein identifies many common elements but also significant disagreements, some of which "reflect the bitter differences of opinion between the two authors."[40] Judas quickly achieves some military success and 8:5 explains this saying, "the Gentiles could not withstand him, for the wrath of the Lord had turned to mercy." The early success of Judas causes Ptolemy to appoint a man named Nicanor and send him with twenty thousand troops to suppress the revolt. In addition, Nicanor begins to institute a plan to sell Jews into slavery, "not expecting the judgment from the

---

39. On this point, see Gerry Wheaton, "The Festival of Hanukkah in 2 Maccabees: Its Meaning and Function," *Catholic Biblical Quarterly* 74 (2012): 253–55.
40. Goldstein, *2 Maccabees*, 321. He also adds that each of the two authors "would have been glad to discredit the other." It would be easy to read such statements as claims that there was actual conflict between these two authors outside of their texts, but there is no evidence of that.

Almighty that was about to overtake him" (8:11). Second Maccabees 8:12–18 portrays the varying responses to Nicanor's threat by members of the Jewish community in terms of their faith in God's actions. Some are "cowardly and distrustful of God's justice" (v. 13), so they run away, while others pray for God to remember the ancient covenants and rescue them (v. 15). The group led by Judas seems to strike the perfect balance of faith and action in the view of the writer, as they build an army but declare that "we trust in the Almighty God, who is able with a single nod to strike down those who are coming against us, and even, if necessary, the whole world" (v. 18). Judas then encourages his troops by telling two illustrious stories of the past in which God struck down the enemies of the Israelites. One of these is the story of the mysterious death of one hundred eighty-five thousand Assyrian troops in Sennacherib's army during the days of Isaiah and Hezekiah, reported in 2 Kgs. 19:35–37 and Isa. 37:36–38. Judas's reliance on such a dramatic story of miraculous victory in the past is surprising, especially considering the later attempt by the writer of Chronicles to downplay the event (2 Chron. 32:20–23).[41] The other war story Judas tells is otherwise unknown in the biblical tradition and involves a "battle against the Galatians that took place in Babylonia" (2 Macc. 8:20).[42] In this case "help from heaven" defeated one hundred twenty thousand enemy soldiers. Given this introduction to the battle it is no surprise that Judas prevails, and the report of the battle in 8:21–29 is filled with attributions to the divine. The story comes full circle at the end when Judas's troops take the spoils attained in the battle, distribute

---

41. See the discussion of this tradition and its effect on the development of the divine character in the Tanak in McEntire, *Portraits of a Mature God: Choices in Old Testament Theology* (Minneapolis: Fortress Press, 2013), 144.
42. The report does seem to reflect an actual battle, though some of the details here are of the type that cannot be confirmed. For more on the historical background, see Goldstein, *2 Maccabees*, 331–34.

them among "those who had been tortured and to the widows and orphans" (v. 28), and then close the affair with a final prayer. The next victory for Judas and his army leads to one of the texts that makes use of retributive balance. First, the enemies who had burned the gates of Jerusalem, including a person named Callisthenes, are themselves burned in the house to which they had fled (8:33), then Nicanor, whose most serious offense had been selling Jews into slavery, is forced to strip off his uniform and run away like a fugitive slave. The final text does not use language of worship and conversion as specific as in the case of Heliodorus in 3:36–39, but reports concerning Nicanor, "So he who had undertaken to secure tribute for the Romans by the capture of the people of Jerusalem proclaimed that the Jews had a Defender, and that therefore the Jews were invulnerable, because they followed the laws ordained by him" (8:36).

A decisive turn takes place in 2 Maccabees 9–10, and divine behavior plays a crucial role. The divine character exhibits little direct behavior in 1 Maccabees, as noted above, and in 2 Maccabees divine action receives more overt attention, but is somewhat limited in its scope until 9:1–12. The narrative of 2 Maccabees has been working its way through Seleucid officials, making its way to the top, and it has become Antiochus's turn to take the stage. The people of Persepolis in Persia defeat Antiochus and force him to flee their land in 9:1–4, and he decides in response to turn his attention to the Jews, declaring, "When I get there I will make Jerusalem a cemetery of Jews" (9:4). Antiochus's plan elicits a direct divine response: "But the all-seeing Lord, the God of Israel, struck him with an incurable and invisible blow" (9:5). The result of the blow is debilitating pain to his abdomen. After this, Antiochus is stricken with all kinds of maladies, which the writer of 2 Maccabees considers to be divine judgment. God's torture of Antiochus results in his vow to set Jerusalem free, furnish the temple, and declare God's power (9:14–17), so the king succumbs in a way that none of the Jews he had tortured ever did.[43] Eventually, Antiochus dies a painful death, according to 9:28, having suffered pain like he had inflicted on others. Perhaps this is a reference back to the torture and killing of Eleazar and the seven brothers in 2 Maccabees 6–7.

Following the death of Antiochus, Judas and his army capture the temple in Jerusalem and begin its purification, a story that is the focal point of 2 Maccabees, bringing its first major section to a close. The Hanukkah story is linked to the death of Antiochus Epiphanes by the preceding story in 9:19–29 and concluding statement in 10:9. Gerry Wheaton argues that the Hanukkah story reasserts God's identity as the one true deity, over against Antiochus who claimed divine status. The demonstration of God's power in the support of Judas Maccabeus, resulting in the death of Antiochus and the purification of the temple, is a grand occasion for the Jewish people that they should celebrate and remember not just in Jerusalem but also in the diaspora, as the letters at the beginning of the book encourage.[44]

Second Maccabees 14–15 reports a sequence of events parallel to those in 1 Maccabees 7, indicating the significantly earlier ending of 2 Maccabees. One of the Seleucid opponents is named Nicanor, which creates some confusion because of the earlier appearance of "Nicanor son of Patroclus" in 2 Maccabees 8, who had fled the region in defeat and disgrace. This Nicanor is introduced in 14:12 as one "who had been in command of the elephants," so it would seem to be a different person.[45] This Nicanor at first befriends Judas, but turns against him

---

43. For more on the precise sense of retribution in God's treatment of Antiochus, see Doran, "Second Book of Maccabees," 254.
44. Wheaton, "Festival of Hanukkah," 259–62. Wheaton argues that the placement of the death of Antiochus in 2 Maccabees 9, outside of its logical place earlier in the book, was part of the original work of the writer who summarized Jason. Schwartz on the other hand asserts a two-stage development that inserted the Hanukkah story into the book and rearranged the death of Antiochus around it (Schwartz, 2 Maccabees, 8–9). While these are two different views of how the book reached its current form, their views of what the current form is doing are similar.

when news of their friendship causes the king to pressure Nicanor to arrest Judas. The threat of Nicanor's new behavior intensifies the conflict, and when he threatens the temple, the priests respond by praying to "the constant Defender of our nation" (14:34). They specifically pray that the temple remain pure.

Before the impending battle, 2 Maccabees reports one more gruesome event that may be understood in terms of martyrdom in 14:37–46. The author places the story of the martyrdom of Razis, a Jewish elder, within a sequence of battles in a manner similar to the placement of the martyr stories in 2 Maccabees 6–7.[46] Pursued and surrounded by Nicanor's troops, Razis attempts to kill himself with a sword and fails. His further attempts to end his own life while being pursued are almost comical, as he finally dies tearing out his own intestines to throw them at the crowd. Like the third brother in 2 Maccabees 7, Razis implies a bodily resurrection when he calls upon God to return to him the body parts he offers up. The death of Razis leads to the final conflict between Judas and Nicanor. The speech of Judas, encouraging his troops for the battle, is the occasion for the final supernatural event in 2 Maccabees. At the conclusion of the speech Judas has a vision of the priest Onias, and Onias introduces Jeremiah, who gives Judas a golden sword as "a gift from God, with which you will strike down your adversaries" (15:16). The vision prompts a prayer by Judas, in which he again recalls the angel slaying the Assyrian army of one hundred eighty-five thousand in the days of King Hezekiah, as he had in 8:19; and when the battle finally occurs, Judas and his troops kill thirty-five thousand Seleucid soldiers, including Nicanor himself.

---

45. Goldstein notes that Nicanor was a common name but allows that this could still be the same person. See Goldstein, *2 Maccabees*, 327.
46. For more on this parallel structure, see ibid., 291.

The Jewish characters in 2 Maccabees suffer greatly, particularly at the hands of the Seleucid king Antiochus IV. The book eventually spends much of its time reporting the revolt of the Jews against this king. Both the suffering and the eventual success of the revolt require theological explanation. As Goldstein expresses it, "For the Jews, the events cried out for an interpretation in accord with the teaching of the Torah and the Prophets. . . . If now God's favor had fully returned after the harshest time of troubles, it was necessary for the people to know how and why, otherwise they might again lose his favor."[47] Nevertheless, divine favor is no straightforward concept but must be shaped around very difficult events. Martyrdom poses an enormous challenge to any theological system or any understanding of God's character. Literature and theological thinking of the apocalyptic variety would seem better equipped to deal with the difficulty than 2 Maccabees, an observation that raises questions about why martyrdom is completely absent from 1 Maccabees.

Conclusion

Jan Assmann argues that the Maccabean revolt brought together five "interrelated religious phenomena." The first two of these, zealotry and martyrdom, are two sides of the same coin, being willing to kill for the faith and willing to die for it.[48] The former goes back to the wilderness experience of Israel, not only in the Phinehas story of Numbers 25 but also in the actions of the Levites in Exod. 32:25–29. Martyrdom, however, is a new idea here. The closest the Tanak comes to such a notion is the suffering of the servant in

---

47. Ibid., 3.
48. Jan Assmann, "Martyrdom, Violence, and Immortality: The Origins of a Religious Complex," in *Dying for the Faith, Killing for the Faith: Old-Testament Faith-Warriors (1 and 2 Maccabees) in Historical Perspective*, ed. Gabriela Signori (Leiden: Brill, 2012), 39–40.

Isaiah 40–55 and of prophets like Jeremiah and Ezekiel. The third phenomenon, immortality, was also a new direction in Judaism, but provides obvious support for the promotion of martyrdom. The fourth and fifth phenomena both involve more problematic understandings of warfare. Assmann contends that the revolt was the "first purely religiously motivated war."[49] It is easy to understand why nothing in the Tanak would fit such a definition, since all of Israel's warfare therein involves taking and holding land, but it seems difficult to remove all political motivation from the warfare of the Hasmoneans. The fifth phenomenon is "a religious war carried out according to the principle of fulfilling scripture."[50] The Hasmoneans carried out this last aspect particularly in the killing of assimilators,[51] Jews who had accepted and adapted to the religion and culture of the occupying Seleucids; but, as demonstrated above, the Hasmoneans were willing to make at least one adjustment to torah in order to be successful in the practice of warfare. Two occasions in 1 Maccabees report failures in the revolt because of strict torah observance. In the first instance, Mattathias and his followers decide in 2:39–41 to abandon strict observance and defend themselves if attacked on the Sabbath in the future. In the second instance, the text reports no adjustment to the problem created by lack of food stores in the year of the land Sabbath in 6:53, but such an adjustment could only have come seven years later. Strict obedience to the law leading to death rather than divine rescue raises difficult questions about the character of Israel's God. Second Maccabees takes the opposite position on the issue, reporting the death of those who did not defend themselves on the Sabbath in 6:11, followed by a contorted attempt to explain the implications of such deaths for the character of Israel's

49. Ibid.
50. Ibid.
51. Ibid., 56–59.

God in verses 12–17. After the explanation, 2 Maccabees extols the courage of martyrs who refuse to compromise torah observance even to avoid the most grisly deaths, and has Judas Maccabeus use the suffering of the martyrs to implore Israel's God for assistance in 8:3–4.[52] The theological adjustment in 2 Maccabees is the change of divine behavior in response to the death of martyrs in language that may be reminiscent of Israel's past, portrayed in stories of "cry and response" in Exodus and Judges. But the addition of the martyrs, who suffer for obedience rather than disobedience, changes the equation.[53] A God roused by the blood of martyrs looks different than one who responds to the crying out of people suffering because of their disobedience. This may be why the connection to the exodus in 1 Enoch, which will be explored in the next chapter, may have been more useful than a connection to later stories in Israelite tradition, such as the wilderness complaint stories or those in the book of Judges.

The presentations of martyrdom stories in 2 Maccabees 6–7 are shocking, but the idea of faithful death is present throughout 1 and 2 Maccabees, even if the details differ. The discussion above called into question the common interpretive assumption that 2 Maccabees presents a Deuteronomic version of the revolt. This does not mean that elements of a Deuteronomic view are not present, but the framework is different, and the differences have a profound impact on the divine portrayal. Candida Moss states the transformation in the Maccabean tradition in expansive terms: "These accounts of persecution involved the formation of a particular, distinct, and

---

52. For more on this development in 2 Maccabees, see Jan Willem van Henten, *The Maccabean Martyrs as Saviours of the Jewish People: A Study of 2 and 4 Maccabees* (Leiden: Brill, 1997), 140–44.
53. For more on the "cry and response" tradition and how it functions in the Maccabean literature and the portrayal of Judas Maccabeus in 1 Enoch, see Anathea E. Portier-Young, *Apocalypse against Empire: Theologies of Resistance in Early Judaism* (Grand Rapids, MI: Eerdmans, 2011), 376–81.

coherent Jewish identity in which Jewish history was reframed as a history of obedient suffering."[54] Moss argues for a greater sense of continuity between the martyrs of 2 Maccabees 6–7 and other deaths in 2 Maccabees, particularly the death of Razis. Razis's death may be problematic because of its suicidal nature, but Moss is likely correct that the writer of 2 Maccabees did not view these deaths differently.[55] We may even extend the continuity to the deaths of the Maccabean heroes like Mattathias and Judas. The continuity more difficult to accept is between the martyrs in 2 Maccabees and would-be martyrs in texts like Daniel 1–6.

One explanation for the differences in the accounts of the revolt in 1 and 2 Maccabees is that the former is for an audience living in the Jewish homeland while the latter is directed at an audience in the Jewish diaspora.[56] Arguments for this view are not fully convincing but have enough merit to make it worth asking how their differing divine portrayals might fit into it. This chapter highlights the differences in the portrayals of God, but argues they are not as stark as some interpreters present them. The God of Israel is present in 1 Maccabees and assists the leaders of the revolt, but the language about God is subtle, and the assistance is not plainly visible. In contrast, 2 Maccabees is overt in its God language, and divine assistance occasionally erupts in visible phenomena; nevertheless, it fails to appear at crucial moments. Direct claims about divine assistance are certainly safer when both time and space lie between the events and the audience. This would be the case with 2 Maccabees if it was written later, its story ended earlier, and its intended audience was several hundred miles away.

---

54. Candida Moss, *Ancient Christian Martyrdom: Diverse Practices, Theologies, and Traditions* (New Haven, CT: Yale University Press, 2012), 37.
55. Ibid., 40–43.
56. See the case for this view in Schwartz, *2 Maccabees*, 45–56.

The absence of any manuscript of Esther is one of the most well-known facts about the Dead Sea Scrolls, but 1 and 2 Maccabees are also a striking gap in the collection. Arguments from such absence are hard to make because they could be merely accidental—such scrolls may have disintegrated entirely or have not yet been found. The presence of about a dozen copies each of books like Jubilees and 1 Enoch, however, make it seem unlikely that the Maccabean books were present significantly. The Hasmonean dynasty, even though it had collapsed long before all of the Dead Sea Scrolls were written and placed in the caves, was still likely a major component of the Jerusalem hierarchy that the Qumran community considered its enemy. It is possible that the "Wicked Priest" of the scrolls was one of the later Hasmoneans.[57] Any division between the Qumran community and the Hasmoneans was likely the result of a complex combination of theology and politics that cannot be named with precision. First and Second Maccabees and their reports of events initiated by humans in the past have a very different feel from the literature of the Qumran community. The neglect of the Maccabean literature and the revolt it describes was not an act in which the Qumran community was alone. The preservation of 1 and 2 Maccabees is dependent almost entirely upon Christian tradition. Josephus, writing toward the end of the first century of the Common Era, obviously had access to the Maccabean literature in some form, so it is incorrect to say it had not been preserved at all; but it was also Christian tradition that preserved the works of Josephus. So it is difficult to say what lasting impact the theological thought of 1 and 2 Maccabees had on rabbinic Judaism based on its literature, but a sense of Jewish nationalism compatible with the Maccabean revolt persisted

---

57. On this possibility, see Michael Wise, Martin Abegg Jr., and Edward Cook, *The Dead Sea Scrolls: A New Translation* (San Francisco: Harper Collins, 1996), 28–34.

into the second century of the Common Era and the revolt of Bar Kokhba.[58]

---

58. For a more detailed discussion of the Maccabean revolt and its place in Jewish and Christian tradition, see Michael E. Stone, *Ancient Judaism: New Visions and Views* (Grand Rapids, MI: Eerdmans, 2011), 18–19.

6

God of Dreams and Visions

It has been impossible to ignore entirely the phenomenon known as apocalyptic literature up to this point, because some of the books I have already examined have an apocalyptic backdrop shaping the entire work. This is particularly true of Daniel and 1 Enoch, parts of which are the subject of chapters 2 and 3. The remainder of those two books will be the starting point for this chapter, which will focus on 1 Enoch 72–108, the three most prominent sections of which are most often labeled the Astronomical Book (72–82), the Dream Visions (83–90), and the Epistle of Enoch (91–105), and Daniel 7–14. These are not the only works of the period that might fit the category, and some literature in other categories may have apocalyptic features, but these are the two clearest and probably most influential examples. The apocalyptic sections of Jubilees, particularly Jubilees 23, will also receive brief attention.

God's Heavenly Messengers

Apocalyptic literature has been difficult to define in part because the same adjective has been used to describe communities of the time period and certain ways of thinking that seem to have characterized them. Retaining the adjective just to describe literature allows for a reasonable precision in its use. The best definitions of apocalyptic literature focus on its use of space and time.[1] Apocalyptic literature uses a divided or dual sense of space, creating two realms of existence and activity. One realm is the normal world of human existence, and the other is a hidden realm which is the place in which God and other heavenly beings exist and act. Certain heavenly beings, such as angels, can cross into the world of human beings and help them, and rare human beings, like Enoch, can ascend into heaven within visionary experiences in order to report back what they see. This feature is particularly important for a study like this one that is focused on divine behavior, because the unseen realm is the setting for that behavior. In the books of the Hebrew Scriptures with which readers are more familiar, like Genesis, Exodus, and 1 Samuel, the divine character frequently enters the story to interact with the human characters, but it is seldom clear where the divine character goes when he departs from these scenes. The idea that the God of Israel is connected to certain locations within the world of human existence, such as Mount Sinai, Shechem, or Bethel, is present in certain texts, but the Tanak never directly discusses or explains the idea of locality in reference to YHWH. YHWH is not limited to those places and is able to visit and talk to Abram in Haran in Genesis

---

1. A highly influential and effective working definition of "apocalypse" as a literary genre was the great accomplishment of the now famous volume 14 of *Semeia* published in 1979. This collection of essays clarifies the use of a spatial axis and a temporal axis as the defining elements of the genre. See especially John J. Collins, "Introduction: Towards the Morphology of a Genre," *Semeia* 14 (1979): 1–20.

12, or Hagar in the wilderness in Genesis 16. Still, God's presence in these places is only expressed in stories of divine encounters with human characters. A location to which God might return in between these encounters receives little attention. The lack of some other place to which YHWH goes when not part of an encounter with humans forms a major part of the answer to the profound question Jack Miles asks in *God: A Biography*—"What makes God god-like?" Miles's answer to this question in his reading of the early books of the Hebrew Scriptures is God's "lack of a private life."[2] Texts within the Tanak also operate with the assumption of divine absence and various degrees of intensification in God's presence. Joel Burnett develops the concept of "structural divine presence" and a corresponding "structural divine absence" as a way of characterizing the understanding of God's location in both the Tanak and other literature of the ancient Near East.[3] The structure of the cosmos and the nature of Israel's God meant that this deity could not occupy the "realm of death" or a place characterized by disorder or chaos.[4]

When the Israelites arrive at Mount Sinai in Exodus 19, the text reports that YHWH comes down on Mount Sinai, but there is no indication of where he comes down from. It might seem that this is a change allowing YHWH a place to be without human interaction, but the reason for coming down is so that the Israelites can see and hear the evidence of YHWH's presence in the lightning and thunder on the mountaintop, and so that Moses can go up to meet YHWH. Eventually YHWH comes down from Sinai to dwell in the tabernacle constructed by Moses and then travels with the Israelites

---

2. Jack Miles, *God: A Biography* (New York: Vintage, 1995), 86.
3. Joel S. Burnett, *Where Is God? Divine Absence in the Hebrew Bible* (Minneapolis: Fortress Press, 2010), 59–74. See also the discussion of the spatial aspect of the divine character in McEntire, *Portraits of a Mature God: Choices in Old Testament Theology* (Minneapolis: Fortress Press, 2013), 68–69.
4. Burnett, *Where Is God?*, 84.

AN APOCRYPHAL GOD

through the wilderness; in this period, Moses goes in and out of the tabernacle to communicate with YHWH. Once the Israelites arrive in the promised land, God's presence is still never fully explained or defined, but seems to be associated with the ark of the covenant, which is located in Shiloh until it is brought to Jerusalem by David. Solomon completes the task of housing YHWH by moving the ark into the completed temple. Texts in 1 Kings 8 and 2 Chronicles 7 depict YHWH's entrance into the sanctuary by means of a cloud that represents the divine glory, an idea related to the cloud by which YHWH led the Israelites through the wilderness in Exodus 13 and Numbers 11, and entered the tabernacle in Exodus 40.

Ancient Israelite tradition appears to have possessed a growing discomfort about the presence of YHWH and found ways to deflect the idea, at least in its language. Thus Deuteronomy uses the phrase "the place that YHWH will choose as a dwelling for his name" as a way to refer to Jerusalem, a circumlocution that also allows Deuteronomy to avoid violating the narrative logic of the Tanak. Other books, like Ezekiel, choose to talk about the "glory [*kabod*] of YHWH" dwelling in the temple, allowing the divine presence to depart temporarily while Babylonians destroyed the temple in order to be present with the exiles in Babylon. Texts like Joshua 6 and 1 Samuel 3 attach the divine presence to the ark of the covenant prior to the building of the temple, but the apparent loss of the ark removed the need to associate divine presence with any particular object. Along with the notion of the name, introduced in Deuteronomy, the concept of the *shekinah* also became a way of talking about YHWH's presence, though this exact word does not appear in the Tanak.[5]

---

5. *Shekinah* derives from the Hebrew word for "dwell," a verb whose subject is YHWH in the Tanak (e.g., Exod. 25:8), and it appears most prominently in Aramaic translations known collectively as the targumim.

It is tempting to associate apocalyptic literature with the use of symbolic visions, but this is better understood as an overlapping feature rather than a defining one. The famous *merkabah* vision of Ezekiel 1 is a case in point. This text makes use of images of storms, strange creatures, and jewels, and the four creatures of Ezek. 1:5–14 make an appearance in the book of Revelation (4:6–8) in the Christian New Testament. The latter is undoubtedly an apocalyptic book, and this imagery is part of a separate world where God exists and acts. In Ezekiel, however, this vision appears to the prophet in the world of human existence. The primary point of Ezekiel 1 is that Ezekiel sees the vision, representing divine presence, when he is in Babylon with the exiled people of Judah. The prophet sees the divine chariot rise up and depart from the temple in Jerusalem in Ezekiel 8–10, and sees it return in the vision of the new temple in Ezekiel 40–48. These texts are best understood as theophanies, encounters with the divine presence in the world of human existence, even though they are not part of ordinary human existence. Ezekiel seems to enter a trance-like state when he has these visions. It is not surprising that apocalyptic literature would take up elements of a theophany like this one, because a theophany and an apocalyptic vision are mirror images of one another; but this should not lead to the projecting of the concept of apocalyptic literature back onto a book like Ezekiel.

The other central aspect of apocalyptic literature is the related chronological dualism. If the authors of the literature portray a spatial divide separating the full divine presence from the world of human beings, then it follows that they presume and hope for an end to that situation. So there is a present time in which forces of good and evil struggle in the world, and there will be a future time when the spatial dualism ends and God finally defeats the forces of evil. The exact nature of the eschatological element varies among apocalyptic texts. If the purpose of apocalyptic literature is to provide hope and comfort to its audience in the midst of suffering and difficulty, then it is logical that such texts always portray the end as near; so it is as much, or more, a near end as an actual end that is the focus of apocalyptic literature.

The precise origins of apocalyptic literature are difficult to determine. Interpreters have looked both outside of Israel's tradition to influences from other cultures, particularly Persian, and inside Israel's traditions, especially to the connections between apocalyptic and prophecy. Michael Stone argues that there is no single set of influences or point of emergence. He points particularly to the periodization of history and use of typological numbers, derived from Jeremiah, Zechariah, and Chronicles, as a sign that apocalyptic literature arose from the attempt to determine a sense of order to history and a divine plan for bringing justice into the world.[6] The portions of 1 Enoch, Daniel, and Jubilees examined below will make significant use of this periodization and its characteristic numerology.

Chapter 7 will address texts that identify a messianic figure who partially or fully overcomes the divide between heaven and earth. The material and ideas within this chapter and the next overlap significantly, and the division between them is primarily for convenience of the discussion. The central question of this chapter will not be precisely what the eschaton looks like or who brings it about, but how the idea of one shapes the understanding of the divine character and the way the writers portray this character to their audiences.

---

6. Michael E. Stone, *Ancient Judaism: New Visions and Views* (Grand Rapids, MI: Eerdmans, 2011), 75–89.

1 Enoch 72–108

The second chapter of this book introduced 1 Enoch, which is much better understood as a collection of literature than a single work. That chapter addressed the first major portion, the Book of the Watchers (1–36), and the next chapter will examine the Parables of Enoch (37–71), leaving the Book of the Luminaries (72–82), the Animal Apocalypse (83–90), and the Epistle of Enoch (91–105) for this chapter.[7] The Book of the Luminaries (or simply, Luminaries) requires only brief discussion here because it displays very little divine action. First Enoch 72:1 labels it Book 3 of the collection, provides its title, and describes the text as the product of a guided tour provided to Enoch by the angel Uriel.[8] Some of the ideas in Luminaries appear earlier in summary form in 1 Enoch 33–36 as a conclusion to the Book of the Watchers. Most scholars presume that Luminaries draws heavily upon Mesopotamian astronomical sources but shapes them into a distinctly Jewish perspective.[9] Two ideas about the divine character emerge from the Luminaries, the first of which is stated most explicitly in 75:3, where Uriel is the one appointed by God over all of the heavenly bodies so they can function properly to guide the world. The second idea exists more in what is absent from the text, making Luminaries unique. Randall Argall describes Luminaries as

---

7. There is some dispute about the arrangement of chapters within the five-book scheme of 1 Enoch and the continuity of 91 and 106–8 with the rest of the final section. First Enoch 91 forms a transition between the Animal Apocalypse and the Epistle of Enoch; a precise settlement of the issues surrounding its placement is not essential to this study. Similarly, 106–7, an account of Noah's birth, and 108 appear to be appendices; whether to understand them as such in relation to the whole book or its final major section will not have a major impact on the discussion here. For a more thorough discussion of the issues of organization and composition, see George W. E. Nickelsburg, *1 Enoch 1: A Commentary on the Book of 1 Enoch, Chapters 1–36; 81–108* (Minneapolis: Fortress Press, 2001), 410–15, 539–60.

8. J. T. Milik and Matthew Black demonstrate the likelihood that the Book of the Luminaries existed in a more expansive form independently at Qumran. See Milik and Black, *The Books of Enoch: Aramaic Fragments of Qumran Cave 4* (Oxford: Clarendon Press, 1976), 273–97.

9. On this subject, see James C. VanderKam, *Enoch and the Growth of an Apocalyptic Tradition* (Washington, DC: Catholic Biblical Association, 1984), 89–101.

"truly revolutionary in the sense that the observed regularity excludes any forecasting of future events."[10] The timing of future events must be revealed in special visions to Enoch, not simply derived from astronomical patterns. It is impossible to say exactly why the Book of Luminaries was placed just prior to the portions of the book that contain apocalyptic visions of the future, but one effect of the placement is to put the timing of future events fully in divine control, rather than subject to the timing of the natural world.

A discussion of the apocalyptic material and character of 1 Enoch may begin with the small element known as the Apocalypse of Weeks, which most interpreters identify as the current 93:1–10 91:11–17. Together these texts present a ten-week scheme of human history as the teaching of Enoch to his descendants. Enoch's normal earthly life was in the first week of the scheme; the writer and audience of the Apocalypse of Weeks appear to live at the end of the seventh week. The relationship of this portion to the entire book of 1 Enoch is a matter of dispute, which is further complicated by the mystery of how it became placed in a fragmentary condition in the Ethiopic form of the book. The Qumran fragment called 4QEng contains 93:9–10 followed immediately by 91:11–17, so the Apocalypse of Weeks was a unified text that circulated among Jewish communities in Palestine in the first and second centuries BCE.[11] The Apocalypse of Weeks shows signs of dependence on the Book of the Watchers in 1 Enoch 1–36, placing it within the Enoch tradition. Anathea Portier-Young argues for a date around 167 BCE, just prior to the beginning of the Maccabean revolt, making the Apocalypse of Weeks perhaps the earliest historical apocalypse, though this date

---

10. Randall A. Argall, *1 Enoch and Sirach: A Comparative Literary and Conceptual Analysis of the Themes of Revelation, Creation and Judgment* (Atlanta: Scholars Press, 1995), 50.
11. For a more thorough discussion of the date and provenance of the Apocalypse of Weeks, see Nickelsburg, *1 Enoch 1*, 440–41.

would make it only slightly earlier than Daniel 7–12, a text with which it has much in common.[12]

A remarkable feature of the Apocalypse of Weeks is the almost complete lack of divine designations. The one likely exception is the reference to the "Great King" in 91:14 during the description of the building of a new temple during the eighth week. The text is filled with passive verb constructions having direct or indirect divine agency. A list of verbal clauses in table 6-1 consists mostly of such passive constructions.

Table 6-1

Verbs with Divine Cause in the Apocalypse of Weeks[13]

93:2	"The vision of heaven was shown to me"
93:4	"a man will be saved"
93:4	"a law will be made for sinners"
93:5	"a man will be chosen"
93:6	"a covenant . . . and a tabernacle will be made"
93:10	"the chosen will be chosen as witnesses"
93:10	"to whom will be given sevenfold wisdom"
93:12	"a sword will be given to all the righteous"
93:12	"and they will be delivered into their hands"
93:14	"the righteous law will be revealed"
93:15	"the eternal judgment . . . will be executed on the watchers"
93:16	"the first heaven will pass away"
93:16	"a new heaven will appear"
93:16	"the powers of heaven will shine forever"

---

12. See Anathea E. Portier-Young, *Apocalypse against Empire: Theologies of Resistance in Early Judaism* (Grand Rapids, MI: Eerdmans, 2011), 313–19.
13. All translations of 1 Enoch here and elsewhere, unless otherwise noted, are from George W. E. Nickelsburg and James C. VanderKam, *1 Enoch: The Hermeneia Translation* (Minneapolis: Fortress Press, 2012).

Assumptions throughout 1 Enoch make it possible that divine agents, specifically angels, perform some of these actions, but a plot emerges that includes the work of Israel's God in the past and projects into the future. The schematization of history in the Apocalypse of Weeks has received a great deal of scholarly attention, both because of its prominence here and the way it became a common feature of apocalyptic writings. Many interpreters relate the ten-week scheme here to the seventy generations of 1 Enoch 10; the following section of this chapter will examine how a similar scheme functions in Daniel. The Apocalypse of Weeks pays less attention to the spatial dualism than to temporal concerns. The scheme assures the audience that God and God's agents were in control of time and historical events in the past and will assert the same kind of control in the future. The audience, as the chosen and righteous ones, has an assured place in the divine timing.[14]

The extent to which the Apocalypse of Weeks encourages its audience to wait patiently for divine intervention or to take matters of resistance into their own hands is a matter of dispute. The previous chapter raised questions about the absence of the Maccabean literature from the Dead Sea Scrolls. There are many possible explanations for this, beyond just a mere accident of history. The Hasmoneans and the community that produced the sectarian material in the Dead Sea Scrolls would likely have had many points of disagreement, including the proper operation of the temple and interpretation of the Torah, but the timing of active, armed resistance may have been another one. A periodized system of time like the one in the Apocalypse of Weeks might have rejected such active revolt

---

14. See John J. Collins, *The Apocalyptic Imagination: An Introduction to the Jewish Matrix of Christianity* (New York: Crossroad, 1984), 50–52.

until the eighth week.[15] The immediacy of the armed conflict in the Maccabean tradition presents a very different view.

The fourth "book" in the 1 Enoch collection (chs. 83–90), sometimes called the Dream Visions, contains two visions. The first vision (83–84) presents itself as a dream Enoch has as a young man and later reports to his son, Methuselah. The dream describes the destruction of the earth and Enoch's terror, which he had described at the time to his grandfather, Mahalel. With his grandfather's encouragement, Enoch prays to God to spare some of his family from the destruction so they might continue the human race and his own genealogical line. Not all interpreters agree that the dream deals with Noah and the flood, but that seems to be the most likely reference.[16] Enoch's prayer in 84:2–6 calls God the "great King," extols God's power and control over creation, and approves of God's plan to destroy the humans who have made God angry, but begs for the preservation of the righteous. The temporal dualism of apocalyptic literature sometimes leads to the fusion of ancient traditions and future events in a way that creates new meanings and new uses of mythic imagery from the past, which might lead interpreters to different conclusions about how to read such texts in reference to the flood story in Genesis and its antecedents.[17] The troubling implication of the prayer is that there are righteous people, but God intends to destroy them with the wicked. Enoch's prayer thus reflects the prayer of Abraham concerning Sodom in Genesis 19,

---

15. On this issue, see Portier-Young, *Apocalypse against Empire*, 334–40.
16. Collins makes the puzzling claim that the first dream refers only to a general idea of the destruction of the earth and that "[i]t need not refer to any particular crisis" (*Apocalyptic Imagination*, 53–54). Nickelsburg, on the other hand, observes the connections to the Noah story, particularly parallel passages in 1 Enoch 65 and 106–7. See Nickelsburg, *Jewish Literature between the Bible and the Mishnah*, 2nd ed. (Minneapolis: Fortress Press, 2005), 83. On the relation to the flood story, see also Portier-Young, *Apocalypse against Empire*, 346–47.
17. On this function of ancient myths in apocalyptic literature, see D. S. Russell, *The Method and Message of Jewish Apocalyptic* (Philadelphia: Westminster, 1964), 122–26.

even if Enoch is not quite as direct as Abraham in his challenge to God's moral decision making. The similarities between Enoch's prayer before the flood in 84:2–6 and the prayer of the angels in 1 Enoch 9 also invite discussion.[18] The contrast between the tone of the two prayers further highlights Enoch's reverence. Whereas the petitions the angels bring in 9:3 are presented as lawsuits, Enoch makes a humble plea in 82:6.[19] The first vision ends without reporting God's response, but the assumed background of the Noah story may make a response unnecessary, and leaving the matter unresolved creates an introduction to the second dream.

The second dream-vision is the intriguing Animal Apocalypse (85–90), which is also related to the flood story of Genesis and is also presented as Enoch's report of a dream to his son, Methuselah. The Animal Apocalypse makes use of a periodization of history not as clearly divided as the one framing the Apocalypse of Weeks. Nickelsburg understands the Animal Apocalypse to present three periods: 1) the time up to and including the flood (85:3–89:8), 2) after the flood until the great judgment (89:9–90:27), and 3) a time of transformation after the judgment.[20] It is possible to divide the long second period into smaller subdivisions, as John Collins does.[21] The lack of clear markers in the text for such divisions, however, makes the process uncertain and less helpful when pressed for too much detail. The vision receives its name because the major characters in the vision, most corresponding to figures in Israel's past, appear as

---

18. See the detailed discussion in Nickelsburg, *1 Enoch 1*, 351–52.
19. See the discussion of the difference in tone in Portier-Young, *Apocalypse against Empire*, 361–62. Though Portier-Young generally describes the difference well, she goes too far in insisting that "[r]ather than calling God to the task of justice, Enoch appeals for mercy" (361). Enoch makes a clear distinction between the wicked humans he wants God to destroy and the righteous and upright ones for whom he pleads.
20. Nickelsburg, *Jewish Literature*, 83–84. See this division spelled out in greater detail in Patrick A. Tiller, *A Commentary on the Animal Apocalypse in I Enoch* (Atlanta: Scholars Press, 1993), 15–20.
21. Collins, *Apocalyptic Imagination*, 54–55.

animals, beginning with Adam as a white bull, Eve as a heifer, and Cain and Abel as black and red calves. The story of the first family in 85:3–10 is followed by the story of the Watchers in 86:1–6, who are stars that fall from heaven to live among the cows and impregnate them, producing elephants, camels, and donkeys. Violence ensues among the animals until the four angels appear in 87:1–4 to rescue Enoch. This is the first hint of even a mediated divine presence in the Animal Apocalypse. In 88:1–3 the angels bind the fallen stars and throw them into the abyss. Noah appears in 89:1–9 as a cow given a secret by one of the angels; he turns into a human, builds a boat, and survives the flood with three cows representing his sons.

The first direct divine appearance occurs at 89:14. The proliferation of animals after the flood includes twelve sheep, who give away one of their members to live among wolves (Joseph in Egypt); God gathers the other eleven to dwell with him and multiply, but they are also surrounded by wolves. In 89:15–27 God responds to the pleas of the sheep and rescues them from the wolves in a lengthy representation of the exodus story. The wilderness period also receives a fairly detailed treatment in 89:28–40, followed by a fairly rapid report of the entry into Canaan leading up to the building of the temple in 89:41–50. Within this section God promotes certain sheep to be rams, representing Israel's early kings, and 89:51–67 presents the division of the monarchy, the failure to listen to the prophets, and the resulting rise of predators who eat the sheep. In the midst of this part of the dream, Enoch reports crying out to God because of the lions devouring the sheep in 89:57, and God appoints seventy shepherds in 89:59 to look after the sheep. The identity of the seventy shepherds has been a point of difficulty in interpreting the Animal Apocalypse. Their number and characterization make them unlike the angels, who are represented as stars. As human beings in the allegory, they are unlike the animals who represent actual human beings. Only Noah and Moses have been transformed into humans for their specific tasks, and even the kings of Israel are only elevated by God to the status of rams. The period of the shepherds corresponds to the exile and the dispersion of the people of Israel, so the proposal of R. H. Charles that they represent angels rather than any human ruler seems most likely.[22] Their number may also be connected to the assignment of seventy years of punishment in Jer. 25:11–12 and 2 Chron. 36:21.[23] The Animal Apocalypse thus portrays God's actions toward Israel as both punishment and caretaking at the same time by putting them in the hands of shepherds who are negligent, but under whom Israel survives. The more comprehensive presentation of divine behavior in this section at 89:58 is troubling, as God is "silent" and even "rejoices" when the sheep are devoured.[24]

Beginning at 1 En. 89:72 the sheep return and rebuild Jerusalem, but the writer of the Animal Apocalypse does not view the rebuilding of the temple positively. The text portrays the sheep as blind and their practices as impure in 89:73–74. Moreover, the divine silence of 89:58 continues in 89:75, and opposition to the Israelites continues in the portion of the story corresponding to the Hellenistic period. As at other points the scribe shows the book he is writing to God and pleads with God on behalf of the sheep, but God pays no attention, sets the book aside, and leaves. So the divine response to Enoch's pleas diminishes from listening and appointing the shepherds (89:58), to reading the book but sealing it (89:71), to refusing to read the book

---

22. R. H. Charles, *The Apocrypha and Pseudepigrapha of the Old Testament*, vol. 2 (Oxford: Clarendon, 1913), 255. There is even some disagreement on how to read Charles on this point. Collins points to an association with the patron angels of the nations, but this is not explicit in Charles's statement (*Apocalyptic Imagination*, 54–55). Tiller points to Charles in his outright denial that the tradition of the angelic patrons of the nations (e.g., Deut. 32:8–9) are involved. See Tiller, "*A* Commentary," 51–60. Nickelsburg's view that the image here is an amalgam that might include the angelic patrons in some way seems like a well-balanced position (*1 Enoch 1*, 391–92).
23. On this connection, see Nickelsburg, *1 Enoch 1*, 391–92.
24. Ibid., 385–86.

and departing (89:77).²⁵ Portier-Young argues that Enoch's success in supplicating God during the flood account in the Book of Dreams serves as a model for readers to pray for deliverance, while his failure at later points leaves their own prayers as their only hope.²⁶

In 1 Enoch 90 the shepherds are still in place and a variety of birds attack the sheep in a confusing portrayal that likely corresponds to the years leading up to the Maccabean revolt. The story finally begins to turn with the appearance of a sheep with a large horn in 90:9, representing Judas Maccabeus.²⁷ Part of the shift in the story here is the ability of the horned sheep to fight back and defend themselves, and this action seems to be part of what brings the divine character into the action when the scribe appeals to God again in 90:14. At this point the narrative becomes confusing in its referent. In 90:18 God finally arrives in the midst of the sheep with "the staff of his wrath," and in 90:19 the sheep receive a great sword with which to attack their adversaries. A throne of judgment appears in 90:20 and the final judgment begins in 90:24. It is difficult to say when the work of Judas Maccabeus, in the past of the original audience, ends, and a final judgment, which is in their future, begins. Nickelsburg blames the confusion, in part, on an editorial process that emended an earlier version of the vision in 90:17–19.²⁸ Our earlier discussion raised a question about the possibility of an active revolt like that of Judas by a group like the Dead Sea sect that embraced an apocalyptic view. That sort of dispute between acting and waiting could have been the kind of issue that is contested in the alternative versions of 1 Enoch 90 that Nickelsburg suggests.

The portrayal of the judgment and its resulting new period become clearer in 90:20–37. God begins punishing the shepherds

---

25. Ibid., 395.
26. Portier-Young, *Apocalypse against Empire*, 374.
27. On the identity and role of Judas Maccabeus, see Tiller, *Commentary*, 355–57.
28. Nickelsburg, *1 Enoch 1*, 401.

for killing more of the sheep than God had ordered them to kill (90:22). At this point the Animal Apocalypse struggles with some of the same ambiguities of divine punishment as the prophetic literature in the Tanak. The understanding of other nations as the tool of God's judgment creates moral contradictions demanding some resolution. As far back in the prophetic tradition as Isaiah 10, the Assyrian Empire is both God's "rod of anger" (10:5) and the object of God's judgment because of the arrogance of the Assyrian king (10:12). The judgment of God is complete in 1 En. 90:24–26 when it includes the stars representing the fallen angels, the shepherds representing foreign nations, and the blinded sheep representing unfaithful Israelites. As the vision moves toward its conclusion, the surviving sheep fall down and worship in 90:30, lay down the sword in verse 34, and enter the Lord's house in verse 35. The house, according to verse 36, is full of returned sheep. The final elements of the vision in verses 37–39 are difficult to interpret, as a great white bull appears, which Nickelsburg interprets as a messianic figure. The end of the Animal Apocalypse reflects the beginning in which Adam was a white bull, but now all the cows become white, unlike the differing colors of the sons of Adam and Eve at the beginning. The divisions of humanity appear to be healed so that they are all reunited, and with this Enoch awakes and worships God (v. 40).

The Epistle of Enoch takes up the difficult issue of waiting directly in chapter 92, along with its implications for understanding the behavior of the divine character. To his descendants Enoch declares in 92:2 that "the Great Holy One has appointed days for everything." After the interruption of the portion of the Apocalypse of Weeks in 93:1–10, most of the Epistle of Enoch consists of two kinds of literature addressing the difficulties of living and waiting for God's intervention. The most common type is the statement of woe. While the woes use direct second-person language to address sinners and describe the punishment they will receive in the divine judgment, they are addressed to the children of Enoch primarily as words of comfort, though there can be an aspect of warning to them. The corresponding, somewhat less common type of unit is the statement of exhortation, which often begins with "Fear not" or "Take courage." The juxtaposition of these kinds of statements reveals the primary theme of the Epistle of Enoch, in which even the parts that do not use the formal language of woe and exhortation participate. The judgment of God is coming and Enoch's audience is suffering in the current age, but they will be rewarded while the sinners will be punished. Samuel Adams documents the situation of economic inequality of the period and finds in the Epistle of Enoch a text that "stands in solidarity with those who face oppression under a system marked by elitism and corruption."[29] The result is a stark contrast between two different ways of life and the manner in which God will act toward those who choose the two different ways.[30] Though the woes outnumber the exhortations, the latter exert more control toward the end of the epistle. A characteristic statement of divine judgment is in 100:4–5: "The angels will descend, going down into the hidden places on that day; and those who aided iniquity will be gathered into one place. And the Most High will be aroused on that day to execute great judgment on all. He will set a guard of the holy angels over all the righteous and holy; and they will be kept as the apple of the eye, until evil and sin come to an end." Thus God is portrayed as the vindicator of the righteous, and Enoch's audience is assured that the current divide between heaven and earth will collapse in a great act of judgment at the end.

29. Samuel L. Adams, *Social and Economic Life in Second Temple Judea* (Louisville, KY: Westminster John Knox, 2014), 159–60.
30. For a more detailed description of these forms and how they function in the Epistle of Enoch, see Nickelsburg, *1 Enoch 1*, 416–29. Nickelsburg presents charts that delineate about thirty woes (417) and about ten exhortations (419).

Daniel 7–14 (Greek)

The Greek version of Daniel contains three major additions, the first of which, the Prayer of Azariah and the Song of the Three Jews, is inserted into the middle of Daniel 3 in the version of the story in the Masoretic Text. The other two additions, Susanna and Bel and the Dragon, appear at the end of the book and are typically numbered as Daniel 13 and 14.[31] The content of all three stories was part of the discussion in chapter 3 of this book because even the last two additions appear to be more closely associated with the stories in Daniel 1–6, but their appearance at the end of the book, framing the apocalyptic material in 7–12, will receive further consideration here. The additions to Daniel in the Greek versions are far from being the end of the tradition. Additional Daniel material appears, in fragmentary remains, among the Dead Sea Scrolls, and a new wave of writings connected to Daniel appeared in Christian writings of late antiquity and the early Middle Ages. The continuing traditions match both the legendary tales of Daniel 1–6 and the apocalyptic visions of 7–12 in form.[32] Thus the Greek versions of Daniel stands in the center of the Daniel literary tradition rather than at its end. The extent of this material and the many ways Daniel has been interpreted far beyond its canonical scope up to the present day indicate it is a book that invites expansion even more than others.

---

31. There is some variation in the placement of Susanna and Bel and the Dragon. In the Theodotion text Susanna is placed at the beginning of Daniel, but the Old Greek and Vulgate place it at the end. Bel and the Dragon is always at the end of the book, though in Papyrus 967 Susanna is after it. See the discussion of these manuscripts and arrangement of these texts in John J. Collins, *Daniel: A Commentary on the Book of Daniel* (Minneapolis: Fortress Press, 1993), 3–4. On the placement and possible dates of the expansions, see also Timothy Michael Law, *When God Spoke Greek: The Septuagint and the Making of the Christian Bible* (Oxford: Oxford University Press, 2013), 72–74.
32. Lorenzo DiTommaso, *The Book of Daniel and the Apocryphal Daniel Literature* (Leiden: Brill, 2005), 6–14.

Another difficulty presented by the Greek version of Daniel is its existence in two different versions, usually called the Old Greek and Theodotion. According to St. Jerome the Theodotion text had replaced the Old Greek in Christian usage by the fourth century, and this text is reflected in the early Greek manuscripts of the Christian Bible.[33] The discussion below will distinguish between the two only if the textual differences create different portrayals of the divine character, with preference given to the Old Greek version, the one that would have been in existence before the turn of the eras.[34]

Daniel 7 opens with Daniel's vision of the four beasts. The lack of an introduction to the character named Daniel assumes the reader is familiar with the character from the preceding stories in the book of Daniel, but the timing of the initial vision in the first year of the reign of Belshazzar/Baltasar of Babylon harkens back to Daniel 5, before Darius kills Baltasar in 5:31. Thus the setting of Daniel's dream experience is at the very end of the Babylonian Empire. In Daniel 7:1 a narrator reports that Daniel had a dream and wrote it down, then the language switches in 7:2 to Daniel's description of the dream in the first person. After the description of the four beasts, God appears in the vision in 7:9 as "an Ancient of Days" on a flaming throne with white hair and in a white robe. Tens of thousands of servants surround the divine figure, and the end of 7:10 reveals the scene as a court of judgment. The description of God in 7:9 is striking in two ways, the first of which is that a physical

---

33. The most important manuscript of the Old Greek, Papyrus 967, was rediscovered in 1931. On the significance of this manuscript and its relation to the Theodotion text, see Tim McLay, *The OG and TH Versions of Daniel* (Atlanta: Scholars Press, 1996), 1–7.
34. On the differences between the two texts and how they operate as translations, see R. Timothy McLay, "Daniel," in *A New English Translation of the Septuagint*, ed. Albert Pietersma and Benjamin G. Wright (New York: Oxford University Press, 2007), 991–92. There is now general agreement that the Theodotion text is an independent translation of a Hebrew text, but whether the two Greek versions used the same Hebrew text is uncertain. See Collins, *Daniel*, 220.

portrayal is present at all. The Tanak and, subsequently, Judaism as a whole resist descriptions of God, most likely as an extension of the command against making images. The verbal image is also surprising because it depicts God as an old man, with white hair. While not describing physical characteristics, depictions of YHWH in the Tanak frequently make use of the divine warrior image, which would seem to require a youthful, vigorous deity. Louis Hartman points to a "popular notion of God as an old man," but offers no support for such a notion at the time Daniel was written, other than the possible transfer of bearded images of Zeus in surrounding Greek culture.[35] Jason Bembry demonstrates that the metaphorical attachment of God to the human life cycle, using the language of husband and parent, made the understanding of a God who could age possible. Bembry argues further that the function of time in apocalyptic literature made "refracted portrayals" of God possible, such as old age.[36] The behavior of YHWH in Daniel 1–6, leading up to the aged portrayal in 7:9–14, fits the image of a wise, grandfatherly figure.[37]

The other major interpretive challenge of Dan. 7:9–14 is the appearance of the "son of man" figure. Chapter 7 of this book will address the use of this title in relation to messianic portrayals, but does the figure in Daniel fit that idea? The concept of a messiah figure and its explicit terminology do not appear in Daniel, and the most common understanding of the "son of man" among scholars has been that this is a human figure, which may or may not correspond to any actual human being outside the text. Collins argues for identifying

---

35. Louis F. Hartman and Alexander A. Di Lella, *The Book of Daniel: A New Translation with Introduction and Commentary*, Anchor Bible 23 (Garden City, NY: Doubleday, 1978), 218.
36. Jason Bembry, *Yahweh's Coming of Age* (Winona Lake, IN: Eisenbrauns, 2011), 148–50.
37. For more on the narrative portrayal leading up to the appearance of the Ancient of Days, see Mark McEntire, "The Graying of God in Daniel 1–7," *Review and Expositor* 109 (2012): 569–79.

the son of man figure here as an angelic being, specifically Michael, in part because "the holy ones of the Most High" of verse 22 are angels elsewhere in the book of Daniel.[38] The nature of the son of man figure may be impossible to resolve, and it is more important to identify the function of this figure, particularly in relation to God. If 7:9–10 portrays the setting up of God's throne on earth as a seat of judgment, then there are two possibilities concerning what God gives to the son of man figure in 7:14.[39] When Daniel ponders and asks about the vision in 7:15–22 the answer to this question becomes clear, as he describes the Ancient of Days giving the verdict for "the holy ones of the Most High." God's act of judgment gives dominion and kingship to the son of man figure, and this gives the holy ones possession of the kingdom. The arrival of God on earth for the judgment scene marks the end of the period of spatial dualism characteristic of apocalyptic literature. The continuing divine communication to Daniel in verses 23–27, however, reveals that the time for this arrival will not come until after a fourth kingdom. The first three beasts of Daniel's vision represent the empires of the past—the Babylonians, the Medes, and the Persians. The fourth beast, depicted in the most detailed and horrifying language, is the Greek/Seleucid Empire under which the audience of the book suffers. Daniel 7 must portray the final victory and

---

38. Collins, *Apocalyptic Imagination*, 82–83. See also Collins, *Daniel*, 312–18. For an interpretation of the son of man and the holy ones as symbolic humans, see Hartman and Di Lella, *Book of Daniel*, 218–19. Collins's argument that the angelic identity is confirmed by later texts like the Parables of Enoch and the War Scroll seems strained since those texts have a messianic son of man, which he argues is a later development and not present in Daniel.
39. Some interpreters understand the judgment scene to be in heaven, but Kathryn M. Lopez argues persuasively for an earthly location because of the need to set up God's throne (7:9) and the need for God to come to the location (7:22). See Lopez, "Standing before the Throne of God: Critical Spatiality in Apocalyptic Scenes of Judgment," in *Constructions of Space II: The Biblical City and Other Imagined Spaces*, ed. Jon L. Berquist and Claudia V. Camp (New York: T&T Clark, 2008), 147–48.

judgment of God before describing the beast that really matters to the audience, which even then leaves Daniel "seized with great dismay."[40]

The vision in Daniel 8 receives a date two years after the first vision and is similar in content and reference to the first vision. Again the succession of empires is represented by horns on a ram until eventually a "little horn," representing Antiochus Epiphanes, emerges in 8:9. No direct divine presence appears in the second vision, and when it is complete Gabriel comes to explain it to Daniel in verse 17. Gabriel's explanation implies that the suffering of the Jews at the hands of the empires is a result of divine wrath, though the Old Greek text makes this point a bit more clearly than the Theodotion text in verse 19.[41] The vision and its explanation end in 8:27 and have a physical impact on Daniel, who becomes sick for several days.

The third "vision" of Daniel, which is placed in a very different context in the reign of Darius the Mede, differs from the first two in two important respects. First, the opening of the chapter is a long prayer spoken by Daniel. In the prayer Daniel acknowledges the power of God (9:4, 15), the righteousness of God (vv. 7, 13), and the mercy of God (vv. 4, 9, 18). He also confesses that Israel has violated the law and forsaken God (vv. 5, 8, 11), and concludes the prayer by asking God not to delay in coming to help Israel. Collins points to the tensions between the prayer and the visions in Daniel 7–8. The apocalyptic view in the first two visions understands all of the events they portray as predetermined, but Daniel's prayer in 9:1–19 seems to presume the standard Deuteronomic view of much of the Tanak, that the events are punishment for sin and that repentance might forestall

---

40. This is McLay's translation of the Old Greek in 7:28, in which the language is stronger than the Theodotion text, which he translates as "my thoughts were greatly troubling me" (McLay, "Daniel," 1014). English translations of Daniel in this chapter will be from McLay, unless otherwise noted.
41. The Old Greek says "wrath against the sons of the people," while Theodotion just says "wrath" (ibid., 1015).

them. Moreover, verse 23 indicates that the divine word went out at the beginning of the prayer, and not as a result of it.[42]

The second difference is the lack of a true vision experience. The response to Daniel's prayer is the arrival of the angel Gabriel to speak to him. At issue in the discussion is the meaning of the seventy weeks of punishment, an idea from Jer. 25:11–12 concerning the Babylonian exile that the interpretation from Gabriel schematizes in a manner similar to the Apocalypse of Weeks in 1 Enoch. Daniel had raised this point in 9:2 at the introduction to his prayer. The seventy years of Jeremiah become seventy weeks of years (490 years) in 9:24, and Daniel is searching for a sign of the end of the period. Gabriel provides an explanation in verses 25–27, but not one easy to follow.[43] More significant than any attempt to make the arithmetic of the section match any historical chronology outside the text is the sense that the flow of history is predetermined. The absence of God in the passage is striking. The "ordinance" went out from the Lord, according to verse 23, but the people for whom Daniel prays seem caught in its scheme with little or no hope for divine assistance until it is over.

The vision in Daniel 10 moves to another time, the first year of King Cyrus of Persia, which connects this text back to the introduction of Daniel in 1:21.[44] Daniel's description of his mourning in 10:2 fits as a response to the devastating news of the previous chapter. The angelic being Daniel sees and describes in 10:5–6 is significantly different from earlier appearances of Michael and Gabriel, and the differences have led to disagreements about the identification of this being. Later in the Old Greek text he says

---

42. Collins, *Apocalyptic Imagination*, 86–87.
43. For a more detailed discussion of the possibilities for understanding the scheme, see Hartman and Di Lella, *Book of Daniel*, 246–53.
44. The Hebrew text has "third year of King Cyrus of Persia," which seems to contradict a strict reading of 1:21. See ibid., 262.

that "one of the holy angels helped me," but the Theodotion text inserts Michael's name there, making an identification with Gabriel in 10:5–6 more likely. Both Greek texts identify Michael as the helper by name later at verse 21.[45] Perhaps a more important mystery is the identity of the Persian and Greek figures with whom the angels contend in verses 13–21. Some interpreters understand these as heavenly beings, so the vision is of a battle entirely in heaven which the struggle of the Jewish people on earth reflects.[46] Others understand the Persian and Greek leaders to be earthly figures, but why would they be fighting with heavenly beings? Tim Meadowcroft argues that this is the kind of interaction between earth and heaven that apocalyptic visions are about, so that precise distinctions between heavenly and earthly beings are not necessary.[47] Two important theological points are present at the end of Daniel 10. First, the angelic being tells Daniel that he has left the battle in order to come speak to and reassure Daniel, and he must return to it quickly. This appears to be a subtle indicator that Daniel should not request any more explanations. He has all he needs and such requests are a distraction. Second, though the power of heaven is involved in the struggle, it is still mediated, involving only angels, for whom the Persian and Greek rulers (whether of heaven or earth) appear to be close to an even match.

The return to stories in Daniel 13–14, after the apocalyptic visions, may be incidental, but in the final Greek form of the book the

---

45. McLay, "Daniel," 1018. The Theodotion insertion looks like a response to an Old Greek text that leaves the identity too uncertain for a while, but the Masoretic Text also includes Michael's name.
46. This is the position, for example, of G. B. Caird. See Caird, *The Language and Imagery of the Bible* (Grand Rapids, MI: Eerdmans, 1997), 238. D. S. Russell sees the struggle here between the guardian angels of the nations as one between the "heavenly counterparts" of the earthly nations (*Method and Message*, 245).
47. Tim Meadowcroft, "Who Are the Princes of Persia and Greece (Daniel 10)? Pointers toward the Danielic Vision of Heaven and Earth," *Journal for the Study of the Old Testament* 29 (2004): 101–5.

reconnection to Daniel 1–6 has a subtle impact on the way the book portrays the divine character. The ending of Daniel in chapter 12 is uncertain and the visions have often left Daniel bewildered, troubled, or even sick. The messenger in 12:12 tells Daniel, "Happy is the one who continues" (Theodotion: "perseveres"). But how is one to do that? If Daniel is to function as a book, then the stories at the beginning, which are all about continuing through times of difficulty and persecution, may be the answer, but remembering them after the horror of the visions is difficult. The story of Susanna not only offers a remedy for this by portraying a young woman who survives, but it also includes the Daniel character, whose cleverness helps to save Susanna and also points back to his own struggles in the first half of the book. If the end of Daniel 12 left the reader wondering whether divine help was still available, the story of Susanna reasserts that it is. Much the same is true of Bel and the Dragon, which even includes another version of Daniel in the lions' den. In this version, God does more than just keep the mouths of the lions closed, but sends Habakkuk from Israel to bring food to Daniel. Divine provision is possible, and the story ends with the Babylonian king declaring faith in the God of Israel.

Jubilees 1 and 23

The majority of Jubilees received treatment in chapter 2 because it is primarily a retelling of the past that portrays the divine character differently than the book of Genesis. Two portions of Jubilees, some of chapter 1 and most of 23, extend into the future in such an overt way that commentators have labeled them either eschatological or apocalyptic. The former term is the choice of James VanderKam.[48] Michael Segal, on the other hand, uses "apocalyptic" to describe

---

48. James C. VanderKam, *The Book of Jubilees* (New York: T&T Clark, 2001), 57.

these parts of Jubilees.[49] The spatial dualism of apocalyptic exists throughout Jubilees, so the key question is whether a sense of temporal dualism exists in this text. While it almost certainly does, it expresses itself in an odd way. The death of Abraham in Jubilees leads into an apparent diversion concerning the changes in the human life span. The primary argument of Jubilees 23 is that human sin led to a decrease in life spans after the flood, but that in the distant future, following a period of intense divine punishment, human obedience and divine mercy will lead to a gradual restoration of the long life spans of early human beings in Genesis. Perhaps the decisive verse is 23:29, which declares, "And all of their days will be complete and they will live in peace and rejoicing and there will be no Satan and no evil (one) who will destroy, because all of their days will be days of blessing and healing."[50]

James Scott delineates the chronological scheme of Jubilees and finds a significant similarity between its scheme and that of the Apocalypse of Weeks in 1 Enoch. Jubilees 23 divides history into three periods, producing a strong symmetry between the first and last eras. The decreasing life spans of the first period are gradually restored in the third.[51] In both 1 Enoch 93 and Jubilees 23 the gradual restoration of the world to an ideal state is "expressed in terms of sabbatical chronology (the 490-year 'week' and the 49-year 'jubilee,' respectively) whose periods are engraved on heavenly tablets (cf. 1 Enoch 93:22; Jub. 23:32)."[52] Jubilees 23:30–31 uses direct language to attribute acts of healing and mercy to the divine character, thus

---

49. Michael Segal, *The Book of Jubilees: Rewritten Bible, Redaction, Ideology and Theology* (Leiden: Brill, 2007), 320–21.
50. Quotations of Jubilees come from O. S. Wintermute, "Jubilees," in *Old Testament Pseudepigrapha*, ed. James H. Charlesworth (Garden City, NY: Doubleday, 1985), 35–142.
51. James M. Scott, *On Earth as in Heaven: The Restoration of Sacred Time and Sacred Space in the Book of Jubilees* (Leiden: Brill, 2005), 103–22.
52. Ibid., 126.

the temporal dualism is collapsed and God is active in the world of human beings again.

Conclusion

The depiction of God in apocalyptic literature addresses the challenge of divine hiddenness in a particular way. Most importantly for the communities to whom such writings are addressed, hiddenness is a matter of divine choice that is not permanent. The apocalyptic approach draws a sharp contrast with the divine character in books like Ezra-Nehemiah. In the latter, YHWH is able to act in subtle, invisible ways to influence human beings, even foreign leaders who might otherwise be enemies of Israel. Texts like Nehemiah 9 claim that God has not always acted this way, but was more direct and observable in the past, yet there is no indication that an end to the hiddenness will come. It is not difficult to understand how the continuing struggles of the Jewish people throughout the Persian and Hellenistic periods would pose serious challenges for theological claims like those found in Ezra-Nehemiah.

At first glance the Maccabean story of armed revolt, examined in chapter 5, seems incompatible with an apocalyptic view that assumes a dramatic divine intervention in the near future. The former approach portrays a deity who inspires and assists human beings who fight back against oppression using human, military means. The accounts in 1 and 2 Maccabees differ from each other in terms of how explicitly they speak of the divine character and the heavenly assistance the Maccabeans receive, and 2 Maccabees portrays the role of martyrs and the failure of divine assistance, but Israel's God still assists armed resistance in both narratives. The appearance of Judas Maccabeus in 1 Enoch 90 may be something of a surprise, and the discussion earlier in this chapter dealt with the possibility that it is a later insertion. Nevertheless, eventually the question of compatibility between apocalyptic eschatology and active military revolt against oppressors demands some sort of resolution. Is it possible that the Enoch tradition at this point made some attempt to bring them together, despite the possibility that the two approaches parted ways entirely in the views of the group that produced the Dead Sea Scrolls? Portier-Young emphasizes the joining of war traditions involving Judas Maccabeus and Joshua in 1 Enoch in a way that highlights faithfulness to God's covenant more than successful overthrow of the oppressor.[53] The military exploits of Judas remain within the visionary realm, linked to a mythical past. For the vision of Enoch to tell the story of Israel, ignoring the work of the Maccabeans would have been a problematic choice, but perhaps the writer of the Dream Visions of Enoch found a way to make them part of a different kind of resistance to foreign domination.

The apocalyptic portions of Daniel and 1 Enoch represent the most important exemplars of this important genre of literature from the last two centuries before the Common Era. Other pieces of literature are sometimes included in the discussion, but present various difficulties. The Testament of Moses is an apocalyptic work whose date is very difficult to determine. Nickelsburg argues for a second-century BCE date for an earlier version of the work, which was then updated after the turn of the eras.[54] There is, however, only one extant copy of the Testament of Moses, a poorly preserved Latin manuscript from the sixth century, which makes firm conclusions about this text and its origins difficult to draw.[55] Fourth Ezra is an important apocalyptic work, but it is clearly a product of the Common Era,

---

53. Portier-Young, *Apocalypse against Empire*, 377–79.
54. Nickelsburg, *Jewish Literature*, 74–77. Given the manuscript evidence, the conclusion that the Latin version was translated from a Greek text which had been translated from Hebrew or Aramaic seems highly speculative.
55. J. Priest, "Testament of Moses: A New Translation and Introduction," in *The Old Testament Pseudepigrapha*, ed. James H. Charlesworth (Garden City, NY: Doubleday, 1983), 1:920–21.

and the extant manuscripts exhibit Christian influence, even if there was an earlier Jewish version behind it. The Sibylline Oracles are a massive collection of material, much of which falls into the category of apocalyptic, but their transmission and present status make isolating portions of the collection and dating them to a time before the turn of the eras very difficult.[56] I sight these examples, among many others, to indicate the heavy influence of apocalyptic thought and literature in the period with which this study is concerned and beyond, which would include the Apocalypse of John in the New Testament.

Apocalyptic literature elicited a distinctive fascination that continues to the present day, and part of the fascination has to do with the way it portrays the divine character. The end of the Tanak presents a hidden divine character, whose activity in the world is limited to the internal influencing of human beings. Apocalyptic literature appears to be less than fully satisfied by such a theology, and during times of great struggle and suffering for the Jewish people this is understandable. By establishing a spatial dualism and attributing the subtle divine influence on earth to mediating angelic beings, apocalyptic literature could leave the divine character unchanged, still possessing all of the raw power that had initially created the world. The chronological dualism was also necessary to make this understanding possible and not permanent, but the writers struggled with presenting some sense of timing.[57] The portions of 1 Enoch and Daniel examined here frequently delve into schematized versions of history, but these always seem malleable, as even contemporary efforts to match them with events and times outside the text prove. The scheme in Jubilees 23 differs in its arithmetic details but moves in

---

56. Nickelsburg attempts to do this with much of Book 3 of the Sibylline Oracles, but his dating is disputed. See Nickelsburg, *Jewish Literature*, 193–94.
57. For a more detailed discussion of these developments, see Stone, *Ancient Judaism*, 83–89.

similar directions and accomplishes the same goal as it works out the restorative results of the end of the spatial divide between the realm of God and the world of human beings.

In another sense, the visions themselves become the divine presence in the world. Both 1 Enoch and Daniel also require a human mediator who is able to transcend the spatial dualism in order to perceive divine mysteries. These two characters connected the situation of Jews in the Hellenistic empire with important points in Israel's past. Enoch had been able to help humanity, through Noah, to survive the flood, the greatest act of divine punishment, and Daniel plays a similar role in relation to the Babylonian exile. Establishing the present day of the audience of Daniel as a continuation of the captivity and suffering of the past provided a clearer sense of Jewish identity within the long succession of foreign empires so often depicted in the visions.[58] An additional message could be that Antiochus, like the emperors of the past, would eventually pass away. The question is whether he would be the last tyrant.

The approach of apocalyptic literature placed it in great tension with other traditions, literature, and ways of thinking in Jewish tradition. One relatively minor point is the positive portrayal of the Persian Empire in texts like Isaiah 40–55 and Ezra-Nehemiah, which stands in tension with the portrayal of Persia as one of the beasts in Daniel 8. The discussion above identified the tension between the Deuteronomic view, expressed in Daniel's prayer in Daniel 9, and the apocalyptic view of a periodized scheme of history. More seriously, the prophetic literature, especially Jeremiah and Ezekiel, expended considerable effort renegotiating the understanding of inherited sin and punishment. The declaration of Ezekiel at 18:20–21 is difficult to square with an apocalyptic perspective: "The person who sins shall

---

58. Portier-Young, *Apocalypse against Empire*, 270.

die. A child shall not suffer for the iniquity of a parent, nor a parent suffer for the iniquity of a child; the righteousness of the righteous shall be his own, and the wickedness of the wicked shall be his own." If this is the case, then why does an all-powerful God wait, outside the world of human suffering? The need for a divine entry into the world leads to the texts examined in the next chapter.

7

God of the Future

The development of God's character in the literature used in chapter 6 has left a space that can now be filled in, to some degree. Apocalyptic literature removed the divine presence from the space occupied by human beings through the use of a spatial dualism. The accompanying temporal dualism, which separated the present time of these writings from the time when the spatial dualism would collapse and the two worlds would be rejoined in the distant future, left a middle time, the near future, in which divine presence and activity lacked description. Apocalyptic literature itself was one way of filling this in-between time, with heavenly agents managing the world and heavenly messengers bringing descriptions of the other space. But it becomes apparent from looking at other literature that this way either did not appeal to, or was not enough for, everyone within Judaism at that time. Perhaps there were ways for God to be more present in the world of human affairs during this period. Two means of such presence emerged. One was a divine representative more powerfully connected to God than past or present mediating agents. The other involved further development of written texts through which God could speak more directly.

A God Who Is Coming

It is difficult to talk about the concept of a messiah before and during the turn of the eras without introducing later Christian understandings, so readers of texts from that period and earlier must be vigilant about their assumptions. The noun form of the word, the root of which is the verb meaning "anoint," appears in the Hebrew Scriptures only thirty-nine times, as listed below in table 7-1.

Table 7-1

The Occurrences of the Noun "Messiah" in the Hebrew Scriptures

Book	Number of Uses	Most Common Referent
Leviticus	4 times	Priests
Samuel	18 times	Kings (Saul and David)
Chronicles	2 times	King, Israelite ancestors
Psalms	10 times	King?
Lamentations	1 time	King
Isaiah	1 time	Cyrus
Habakkuk	1 time	Israelites
Daniel	2 times	A prince (Zerubbabel?)

The data demonstrate that the term "messiah" is most closely associated with the Israelite monarchy, but not exclusively so. Other groups, such as priests or even Israelites more generally, can be called anointed one(s), as can a foreign king like Cyrus of Persia. None of the occurrences of the term in the Hebrew Scriptures refer to the type of powerful figure it came to be associated with later, one coming in the near future to deliver God's people. Such a figure does appear, however, in other literature that will be the focus of the first section of this chapter, most notably in the Parables of Enoch (1 Enoch 37–71), the Psalms of Solomon, and certain documents found among the Dead Sea Scrolls. The extent of messianism in Jewish literature from the last two centuries BCE has been a matter of some dispute. Charlesworth's survey of the literature he identifies as Pseudepigrapha yields only five relevant texts, and he dates all but the Psalms of Solomon after the turn of the eras.[1] Collins challenges Charlesworth's conclusions about the lack of widespread messianism within Judaism before the turn of the eras, based on the larger number and greater extent of references among the literature of the Dead Sea Scrolls.[2] Lawrence Schiffman identifies two strands of messianism in Second Temple Judaism, which he labels restorative and utopian.[3] The first is more recognizable in terms of connections to the Tanak, with precursors in some of the prophetic literature related to the Persian period, such as Zechariah and Malachi. The future figure in this strain of messianism was still connected, at least in terms of function, to the Israelite monarchy and would bring about a great reform of the people and nation. The utopian version of messianism appears in the Tanak only in Daniel (e.g., 12:1) and includes a greater sense of disruption with the present age. Utopian messianic thought thus has extensive connections with apocalyptic thought. Eventually some divided the idea of a messiah into two figures, one more political and one more religious. The clearest expression of the two-messiah view is in the Community Rule, which identifies a messiah of Aaron and a

---

1. See James H. Charlesworth, "The Messiah in the Pseudepigrapha," in *Religion (Judentum: Allgemeines, Palästinisches Judentum)*, ed. Wolfgang Haase (Berlin: Walter de Gruyter, 1979), 196–216. The majority of opinion among scholars has now moved the date of composition for the Parables of Enoch back into the first century BCE.
2. John J. Collins, "What Was Distinctive about Messianic Expectation at Qumran," in *The Bible and the Dead Sea Scrolls*, ed. James H. Charlesworth (Waco, TX: Baylor University Press, 2006), 2:71–72.
3. Lawrence H. Schiffman, *Reclaiming the Dead Sea Scrolls: The History of Judaism, the Background of Christianity, the Lost Library of Qumran* (Philadelphia: Jewish Publication Society, 1994), 317–18.

messiah of Israel (9:11–12).[4] Ideas about a messiah, along with figures who would eventually embody such claims, varied tremendously, and some of the more significant understandings will be demonstrated in the discussion of texts below.

The discussion of 1 Enoch 1–36 in chapter 2 of this book provided significant background about the book as a whole. The majority of scholars agree that the Parables section was a later addition to the 1 Enoch corpus, but estimates of the date of composition range from early in the first century BCE to the middle of the first century CE.[5] Some ideas in chapters 37–71 stand in contrast to those in the sections on either side, and the most important of these for the discussion here is the appearance of a messianic figure, though the depiction of that figure is not consistent even within 37–71. None of the fragments of 1 Enoch found at Qumran are from the Parables section, so it is possible there was little or no interaction between the Parables of Enoch and the Dead Sea texts treated below, but, as Nickelsburg argues, this is not conclusive evidence of a late date.[6] Nevertheless, the processes of dating these texts have become intertwined. One part of dating the Dead Sea Scrolls is easy because they were almost certainly put in the caves before the Roman invasion of the area in the sixth decade of the first century BCE. While that boundary point at the late end of the range is easy to establish, though, a boundary at the early end of the range is much more difficult. Some of the scrolls appear to have been two or three centuries old when they were put in the caves. The source of the scrolls is a related problem. Were they all written by the group that hid them, in or around the Qumran area, or were some of them gathered from other places throughout Israel?

---

4. Ibid., 323–24.
5. For details on this debate, see George W. E. Nickelsburg and James C. VanderKam, *1 Enoch 2: A Commentary on the Book of 1 Enoch, Chapters 37–80* (Minneapolis: Fortress Press, 2011), 58–65.
6. Ibid., 254.

Uncertainty about the production and collection of the Dead Sea Scrolls should lead to an independent dating of the Parables of Enoch, and in recent decades a majority opinion placing the composition of the Parables in the last half of the first century BCE has emerged.[7]

A general approach to the Dead Sea Scrolls should start by separating the documents into two groups, those that are copies of books found elsewhere, including the Hebrew Scriptures, and those that seem to be peculiar to the group that collected the scrolls.[8] This chapter will treat four texts—the War Scroll, the Damascus Document, the Community Rule, and the Temple Scroll—all of which fall in the latter, sectarian group. The primary ideas and apparent purposes of these documents are not identical, but do overlap significantly. The War Scroll and the Damascus Document emphasize the approaching end of time and the coming of God, and the latter includes extensive rules for the life of the community in the meantime. The Community Rule makes reference to an approaching change, but puts far more emphasis on laws and regulations concerning the life of members in the sectarian group. References to a messianic figure are explicit in the Damascus Document and the Community Rule, but are a matter of dispute in the War Scroll. The Damascus Document and the Community Rule will function in part as a transition from the "coming God" in the first main section of this chapter and the "written God" in the second section because they also include rules for the daily life of the community, but it will be

---

7. For an overview of the arguments and a case for a date around 30 BCE, see Paolo Sacchi, "Qumran and the Dating of the Parables of Enoch," in Charlesworth, *Bible and the Dead Sea Scrolls*, 2:377–92. Sacchi accounts for the absence of the Parables at Qumran by positing a schism between the Qumran community and Enochism, after which the Parables were composed within the latter movement (390–91).
8. The one scroll that presents problems for the use of these two categories is the one called the Damascus Document. Pieces of as many as eight copies of this document were found in three different caves at Qumran, and these were matched to two medieval documents that had been found near the end of the nineteenth century in the Cairo Genizah.

the Temple Scroll that most embodies this notion of a divine voice present in literature, speaking directly to the reader or hearer.

There is fierce, ongoing debate about the identity of the persons who produced the scrolls. For almost all of their history the scrolls have been linked with the Essenes, a Jewish group mentioned in the writings of Josephus, Philo, and Pliny the Elder, though the writers of the scrolls never refer to themselves by this name. The equation of the two groups has sometimes been little more than an assumption, but Joan E. Taylor makes a more robust case for the Essene hypothesis.[9] Because the concern here is with the portrayal of God in the texts, knowing more about the group that produced them might be of some help, but uncertainty does not place a significant limit on our understanding. Without naming themselves, the writers of the texts reveal a great deal about their understanding of themselves. The establishment of an identity (such as the Essene hypothesis) would tell us what others thought of them and whether they had significant influence outside their own membership, but their portrayal of God emerges from their own texts even if the external identity of the group is uncertain.

1 Enoch 37–71

The large section in the middle of the final form of 1 Enoch most often receives the designation the Parables of Enoch, a title derived from a description within the book at 68:1. Each of the major discourses also introduces itself as a parable at 38:1, 45:1, and 58:1. The Parables (or Similitudes) of Enoch appear to be an originally

---

9. Joan E. Taylor, *The Essenes, the Scrolls, and the Dead Sea* (New York: Oxford University Press, 2012), 244–303. Taylor also revives and revises the "genizah theory" of Eleazar Sukenik. The size and variety of the collection and the dispersal of the scrolls make the common idea of a rapid hiding of the scrolls seem unlikely. Taylor proposes that the caves were temporary sites for preparing old scrolls for burial, and that the scrolls were brought there from Essene groups throughout Israel (272–95). If this is true the influence of the texts may have been much wider than if they were the product of a single sectarian group living in the area of the Dead Sea.

independent work, which eventually became a part of the large literary complex called 1 Enoch. The section has much in common with other parts of the book, particularly when it revisits the story of Noah and the flood and portrays an eschatological judgment.[10] A major factor that distinguishes it from the rest of 1 Enoch, though, is the appearance of a figure called "the Son of Man" or "the Chosen One." The opening of the collection at 37:1 describes what follows as "the vision of wisdom that Enoch saw," and this often seems like a better description of the content because the three discourses describe visionary experiences of Enoch.[11]

The most striking feature of the Parables section, which has drawn most of the interpretive attention, is the presence of a character variously identified as "the Son of Man" or with three other, less frequent titles—"the Chosen One," "the Righteous One," or "the Anointed One." Nickelsburg argues persuasively that images derived from a combination of the Servant Songs in Isaiah, royal poems in Isaiah 11 and Psalm 2, and the vision in Daniel 7 help form this composite figure and account for the variety of designations.[12] The activity of this figure defines the purpose of each of the three discourses. Though the title "Son of Man" does not appear explicitly until 46:3, the other titles in the first discourse (38–44) describe the coming of the same character. The second discourse (45–57) describes the enthronement of the Son of Man and prepares for his judgment of the world, the subject of the third discourse (58–69).[13]

The term "son of man" in the Tanak and other Jewish literature presents enormous problems, and it is clear that use of the term shifted

---

10. See the summary of these literary relationships in George W. E. Nickelsburg, *Jewish Literature between the Bible and the Mishnah,* 2nd ed. (Minneapolis: Fortress Press, 2005), 248–49.
11. On the naming of the section, see Nickelsburg and VanderKam, *1 Enoch 2,* 85. All quotations of 1 Enoch are from George W. E. Nickelsburg and James C. VanderKam, *1 Enoch: The Hermeneia Translation* (Minneapolis: Fortress Press, 2012).
12. Nickelsburg and VanderKam, *1 Enoch 2,* 113–16.
13. Ibid., 119–20.

and evolved in ways that make a single definition impossible. Sabino Chialá traces the development of the term with specific reference to its use in 1 Enoch 46–48 and 71.[14] Initially in the Tanak, "son of man" designates a human being in the third person, but the usage shifts in Ezekiel when YHWH uses the term to address Ezekiel the prophet directly. The biggest shift in the Tanak takes place in Daniel where the occurrence in 8:17 refers to Daniel, while the one in 7:13 refers to a much different figure who is difficult to identify.[15] Chialá concludes about the son of man in Daniel that "there is no trace of a particular figure with the functions later texts were to attribute to him. . . . Nonetheless, the book contains the basic *imagistic repertoire* that was taken up and elaborated in the centuries that followed."[16] In 1 En. 47:3–48:6 God, identified as the "Head of Days"[17] (another image borrowed from Daniel), gives up the throne to the Son of Man, an act unprecedented in the Tanak where YHWH is always the judge.[18] The image evolves one more time in 71:9–14 when Enoch himself is the Son of Man. These examples are enough to demonstrate that occurrences of the term need individual consideration.

Understanding the work of the Son of Man in the three discourses of 1 Enoch 37–71 requires an examination of the God who sends and enthrones him. The dominant divine designation throughout 1 Enoch is "the Lord of the Spirits," and the introductory section prior to the first discourse indicates a shift in divine behavior and attitude. In 37:4 Enoch indicates he has received wisdom that had been withheld before by the will of "the Lord of the Spirits." As the

---

14. Sabino Chialá, "The Son of Man: The Evolution of an Expression," in *Enoch and the Messiah Son of Man: Revisiting the Book of the Parables*, ed. Gabriele Boccaccini (Grand Rapids, MI: Eerdmans, 2007), 159–63.
15. Ibid., 154–59.
16. Ibid., 158.
17. On the background of the depiction of God as aged, see Jason Bembry, *Yahweh's Coming of Age* (Winona Lake, IN: Eisenbruans, 2011), 107–50.
18. Chialá, "Son of Man," 161.

first discourse opens, 38:3 describes the coming appearance of the Righteous One who will drive the wicked away from the righteous and cause the death of kings and rulers, while the Lord will stop showing mercy at that point. In 39:2 divine speech confirms the end of all mercy for the wicked, but the righteous, who are the focus of 39:3–8, will dwell under the Lord's wings. The opening of the first discourse thus announces a new period of divine activity, creating a permanent division between the righteous and the wicked, which a new divine agent will inaugurate.

In 39:9–14 Enoch praises the Lord who strengthened him and who knew all things before creation. The section concludes with Enoch describing a change in the appearance of his own face because of the vision he has seen. He does not describe the change, but the effect of proximity to the divine presence is reminiscent of the change in the face of Moses in Exodus 34. The visible change in both places is confirmation of contact with the divine, and the testimony of Enoch carries the authority of the revelation to Moses on Sinai. A related point of continuity with the Torah is the inability of ordinary humans to have direct contact with YHWH because of the Lord's dangerous, transformative power.[19] The preexistence of God and God's knowledge arises as a new theological issue in this part of 1 Enoch. As if answering an unasked question, 39:11 suddenly states, "In his presence there is no limit; He knew before the age was created what would be forever, and for all the generations that will be." Not only does this directly address a question of divine preexistence left open by Genesis 1, but it is also an overt part of the removal from 1 Enoch of the various texts in the Tanak in which YHWH seems genuinely surprised, especially by human behavior. Given the context within the Parables of Enoch, the primary purpose of God's

---

19. For more on this feature in Exodus 34, see Mark McEntire, *Portraits of a Mature God: Choices in Old Testament Theology* (Minneapolis: Fortress Press, 2013), 73–74.

infinite knowing is to assure the completeness of the coming divine judgment.

Angels are a significant aspect of earlier parts of 1 Enoch and they emerge in the first discourse with faces, voices, names, and tasks (40:1–10). Because the angels mediate divine presence, the tasks they perform are substitutes for divine actions. Michael's task is patient mercy, Raphael's is healing, Gabriel's is strengthening, and Phanuel's is overseeing repentance. Following his introduction to the angels, in the remainder of the first discourse Enoch witnesses other secrets of heaven, the most important of which is the inevitable divine judgment; the secrets of the cosmos and creation undergird God's work of judgment. The separation of the righteous and the wicked reflects the dichotomies of creation like light and darkness in 41:8–9; and the authority of the Lord of the Spirits to judge reflects his ability to command the stars by name in 43:1–4.

A strange interlude about Wisdom as a female character appears in 1 En. 42:1–2. Unable to find a resting place in the world among humans she returns to heaven to live among the angels. Another figure called "Iniquity" goes out to dwell among humans and 42:3 describes her presence in terms of restorative water. So 1 Enoch 42 demands comparison with Proverbs 8–9 in the Tanak and various passages in Sirach and the Wisdom of Solomon that personify wisdom as a female figure. John Collins observes that the behavior of Wisdom in 1 Enoch 42, which he classifies with other apocalyptic literature, stands in contrast to the distinct movement of Wisdom into divine roles in Sirach, and to the specific claim that Wisdom found a home in Israel in Sir. 24:8–12.[20] Nickelsburg and VanderKam describe an even harsher contrast: "The poem can be understood as an outright attack on the notion that the Mosaic Torah embodies

---

20. John J. Collins, *Jewish Wisdom in the Hellenistic Age* (Louisville, KY: Westminster John Knox, 1997), 51.

heavenly Wisdom and, thus, as a denigration of the Torah as an effective catalyst of the righteous life."[21] Nevertheless, they acknowledge that this absolute view does not fit with the Parables of Enoch generally, so the wisdom poem is likely an inserted fragment. The portrayal of Iniquity as life-giving water also seems a contradiction to Sir. 24:12–34 where Wisdom receives a similar description.[22] The first discourse closes with a final confirmation of God's mastery of the universe, including lightning and stars, which represent the holy ones of God.

The second discourse opens with a poem containing a divine speech placing the Chosen One on the throne of judgment (45:3). The prose explanation that follows in 1 Enoch 46 begins with the startling description of God as the one whose head was "like white wool." The depiction of God with a physical description is rare in Jewish tradition, so the image of a white-haired God is striking for two reasons; first, because it is in the text at all.[23] The second startling aspect is the portrait of an aged God, a trait borrowed from the description in Dan. 7:9.[24] Therefore, two questions arise from the theophanic portrait in 1 En. 46:1. Why is God described physically at all, and why in this particular way? In Daniel 7 the aged picture of God fits the way God behaves in the narrative leading up to it, as a grandfatherly source of wisdom and counsel.[25] In 1 Enoch 46 the white-haired God is introducing the powerful and vigorous Son of Man who will assume the throne and the task of judgment. In Daniel 7 God also interacts with a figure described as "like a son of

---

21. Nickelsburg and VanderKam, *1 Enoch 2*, 139.
22. Ibid., 141.
23. On the embodiment of God, see McEntire, *Portraits of a Mature God*, 197–98.
24. On the aging of God and its relation to the text in Daniel, see Bembry, *Yahweh Comes of Age*, 148–49.
25. See the development of this idea in Mark McEntire, "The Graying of God in Daniel 1–7," *Review and Expositor* 109 (2012): 572–77. See also Jack Miles, *God: A Biography* (New York: Vintage, 1995), 365.

man." Given these common elements, the Daniel 7 passage must lie in the background of 1 Enoch 46, though the author of the Parables of Enoch developed the description of a human form, representing a faithful Israel in Dan. 7:13, into a specifically messianic figure in 1 Enoch 46.[26] While it is possible to see an aging God in both Daniel 7 and 1 Enoch 46 having a diminished capacity, it is more likely that God is assuming the role of revered advisor in order to create space for another figure.

The Chosen One or Son of Man, who has a human face in 46:1, receives clearer definition in 1 Enoch 48, which claims he was present before the creation of the world but had been concealed by God until this point. In 1 Enoch 46 and 48 the Son of Man comes to humiliate kings and remove them from their thrones. Between these two depictions of the judgment is the report of the prayer of the righteous ones in 1 Enoch 47. When the prayers of the righteous reach the Lord of the Spirits, 47:4 assures the readers they have been heard, and the revealing of the Son of Man in chapter 38 appears to be the divine response to those prayers. The remainder of the second discourse deals with several subjects. First Enoch 50–51 assures readers of God's great mercy and of the resurrection of the dead, leading up to a gruesome depiction of the great judgment in chapters 53–54. Enoch sees the "angels of plague" preparing chains for the kings of the earth, and the "angel of peace" tells him how Michael, Raphael, Gabriel, and Phanuel will defeat the army of Azazel. The reference to the great flood in 54:7–55:2 comes as something of a surprise, but the reminder of God's repentance after the flood serves as an assurance that the coming judgment will not destroy everyone on the earth. God, as the Ancient One in 55:1–2,

---

26. For a more thorough explanation of the use of the Aramaic phrase meaning "son of man" in Dan. 7:13, see Louis F. Hartman and Alexander A. Di Lella, *The Book of Daniel: A New Translation with Introduction and Commentary*, Anchor Bible 23 (Garden City, NY: Doubleday, 1978), 85–102.

recognizes that such total, indiscriminate destruction was an empty act and repents, vowing never to do it again, as in Gen. 9:8–17.

The third parable begins in 58:1 and portrays the judgment itself. The coming of divine judgment brings with it many of the standard accoutrements of a theophany, including lightning, thunder, and earthquake. Though the second parable had portrayed the enthronement of the Chosen One, this is a repeated emphasis of the third parable in 61:8, 62:1–2, and 69:27.[27] The third parable leaves no doubt that the judgments of the Chosen One are the judgments of God. First Enoch 64:64–69 returns to the subject of the fallen angels and the flood, and one purpose of such recollection appears to be remembering Enoch's prediction of the flood in 65:1–12, which would verify Enoch's pronouncement of the judgment to come. Confusion arises as the third parable draws to a close when Enoch ascends into heaven and sees millions of angels, along with the Ancient of Days, whose hair is white in 71:10 as it was in 1 Enoch 46. In 71:14 an angel approaches Enoch and addresses him as "son of man," and interpreters have disagreed sharply about whether the address identifies Enoch with the messianic figure of the Parables of Enoch.[28] The relationship of the messianic Chosen One or Son of Man to the God of Israel is uncertain in 1 Enoch, and the identification of this character with a human figure like Enoch clouds the relationship even further. The Son of Man receives divine authority, and his appearance is a step toward reestablishing divine presence among human beings, but the Parables seem reluctant to be too clear on this point. This dramatic portion of 1 Enoch comes to an end with a promise to the righteous that they will dwell with

---

27. Nickelsburg and VanderKam, *1 Enoch 2*, 120.
28. E. Isaac, along with Charlesworth, argues against identifying Enoch with the Elect One and insists on the translation "son of man" (71:14) with lowercase letters. See "1 (Ethiopic Apocalypse of) Enoch: A New Translation and Introduction," in *The Old Testament Pseudepigrapha*, ed. James H. Charlesworth (Garden City, NY: Doubleday, 1983), 1:50.

the Son of Man for a long time, but the identity of this figure and his relationship to God remains shrouded in mystery. The role of the Son of Man as companion and helper at the very end (71:17) stands in some contrast to the role that the figure plays as a judge in the Parables of Enoch up to this point.[29]

The War Scroll

The War Scroll, designated 1QM,[30] was one of the original seven Dead Sea scrolls to emerge in the late 1940s. Five other fragmentary copies were later found in Cave 4 at Qumran. It is possible the document had relatively little influence, since the number of copies is fairly small and it appears nowhere else other than the caves. Nevertheless, it provides a more detailed and vivid description of the final eschatological battle than any other writing of the period, so it merits some attention. The central question here is understanding how the War Scroll depicts God's role in the final battle. In the description, the Sons of Light do not generally fare well against the Sons of Darkness and the writer of the scroll appears to be encouraging a similarly beleaguered audience. The present struggle against evil is presented as "God's crucible" in column 17 of the scroll, a necessary part of the ultimate exaltation of the Sons of Light at the time of God's final appearance.[31] Assurance of the divine advent appears early in the document at 1:13–15 and receives confirmation

---

29. The relationship of chapter 71 with the remainder of the Parables of Enoch is a point of contention. Nickelsburg summarizes the arguments and contends for the position that chapter 71 is a later addition to the text (Nickelsburg and VanderKam, *1 Enoch 2*, 329–32).
30. The naming of Dead Sea Scrolls has not always been consistent. Designations like this one indicate first the number of the cave in which it was found with an Arabic numeral, then use a Q (from Qumran) to indicate the location. Sometimes the Q is followed by another Arabic numeral assigned to that particular manuscript, especially with smaller fragments. Some documents received a name based on the content, which is used in the abbreviated designation. In the case the M comes from the first letter of the Hebrew word for "war."
31. Martin Abegg Jr., "The War Scroll," in *The Dead Sea Scrolls: A New Translation*, by Michael Wise, Martin Abegg Jr., and Edward Cook (San Francisco: Harper Collins, 1996), 151.

later in the more detailed account of the final battle in 18:1. For much of the battle, however, God is not directly present, and four angels serve as mediators accompanying the Sons of Light, who use battle towers with the names Michael, Gabriel, Sariel, and Raphael on them (9:10–16).[32] Throughout the battle instructions the author attempts to hold the tension between God's ability to win the battle and God's delay in coming to the direct assistance of the Sons of Light. The speech and prayer of the chief priest in columns 10 and 11 are central to this effort and remind the audience of the great divine warrior of the past, specifically YHWH in his victory over Pharaoh at the Red Sea (11:9–10). The tension between present defeat and future victory is one of many examples of ideas in conflict within the theology of the War Scroll.[33]

The presence of a messianic figure in the War Scroll has been a matter of some dispute. The text in Num. 24:17–19 that often received messianic interpretations in Judaism during this era is quoted at War 11:6 but seems to apply directly to God, not a separate messianic figure.[34] More difficult is the reference to a "prince of the whole congregation" at 5:1. Nickelsburg assumes this to be a royal messianic figure, but others express doubt.[35] In various English translations of the War Scroll there is disagreement about whether to capitalize the title.[36] Even if this disputed possibility is granted, the

---

32. Nickelsburg, *Jewish Literature*, 144.
33. On these tensions, see Jean Duhaime, "The War Scroll," in *The Dead Sea Scrolls: Hebrew, Aramaic, and Greek Texts with English Translations*, ed. James H. Charlesworth (Tübingen: J. C. B. Mohr, 1995), 85–86. Some of the tensions may be resolved by separating the present text into compositional layers, but such a process is complex and creates other difficulties.
34. Ibid., 118–19.
35. See Nickelsburg, *Jewish Literature*, 144. Lawrence Schiffman allows for the possibility that this is the "lay messiah," but still emphasizes the lack of explicit mention of a messiah in the War Scroll. See *Reclaiming the Dead Sea Scrolls*, 325.
36. Duhaime produces an uncapitalized "prince" ("War Scroll," 107). Florentino García Martínez and Eibert J. C. Tigchelaar capitalize "Prince" (*The Dead Sea Scrolls Study Edition* [Leiden: Brill, 1997], 1:121). Abegg translates using the capitalized "Leader" ("War Scroll," 155).

War Scroll falls far short of the Parables of Enoch in developing the idea of a powerful, coming figure separate from God.

The decisive feature of the War Scroll for this study is the depiction of the eschatological war and God's role within it, yet it produces an uncertain picture. Much of the uncertainty is the result of the inconsistency of the scroll's dualism. The war is both a human and divine task, and there is a sense in which it is both a nationalistic war of Israel against its enemies and a cosmic war between good and evil. Philip Davies emphasizes the fantasy element of the depiction of war that is in tension with the precise level of tactical detail, but recognizes that such elements sometimes do coexist. One of the functions of fantasy literature is to resolve the cognitive dissonance between theological claims and lived reality.[37]

The Community Rule

The scroll often called the Community Rule[38] is a relatively complete and coherent document found among the initial set of scrolls discovered in Cave 1 at Qumran, thus it is designated 1QS. Its contents were the primary basis for the early identification of the Qumran community with the Essenes described by Josephus and Philo. Later work located about ten other fragmentary copies in other caves, so use of the scroll seems to have been fairly widespread

---

37. Philip R. Davies, "The Biblical and Qumranic Concept of War," in Charlesworth, *Bible and the Dead Sea Scrolls*, 1:230–31. Davies cautions against oversimplifying distinctions between dualistic terminology and elements that seem more dependent on older Israelite traditions of holy war. These distinctions apply mostly to attempts to separate layers of composition in the War Scroll and determine a trajectory of development of ideas, which fails to produce a consistent development. See Philip R. Davies, "Dualism and Eschatology in the Qumran War Scroll," *Vetus Testamentum* 28 (1978): 25–36.
38. The initial naming of some of the earliest scrolls has created some problems. Some interpreters wish to provide more precise names. Michael Wise, for example, calls this the "Charter of a Jewish Sectarian Association" in Wise, Abegg, and Cook, *Dead Sea Scrolls*, 123–42. Such descriptive names create confusion, however, and I will use the most common designation, the "Community Rule," for 1QS and the other fragmentary copies.

within the community; but like the War Scroll it has not been found anywhere else. There are significant differences between the other copies and 1QS, so interpretations of the Community Rule are best based on the initial, nearly complete copy.[39] Still, Michael Wise is correct to emphasize that the text itself refers to multiple communities in multiple locations, so the idea of a single unified community governed by a standardized text does not fit the evidence.[40] The opening column introduces a teacher who is to instruct the "children of light" to follow God's law in every detail. The extent to which this figure qualifies as a messiah is difficult to say. He forms the connection between God and the written laws in the scroll which instruct the community members. Other texts, like the Damascus Document, may encourage an interpretation in which the teacher is a future messiah.

The description of the initiation process explains the necessity of the community, which provides a place for the elect during the current time in which God has allowed Belial to rule the earth (1:18). The initiates are to follow God's laws as members of a foreordained group. The corresponding group "foreordained to Belial" will receive divine curses and damnation without mercy, and even worse will be the fate of any initiate who is not truly repentant. The divine character is angry and zealous for his laws and the result is a clearly defined system of blessings and curses. Column 3 provides some discussion of the source of the problem. In 3:17–18 the scroll describes God's creation of human beings to rule the world, giving them "two spirits in which to walk until the time ordained for his visitation."[41] The two spirits are truth and falsehood and the choice between them results in two groups of people, the righteous

---

39. On this interpretive practice, see Nickelsburg, *Jewish Literature*, 137–38.
40. Wise, "Charter of a Jewish Sectarian Association," in Wise, Abegg, and Cook, *Dead Sea Scrolls*, 123.
41. This and subsequent translations are Wise's (ibid., 126–42).

governed by the "Prince of Light" and the wicked led by the "Angel of Darkness." The scroll seems to recognize the strangeness of these assertions and the questions that might arise from them, attributing the puzzling human condition to "a situation God in His mysteries allows to continue until his era dawns" (3:23). The direct assertion two lines later that the God of Israel created both the spirits of light and darkness sounds like a direct response to an opposing explanation of the human predicament. The teacher of this community will not accept an explanation that places God's power and control over the world in question. The problem of good and evil persists as the subject in column 4, including the statement at 4:18–19: "In his mysterious insight and glorious wisdom God has countenanced an era in which perversity triumphs, but at the time appointed for visitation He shall destroy such forever." Until the time that God destroys the spirit of perversity, however, it will continue to contend with the spirit of truth in each human heart, and God will judge each person based upon which spirit dominates. Most of the remainder of the scroll consists of laws apparently designed to help the members be sure the spirit of truth wins the struggle within them. The closing section in column 11 is part of a sample prayer, giving credit to God for justification (11:2), for helping those who stumble (11:12), and for teaching all knowledge (11:17–18).

The Damascus Document

The Damascus Document (CD) has a history unlike any of the other sectarian Dead Sea scrolls because copies of the text were found in Egypt earlier in the twentieth century. The two manuscripts found in the genizah of the Cairo synagogue are fragmentary and were produced in the Middle Ages. Fragments of up to ten different copies of CD appeared among the Dead Sea discoveries in the middle of the twentieth century and point toward a date of composition in the early first century BCE. Two of the Dead Sea fragments provide parts of a brief introduction; the largest of the Cairo manuscripts contains most of the first large section of the scroll, which scholars tend to label either the Admonition or the Exhortation.[42] The second half of the scroll consists of a collection of laws for the community.

The introduction to the CD establishes a unique tone from the beginning. The audience of the text understood itself to be "the Children of Light," but, unlike in the War Scroll, their primary adversaries seem to have been other Jews. The community represented by the CD considered their opponents to be followers of a false understanding of the law, while they followed a true version provided to them by the Teacher of Righteousness. The situation created a division within the people of Israel, and it appears that the group behind the CD was the one without political power and access to the present religious institutions.[43] Such a split puts God in a position of taking sides. The CD community claims it will be blessed and saved for following the true law, while God will punish the followers of false ones, a theme that the Admonition elaborates.

The idea of God punishing Israel for disobedience is not new, of course. The beginning of the Admonition section recounts how God turned away from Israel and the temple during the Babylonian invasion. Column 1 juxtaposes the Teacher of Righteousness with a figure known as "the Man of Mockery." As the description of the division of Israel develops, the most challenging theological idea arises in 2:6–13, which claims God knew the identity of the two groups from the beginning, and chose one group to be the faithful remnant while even causing the other group to go astray (2:13). The

---

42. For more on the state of the manuscripts and how they relate to each other, as well as a reconstruction of the scroll, see Joseph M. Baumgarten and Daniel R. Schwartz, "Damascus Document," in Charlesworth, *Dead Sea Scrolls*, 2:1–79. See also the reconstruction in Edward Cook, "The Damascus Document," in Wise, Abegg, and Cook, *Dead Sea Scrolls*, 49–73.

43. Baumgarten and Schwartz, "Damascus Document," 4–6.

Admonition goes on to extend the idea of the predestination of two groups back into Israel's ancient past, as far back as the Watchers in the time of Noah.[44] In the Tanak, the primary understanding of divine punishment is that all of Israel suffers collectively for communal sins, and some of the later portions of the prophetic literature only begin to renegotiate the problem of innocent suffering. Their own personal suffering put prophetic characters like Jeremiah and Ezekiel, presented in books named for them, in a position to negotiate the meaning of sin and punishment. Both characters address issues of sin and responsibility, challenging the proverb that the NRSV translates, "The parents have eaten sour grapes, and the children's teeth are set on edge" (Jer. 31:29 and Ezek. 18:2). Much of the Old Testament presents or assumes the view that suffering results from disobedience, though in texts like Exod. 34:6–7 guilt and punishment can pass from a previous generation to later ones. Ezekiel and Jeremiah experienced suffering because they obeyed divine commands, not because they disobeyed, but neither prophetic scroll completely disconnects suffering from sin when they reject the sour-grapes proverb. Ezekiel states the change most clearly in 18:4, "it is only the person who sins that shall die," rejecting inherited or communal punishment. Ezekiel also asserts that reward and punishment are not immediate, so sinners can still repent and the righteous can become sinful (18:25–29), and he concludes with the divine statement, "For I have no pleasure in the death of anyone" (18:32). The divine character of the CD has worked out the difficulties of communal punishment by dividing Israel into two groups, but the freedom of choice that might allow persons to move from one group to another is limited. Unlike in the prophetic literature, announcements of future judgments function more as

---

44. Nickelsburg, *Jewish Literature*, 123–24.

words of assurance to the righteous than as attempts to get the unrighteous to repent.

The Damascus Document contains specific references to a messianic figure, beginning in 6:10–11 with a description of "the one who teaches righteousness in the End of Days."[45] This figure sounds like an eschatological version of the Teacher of Righteousness whose work generated the scroll's community. The messianic figure receives further attention in the legal section of CD, where 19:10–11 includes the warning, "but all the rest will be handed over to the sword when the Messiah of Aaron and of Israel comes, just as it happened during the time of the first punishment."[46] The future figure will carry out the dividing and punishing work of God. The reference points back to the Babylonian destruction, but the picture seems altogether different this time. Instead of total destruction in response to national sin, a divided Israel will have two very different fates. One more text mentions the messiah explicitly when 19:35–20:21 addresses those who entered the covenant of the community, but might be turning away: "They shall not be reckoned among the council of the people, and their names shall not be written in their book from the day the Beloved Teacher dies until the Messiah from Aaron and from Israel appears. Such is the fate for all who join the company of the men of holy perfection and then become sick of obeying virtuous rules."[47] The coming of the messiah completes a time of testing for the community, which proves its true membership, and 20:3 uses the same "crucible" language to describe the testing as the War Scroll.

---

45. See Schiffman, *Reclaiming the Dead Sea Scrolls*, 323.
46. This is the translation of Cook, "Damascus Document," 58. The two references to the messiah in the legal section of CD, at 19:10–11 and 20:1, are extant only in the Genizah B manuscript.
47. Ibid., 59. On the possible references to two messiahs here, one of Israel (political) and one of Aaron (priestly), see Schiffman, *Reclaiming the Dead Sea Scrolls*, 324.

The Psalms of Solomon

The Psalms of Solomon exist in about a dozen Greek manuscripts, all from the late Middle Ages, but there is common agreement among scholars that their original language was Hebrew. They are listed in the contents of Codex Alexandrinus, but the texts are no longer present in that volume. The Psalms of Solomon owe their preservation primarily to their popularity within Eastern Christianity.[48] Three aspects of this collection of psalms, which sound much like some in the biblical book of Psalms, place it among the literature treated here. First, there is an emphasis on God as judge and on the present suffering within the world of the audience as divine punishment that may lead to future deliverance. Second, an accompanying emphasis portrays two opposing groups within Israel. One of the groups, the righteous or pious, is the primary audience of the psalms, which typically assume a context in which their opponents are in cultural and political ascendancy. The third aspect is the appearance of a royal messianic figure, particularly in Psalms of Solomon 17.[49] It is important to note that, even more than in the canonical book of Psalms, David is the great psalmist.[50] These three in combination connect the collection to the other texts in this section, particularly to those from the Dead Sea collection, so it may be something of a surprise, therefore, that no trace of the collection appears among the Dead Sea Scrolls. There are many explanations for the apparent absence, but the connection between the writing of the psalms and their appearance in the medieval manuscript tradition is a mystery.

---

48. For more detail on the history and preservation of the Psalms of Solomon, see Robert R. Hann, *The Manuscript History of the Psalms of Solomon* (Chico, CA: Scholars Press, 1982), 3–6.
49. On these aspects of the collection, see Nickelsburg, *Jewish Literature*, 238.
50. The most extreme expression of this is the description of David in 11Q5, column 27, which credits David with writing 3600 psalms. See Michael O. Wise, "Apocryphal Psalms of David," in Wise, Abegg, and Cook, *The Dead Sea Scrolls*, 451–52.

Nickelsburg divides the Psalms of Solomon into two groups based on their general themes and tone. The divisions are not perfectly precise, but they provide a useful map for exploring the collection. The group that he calls "psalms of the nation" appear to address the calamity of 63 BCE, the Roman invasion of Jerusalem, but do so in a fairly traditional way.[51] The opening psalm, in the voice of Jerusalem, is reminiscent of the biblical book of Lamentations. The speaker is honest in her distress, but places the blame for foreign invasion squarely on the secret sins of her own children. Psalms of Solomon 2 changes voice to talk about Jerusalem in the third person, but the themes are the same for the majority of the poem. The sins of Israel are to blame for God's righteous judgment, but a turn takes place at 2:22 when the speaker implores God to halt the punishment, not only because it has been enough, but because the instrument is a gentile nation whose own purpose is not righteous.[52] The end of the long second poem only hints at a new movement when it insists in verses 34–36 that God will distinguish between the righteous and the wicked.

The separation theme emerges more clearly in Nickelsburg's second category, "the psalms of the righteous and the pious."[53] The group to and about whom these psalms speak are the true audience of the collection and their opponents are other Israelites rather than foreigners, so these psalms fit life under Roman captivity and the temptations of that context.[54] Psalms of Solomon 3 and 4 compare the two groups, beginning with the righteous, who are not perfect but

---

51. Nickelsburg, *Jewish Literature*, 238.
52. There are competing systems of versification of the Psalms of Solomon. The discussion here follows the verse numbers assigned in R. B. Wright, "Psalms of Solomon: A New Translation and Introduction," in Charlesworth, *Old Testament Pseudepigrapha*, 2:651–70.
53. Nickelsburg, *Jewish Literature*, 244.
54. The tension in 1 and 2 Maccabees between the Hasmoneans and those they viewed as apostates resembles the attitude these psalms express, though, as indicated below, at least one of the psalms might view the late Hasmoneans as enemies.

are in a constant search to find and confess their own sins (3:7–8). The sins of the wicked group are many, but the behavior encompassing these individual sinful acts is an outer life that attempts to please people and gain favor while hiding a secret life of lust, dishonesty, and greed (4:3–13). The divine treatment of the two groups presents a formidable theological problem for the writer/collector of the Psalms of Solomon. The pleas for divine judgment of the wicked in 4:14–22 indicate that present experience does not fit the claims of the poems. One solution to the dissonance is the delay of reward and punishment.[55] The claim that justice will prevail in the future (5:1–4) does not reach the level of eschatological judgment present in many other writings of the period, but it is not inconsistent with them. Psalms of Solomon 6 and 7 describe the suffering of the righteous, but insist upon two types of divine involvement in the experience. First, God accompanies and comforts the righteous in their difficulties and hears their prayers (6:8). Second, the suffering of the righteous is the chastening of God, meant to correct them, and is carefully measured for this purpose (7:4) and always accompanied by God's sufficient mercy (7:5–8). These poems carefully develop a portrayal of God that can function as a confirmation of divine presence with the righteous in times of blessing and adversity.

Through Psalms of Solomon 16 the tone differs little from the biblical psalms, as the deliberate teaching of the righteous emerges as the primary distinction between the two collections. A new direction appears in poem 17, which begins with a declaration of divine kingship, followed by a recollection of the Davidic monarchy. Many interpreters identify the opponents of 17:6–15 as the Hasmonean dynasty, recently overthrown by the Roman emperor who is the foreigner in this section. At verse 23 a new Davidic king emerges, and the poem describes him and his work in a manner consistent

---

55. Wright, "Psalms of Solomon," 644.

with other messianic writings of the period, finally bestowing the title "Messiah" on him at verse 32.

A Written God

The documents examined in the previous section make reference to a messianic figure who embodies a new kind of divine action coming in the future. At the same time, some of them, particularly the Community Rule and the Damascus Document, also commit a lot of energy to delineating sets of rules or laws for the faithful to follow as a means of preparing for the coming of God. One question that the combination of a messianic future and careful attention to written rules raises is how such writing might represent an expression of divine presence. The Torah had provided a mixed response to such a question. After the frightening moment of unmediated divine speech in Exodus 20, the Israelites insisted on the mediation of Moses. Readers of the remainder of Exodus and much of Leviticus and Deuteronomy might encounter the divine voice, but always speaking to or through Moses, or occasionally Aaron.[56] The Dead Sea text called the Temple Scroll takes an important step in diminishing this barrier of mediation. The possibility that writing and reading texts could become a religious experience, even a divine encounter, leads to the idea of the textualization of divine presence, or as Michael Fishbane expresses it, the "displacement of the living divine presence by a textual record of that presence."[57] Hindy Najman refines this idea, describing writing as a divine encounter that is not a replacement but a new mode, and cautions that "textualization and writtenness do not end revelation by announcing its closure."[58] The

---

56. On the mediation of the divine voice in the Torah, see McEntire, *Portraits of a Mature God*, 68—71.
57. Michael Fishbane, *The Garments of Torah: Essays in Biblical Hermeneutics* (Bloomington, IN: Indiana University Press, 1989), 37.

clearest example of this phenomenon lies in the Dead Sea text known as the Temple Scroll.

The Temple Scroll

The Temple Scroll was first published by Yigael Yadin in 1977. About one third of the primary scroll is readable, and other fragments were eventually identified among the scrolls, some of which appear to be from the early second century BCE.[59] The Temple Scroll stands out in two important ways. First, it belongs with the other sectarian texts in the Dead Sea Scrolls collection because it is unique to the group that produced the scrolls, though it contains direct quotations from the Bible.[60] Second, many of the quotations from the Torah change third-person reporting of divine commands to direct first-person language, so that YHWH is speaking directly to the reader. The alteration of Deut. 12:26 will demonstrate this kind of change:

> But the sacred donations that are due from you, and your votive gifts,
>   you shall bring to
> the place that the LORD will choose. (Deut. 12:26)

> You must take up the devoted gifts and all your voluntary offerings and
>   go to the place
> where I shall establish my name. (11Q19 53:9–10)[61]

Yadin's conclusion about this is that "[t]he clear aim of the author is to dispel any doubt that it is God himself who is uttering not only

---

58. Hindy Najman, *Losing the Temple and Recovering the Future: An Analysis of 4 Ezra* (Cambridge: Cambridge University Press, 2014), 15–16.
59. For more on the manuscripts, see Johann Maier, *The Temple Scroll: An Introduction, Translation & Commentary* (Sheffield: JSOT Press, 1985), 1–5.
60. While the Temple Scroll fits in the sectarian category because of its appearance only among the Dead Sea Scrolls, it does not contain some of the most distinctive characteristics associated with the sect, including dualism, determinism, and messianism. See Lawrence H. Schiffman, "The Theology of the Temple Scroll," *Jewish Quarterly Review* 1–2 (1994): 109–10.
61. This is the translation of Michael O. Wise, "The Temple Scroll" in Wise, Abegg, and Cook, *The Dead Sea Scrolls*, 482.

known injunctions in the Pentateuch, even when they are presented in reported speech, but also the supplementary text that appears in the scroll."[62] The last part of this assertion refers to additional legal material in the Temple Scroll but not in the Torah. Michael Wise takes a somewhat different view of the change in voice, based on another effect, the removal of Moses as a mediating figure. The writer of the scroll may have been presenting himself as a new Moses.[63] Yadin is almost certainly correct that one motive of the writer was to transfer the authority of the Torah to additional regulations of the Dead Sea sect, but perhaps something more happens with this move. Bernard Levinson points out that the change in voice occurs not just in relation to Deuteronomy, removing the mediation of Moses in the book most closely associated with him, but also in passages from Numbers (e.g., Num. 30:3 = 11Q19 53:14). The effect is that the Temple Scroll, including the parts from Deuteronomy, is "an immediate divine revelation spoken by God at Sinai."[64] The idea that God can speak directly to the reader of a text yields a new kind of divine portrayal, one that allows a different kind of presence of God in the present and indefinitely into the future, a "written God."

With this possibility established, what sort of deity does the written God portray himself to be? The first column of the scroll is not readable, so observations about its opening need to be tentative. Nevertheless, the material from column 2, drawing upon Exod. 34:10–16 and Deut. 7:25–26, immediately presents the God of the Torah who will drive out all previous inhabitants from the land and demand absolute loyalty from Israel. In the context of the Temple Scroll's time such warnings may have addressed the encroachment of

---

62. Yigael Yadin, *The Temple Scroll: The Hidden Law of the Dead Sea Sect* (New York: Random House, 1985), 65.
63. Wise, "The Temple Scroll," 457–58.
64. Bernard M. Levinson, *A More Perfect Torah: At the Intersection of Philology and Hermeneutics in Deuteronomy and the Temple Scroll* (Winona Lake, IN: Eisenbrauns, 2013), 92.

Hellenism into Jewish culture.⁶⁵ The divine character who emerges from the introduction to speak the law directly demands obedience from Israel and presents a more carefully organized Torah for the faithful to follow. Levinson notes the tension inherent in the work of the scroll: "The Temple Scroll was the work of a community engaged with a scriptural tradition and a scriptural language from which they were long distant and yet whose pristine, revelatory voice they sought." The effort to produce that unmediated voice required human innovation.⁶⁶

One of the areas in most desperate need of logical organization was the Torah's presentation of the cultic/festival calendar. Not only does the Torah contain multiple calendars, but they also do not all agree on the role of a central sanctuary in the practice of festivals. After the very fragmentary columns 3–13 of the scroll present instructions for building the sanctuary and the altar, the more complete columns 14–29 take up the subjects of offerings and festivals and their timing. The calendar in the Temple Scroll matches the one in Jubilees and 1 Enoch's Book of the Luminaries (72–82), perhaps tying together these works and the interest of the Qumran community in them.⁶⁷ The God who tries to speak more directly in the Temple Scroll also tries to speak with more careful order. Once the calendar is established, the Temple Scroll returns to the subject of temple construction so that the temple surrounds the cult both architecturally and literarily. Columns 30–45 provide instructions for building the various courtyards and buildings of the temple complex. The primary question the instructions raise is how they are related to the actual temple in Jerusalem and what the relationship says about the deity who occupies the structure. There has been some dispute about the

---

65. Schiffman, "Theology of the Temple Scroll," 113.
66. Levinson, *More Perfect Torah*, 43.
67. For more on the common festival calendar and connections between these texts, see Nickelsburg, *Jewish Literature*, 155–56.

possible eschatological nature of the temple the scroll depicts. Some have noted its massive size, even compared to the architecturally revered temple Herod would soon build.[68] A visionary temple, unrealistic in real time and space, would not have been unprecedented, but the structure in the Temple Scroll is not as fantastical as the one in Ezekiel 40–48. Schiffman argues that the scroll's author connected his temple design specifically to Deuteronomy, bypassing Solomon's temple, which was not properly designed. The connection to Deuteronomy also includes many specific references to "name" theology, the concept of God's name residing in the temple as a way of talking about God's presence.[69] The dwelling of God's name brings together the emphases on temple design and maintenance of the sacrificial cult and ritual calendar in 11Q19 29:3–4, where proper ritual observance causes the dwelling of the name in the temple.[70] Michael Wise insists, to the contrary, that the entire Temple Scroll is eschatological, and two aspects of this description are important to the present discussion. First, Wise claims that the legal portions of the Temple Scroll formed an "eschatological Deuteronomy." He bases this view, in large part, on connections between the Temple Scroll and the Damascus Document.[71] Second, Wise claims that the temple description is completely unrealistic, labeling it "a magnificent eschatological temple."[72] The eschatological Deuteronomy omitted all parts of Deuteronomy 12–26 not consistent with life in an ideal eschatological age.[73] The maintenance of such a view throughout the Temple Scroll, however, requires

---

68. Nickelsburg notes that the space encompassed by the scroll's temple would be four times that of Herod's (*Jewish Literature*, 156).
69. Schiffman, "Theology of the Temple Scroll," 114–15.
70. Ibid., 116.
71. Wise contends that CD was the most likely source of the expanded ritual laws in 11Q19, 45–51. He then transfers the eschatological concerns of CD to 11Q19. See Michael O. Wise, "The Eschatological Vision of the Temple Scroll," *Journal of Near Eastern Studies* 49 (1990): 156.
72. Ibid., 158.
73. Ibid., 158–59.

a rather elaborate two-stage eschatology in order to accommodate both the temple described in large portions of the document and the temple God would create on "the Day of Creation" according to 29:7–10. Wise develops such a scheme based on ideas in other works like 4 Ezra, 2 Baruch, and the Apocalypse of Weeks (1 En. 93:1–10; 91:11–17).[74] Schiffman seems correct in rejecting Wise's proposal, but offers no significant argument against it or a substitute, other than an unspecified default assumption that the writer and readers of the Temple Scroll really expected to build this temple according to the plans and enact their version of the cult within it.

The argument about the temple described so elaborately in the Temple Scroll and its relation to the present temple and land of Israel of its own time reaches something of an impasse here. I would like to offer one other possibility based upon the growing importance of writing and reading texts during the time period. What if the temple plans in the Temple Scroll were neither actual nor eschatological, but textual? If the voice of Israel's God could take on a direct and unmediated form in the scroll, then perhaps the dwelling place of that God could do the same. If the writer of the scroll and its intended audience had no access to a valid temple, whether for their own ideological reasons or for political reasons imposed by someone else, they could replace being in the temple and performing its rituals with reading and hearing a description of an ideal temple and an ideal cultic practice.[75] A function like this is related to the function of the War Scroll described above as fantasy. It is possible the community

---

74. Ibid., 161–66.
75. A use of ritual texts that is halfway to this one is described by James W. Watts in relation to Leviticus. Watts argues for careful attention to the rhetoric of ritual texts because they are not mere instruction for performing the ritual but persuasion to perform them in a particular way. Thus they have a rhetorical function. The next logical step, in a situation where actual performance was not possible, would be for the reading of the text to replace the performance. See Watts, *Ritual and Rhetoric in Leviticus: From Sacrifice to Scripture* (Cambridge: Cambridge University Press, 2007), 32–36.

that produced the scroll experienced a cognitive dissonance between theological claims and lived reality, which they could resolve through the use of literature.

The last major section of the Temple Scroll is its rewriting of the Deuteronomic code of Deuteronomy 12–26 in columns 52–66. The movement of the biblical text from cultic practice into matters of law in daily life fits the theology of the Temple Scroll, which understands the divine presence to dwell in the temple as the name of YHWH and radiate out in concentric circles to Jerusalem and the whole land of Israel, if proper purity is maintained at the center.[76]

Conclusion

During the last century before the Common Era, did the persons who produced, read, and revered the text presented above expect dramatic divine intervention in the affairs of the world to rescue them from oppression of many kinds, or were they preparing to settle in for the long haul and looking for a way to maintain faithfulness? There may not be a definitive answer to this question or a way to find it. The apocalyptic literature examined in the previous chapter promised a dramatic end to the separation between heaven and earth. The addition of a messianic figure in most of the texts in this chapter provided a means for divine action short of a complete end of the present world, though different understandings of that messiah presented different degrees of continuity and discontinuity with the present age. The sectarian texts among the Dead Sea Scrolls seem to have found a middle ground in their combination of eschatological focus, messianic expectation, and adaptation of divine law for life in the present time, a law spoken directly to the reader/hearer by the literary voice of God.

---

76. Schiffman, "Theology of the Temple Scroll," 119–20.

8

Where Do We Go from Here?

The portrayal of the divine character described in this book may be as fragmented as the literature in which it is found. There have been some recognizable trends, but one of the reasons Second Temple Judaism became a religion made up of sectarian groups in conflict with one another is that there were different ways of understanding and portraying the divine character. Among the theological issues dividing these groups were the degree of God's removal from the world, the ways God is related to human choices and behavior, and the ways God's care for and relation to human beings and the world might extend beyond the present earthly existence. Competing answers to these questions produced portraits of the divine being that fit differing contexts but were not always compatible with each other. The incompatibility may have been a cause of the canonical instability of the writings produced in the last two to three centuries BCE. Even the ultimate winners of the theological competition, rabbinic Judaism and Nicene Christianity, exhibited significant diversity on such issues during the periods in which they emerged, but those developments are beyond the scope of this study. What this final chapter will attempt to illustrate in conclusion is the variety of portrayals of God that were handed to those traditions.

A synthesis like this one must be careful to avoid some common assumptions that have often been central to past scholarship. First, the narrative of the Tanak ends in the Persian period, but the collection of literature did not become final within that period, or even soon after. The books of Daniel and Esther are the most obvious illustration of this, but many other parts of the Tanak were clearly still in progress throughout the Hellenistic period. There is not space here to trace all the recent developments in our understanding of the canonization process, but the old consensus of a tripartite development that had the Torah and Prophets in relatively fixed and authoritative form by the fourth century BCE, with the Writings perhaps only a century behind, has dissolved.[1] It is very important that the literature examined in this study not be understood as a response to or continuation of a fixed and authoritative Tanak. More to the point, there should be no clear line between the production of the Tanak and its reception/interpretation, with the works in the Apocrypha, Pseudepigrapha, and so forth placed in the latter category.[2] Second, while Ezra-Nehemiah presents a fairly unified report of Israel's narrative in the Persian period, even within the literature of the Tanak the portrait of Israel's God begins to move in multiple directions. The clearest divide is between literature directed to those living in the Jewish homeland, with YHWH dwelling in a rebuilt temple and a system of religious practice developed around it, and those in the diaspora seeking to find ways of living faithfully

---

1. For an account of the shifting perspective, see Timothy Lim, *The Formation of the Jewish Canon* (New Haven, CT: Yale University Press, 2013), 17–34.
2. For a more continuous view of textual development in Second Temple Judaism and beyond, see Brennan W. Breed, *Nomadic Text: A Theory of Biblical Reception History* (Bloomington, IN: Indiana University Press, 2014), 1–15.

under foreign political control and without access to centralized religious institutions.³ Third, while we have a lot of literature from the last two or three centuries BCE, there was undoubtedly some that did not survive, along with writings too fragmentary to use. Some of what did survive has come into modern hands through strange and surprising routes, and its transmission may raise questions about its earliest forms. Our picture of Judaism in this era is rapidly developing, and our understanding of how the literature we have relates to the groups of people we know about is only partial.

Revising God's Past

The hidden God at the end of the Tanak stands in stark contrast to the powerful character at its beginning, who speaks directly to the ancestors and intervenes to perform mighty acts on behalf of Israel. During the last three centuries BCE those who produced some of the extant literature seemed to have accepted this plotline, but those who did not had a number of choices. One way to solve the difficulty posed by a shifting character was to change the description of God's behavior in the past. The most successful attempt to do this is in the book of Jubilees, which detached the God of Israel from the world of human affairs from the beginning. The Book of the Watchers in 1 Enoch places this extended divine removal within a highly developed apocalyptic framework that allows the possibility of the reassertion of an active divine character in the future.

The most important effect of revising the past of Israel's God was to remove divine responsibility for the presence of evil in the world. Removing God from the world of human affairs from the

---

3. The needs of the latter group are addressed by the diaspora tales of Esther and Daniel and some, if not all, of the wisdom literature. For a description of the divine character embodied in this kind of literature, see McEntire, *Portraits of a Mature God: Choices in Old Testament Theology* (Minneapolis: Fortress Press, 2013), 191–203.

beginning and expanding the role of the evil beings like Mastema and Shemihaza absolved both God and humans from responsibility for the origins or the propensity of evil in the world. The removal of God from the world of human affairs in the past also required the development of a host of supernatural beings who could act on God's behalf in the human world. The seeds of this development are present in the Tanak in stories like Gen. 6:1–4 and Job 1–2 that contain the "sons of God" and the many appearances of the "angel of YHWH." The use of the latter figure typically signaled God's emergence in the human world, in texts like Genesis 22 and Exodus 3, but the process had to be reversed in order for angels to enable divine withdrawal, and this also left room for the development of angelic characters with names, specialized tasks, and perhaps even personalities.

Expanding God's Present

Some writers who seemed uncomfortable with a God who moved toward silent, subtle behavior exerting internal influence on human beings needed to speak to a broader, dispersed audience. The Tanak had already begun to craft this message for a dispersed Judaism, but the continuing development of Esther and Daniel reveals that it was a work in progress. The actions of the divine character may not be more overt to most of the characters in the story, but the pious characters in Tobit and the expanded characters in the Greek version of Esther are anxious to give credit to God for their deliverance, even if the means of that deliverance look like their own courage and cleverness. Greek versions of Daniel struggle with the conditionality of the statement about God's power in 3:17–18; even that conditionality remnants of it remain, however, they are overwhelmed by the addition of the Prayer of Azariah and the Song of the Three Jews.

The subtle God operating behind and through creation in the wisdom literature of the Tanak was too disconnected from Israel's other religious traditions for the wisdom writers of the Hellenistic period. Sirach explicitly connects wisdom to the torah, and to the traditions of the ancestors, leading up to the high priest Simon and the temple of his own day. The Wisdom of Solomon draws the most explicit connections between wisdom and the exodus tradition. While the connection of wisdom to the nationalistic traditions of Israel may at first seem like a narrowing of geographic scope rather than an expansion, if these traditions had become available to diaspora Jews as textualized traditions, then a wisdom tradition connected to torah, cult, and locations associated with the ancestors would not have been the exclusive property of Jews in the homeland.

Connections to Israel's other traditions also allowed wisdom literature to address additional issues in the Hellenistic period, the most important of which were the closely linked subjects of human free will and the origin of evil. While Sir. 25:24 connects the origins of sin to Eve, even the remainder of that passage implies that sin can be brought under human control. Earlier wisdom literature may have provided counsel to control or avoid sin, but by connecting wisdom to torah, Sirach also provides a way to address it and remove its effects. The many ancestors in honor of whom Sirach sings were obviously not perfect human beings, and the movement of the list toward the priesthood offers the avenue to forgiveness. The inclusion of these traditions thus adds the character trait of forgiveness to the divine character of the wisdom literature

The Maccabean tradition presents good and evil embodied in human behavior in starker terms than any story in the Tanak. Foreign leaders in the Tanak's story of the monarchy were instruments of divine punishment, but the Maccabean literature makes them the embodiment of evil. For the narrators of the

Maccabean story to shift the characters in this way, making the powerful foreign rulers the villains and the suffering Jews victims needing divine deliverance, signals a seismic shift in the divine character. While 2 Maccabees may not be as comfortable jettisoning Deuteronomic theology as 1 Maccabees, Deuteronomic claims ultimately fail. The assertion of the young man in 2 Macc. 7:18 that he is suffering brutal torture because of the sins of Israel is entirely unconvincing and is little more than a refusal to grant any sort of power to his torturers. This reveals the great conundrum of the theology of the Maccabean literature. If God does not wish God's people to suffer, then why are they suffering? Foreign leaders like Antiochus are free to operate outside of the divine will, and even oppose it. Apocalyptic literature offers a picture of a God who temporarily withdraws divine presence and power from the world of human affairs. Without the apocalyptic component, the Maccabean literature can tell its story as long as it is one of success, but it has nowhere to go with failure.

Charting God's Future

The departure of God from the world in dualistic systems, to which even the wisdom tradition was opening, leads to questions about the future of God's relationship to the world. If separation was a divine choice at the beginning, then ending the separation could be a divine choice at the end. The divine departure is not complete, however, since supernatural beings still represent God in the world of human affairs, and events in that world are a reflection of events in heaven, yet the state of the human world creates difficult questions about the future. If the divine beings that God left or inserted in the human world were at war with the forces of evil, then perhaps someday they might win the battle. How much additional divine help might they need to accomplish a decisive victory, and in what form would that additional help come? The most obvious answer to that question comes in the belief that a more powerful figure will emerge in the future. The messianic figures in various texts do not look the same, but the thing they have in common is that they will all tip the current stalemate in the favor of God's people, moving the world toward an inevitable end.

Without a decisive victory in the future, how else might the withdrawn divine character play a role in the human world? At some point, the desperate production of written texts offered its own solution to this perplexing question. In many ways it was a reversion to the distant past when God spoke directly to the ancestors and the prophets of old. If only the text could remove those ancient characters and let the divine voice speak directly to the reader. The Temple Scroll found a way to do this most directly, and may have played a part in the movement of written texts toward their identification as "word of God." If this is what written texts could be then it explains the need to standardize and canonize.

Sectarian Judaism and the Portrayal of God

At crucial points in the story of Israel, it was important for the community called Israel to consolidate itself under a single story. Such a statement refers primarily to the collective character called Israel within the literature of the Tanak; the extent to which it corresponds to a historical entity outside the text is more difficult to say. The narrative consolidation process happens for the first two times in the genealogies of Gen. 5:1–32 and 11:10–32. In each case the book of Genesis contains a prior, parallel genealogy that raises some questions about the lineage of the Israelites. Genesis 4:17–22 presents the mysterious genealogy of Cain ending with Lamech as the father of four children: Jabal, Jubal, Tubal-cain, and Naamah. Because of the descriptions of Jabal and Jubal as a herder of animals and a musician respectively, along with the resemblance of their names to the name of Abel, it might have been possible for Israelites to have understood themselves as descendants of Adam and Eve through Cain.[4] The "Book of the Generations of Adam" in 5:1–31 reroutes this lineage in two important ways. First, it makes Lamech a descendent of Adam and Eve through Seth, and then it makes Noah the significant child of Lamech. The next contested point of lineage involves the two genealogies of Shem. Genesis 10:21–32 traces the family line from Shem to Arpachshad, to Eber, and to Joktan, where it ends in dispersed confusion. The Babel story in 11:1–9 explains the dispersal and accompanying confusion and makes it possible to revisit the genealogy of Shem in 11:10–32, where the line goes from Shem to Arpachshad, to Selah, to Eber, to Peleg, to Reu, to Serug, to Nahor, and to Abram. Once again, groups within Israel that may have understood their ancestry differently are brought together under a single genealogy to agree on Abram as their ancestor.

Another important place where a disparate Israel agrees to a common story is in the final chapter of the book of Joshua. Numerous places in the plot of the exodus and wandering tradition, beginning as early as Exod. 12:38, acknowledge this was a mixed group of people, as others joined in along the way during the journey to and settlement of the promised land. So, when Joshua gathers everyone in Shechem he must tell the story in 24:1–13 to a mixed group, who agree in 24:18 that the exodus will be their story and they will serve the God who made it so. The Tanak does not present the people of Israel as an ethnically pure and exclusive group, but as a narratively pure group, who all lived according to the same story of their origins. The story of the monarchy disrupts the narrative

---

4. This would have been the only possibility in the J source. See Richard Elliott Friedman, *The Bible with Sources Revealed: A New View into the Five Books of Moses* (San Francisco: HarperCollins, 2003), 39–40.

unity, most significantly when Israel divides into two kingdoms in 1 Kings 12 and 2 Chronicles 10. The division comes to an end of sorts when the Assyrian Empire destroys the Northern Kingdom, and some efforts to reconsolidate appear in the story of the Passover celebration sponsored by Hezekiah in 2 Chronicles 30, efforts that require the remnants of the Northern Kingdom to identity with the story of Judah.[5]

During and after the Babylonian exile the struggle to identify a single story for the people of Israel is negotiated intensely again. The prophetic scrolls contain significant elements of conflict among the various groups that survived the Babylonian invasion and the period of exile that followed it. The "good figs and bad figs" sermon in Jeremiah 24:1–10 represents the claim that the story of exile and return is the true story of Israel, rather than a story of remaining in the land; and it would appear the exile story was the winner, whether it was because those who had been taken captive to Babylon included the socially elite and most literate class who could control the production of the story or because exile and return simply make a better narrative, one that looks more like the exodus relived. The political story of the return in the books of Ezra-Nehemiah works out the ideological victory, as those with a different story are excluded from the project of rebuilding in Ezra 4:3, but are able to join once the winning story emerges, as long as they agree to attach themselves to it in 6:21.

In the Second Temple period, evidence suggests sectarian conflict became even greater, and sectarian groups produced competing bodies of literature.[6] Therefore, the final formation of the contents of the Tanak involved the exclusion of literature. Michael Stone presents

---

5. For more on the way that the story of the monarchy attempts to unite all of Israel under the story of Judah, see Jacob L. Wright, *David, King of Israel, and Caleb in Biblical Memory* (London: Cambridge University Press, 2014), 132–47.

a scheme in which an "Axis of Adam and Eve" competed with an "Axis of Enoch" in order to explain the origin and persistence of sin and evil in the world. The victory of the Adam and Eve axis meant the Enochic material was largely excluded from the canon, but this "noncanonical" material was widely preserved among the Qumran material, in the library of a sect that did not survive.[7] Jubilees also appears frequently among the Dead Sea Scrolls, and Stone demonstrates the approximate chronological spread of both Enoch literature and Jubilees among the scrolls. The former seems to have emerged earlier there but did not sustain significance throughout the existence of the group represented by the scrolls. The scrolls of Enoch are relatively old parts of the collection, but the production of manuscripts of Jubilees persisted into the middle of the first century of the Common Era.[8] If the Enoch literature was an alternative to the Torah, then it would make sense that production ended as the Torah became more authoritative. If Jubilees is, rather, a rewritten Torah that does not replace it but solves some of its difficulties, then this might explain its greater resilience, but it eventually vanished within Judaism as well, along with the Dead Sea sect, to be preserved only within Ethiopian Christianity.

There were attempts to tell the continuing story of Israel after the Maccabean period, the most prominent and accessible of which are the two works of Flavius Josephus, *The Antiquities of the Jews* and *The Jewish Wars*. While Josephus's work can be helpful in a study like this one, it is always important to remember that it looks back through most of the monumental events of the first century of the Common

---

6. For a more complete description of the development of Jewish sects in this period, see Shaye J. D. Cohen, *From the Maccabees to the Mishnah*, 3rd ed. (Louisville, KY: Westminster John Knox, 2014), 123–71.
7. Michael E. Stone, *Ancient Judaism: New Visions and Views* (Grand Rapids, MI: Eerdmans, 2011), 47–58.
8. Ibid., 133–38.

Era, reducing its usefulness. One of his most famous passages is the description of the "four sects" of Judaism at the end of book 18, chapter 1 of *Antiquities*. Josephus self-identified as a Pharisee, one of these four sects, so his evaluation of them may be held suspect, but his identification of some of the issues dividing them is likely valid and helpful. And there are two issues among them that are central to the portrayal of the divine character. One is the degree to which God is in control of events happening on the earth, and the effect of this control on human freedom. The other is the immortality of the human soul and the presence of an afterlife, which is a question of God's continuing relation to human beings after their death. In these descriptions Josephus makes no mention of eschatology, which is curious. These groups could not have been in agreement on this subject if the Sadducees denied any sort of afterlife. The Pharisees, who emerged as the only surviving group among these four, claimed the idea of resurrection but seem to have rejected both apocalyptic ways of thinking and apocalyptic literature. It is common to relate the group Josephus describes as Essenes to the group that produced and/or preserved the Dead Sea Scrolls, but the sectarian writings of this group indicate a high degree of affinity with apocalypticism. The case for connecting these two groups is often overstated, but it is far from impossible. Why would Josephus not even bring up this issue? This and other observations reveal that he is not a thorough guide to sectarian Judaism at the turn of the eras, even though his writings offer some useful information.

The end of the era that produced the literature in this study provided several possible paths for future religious movements to choose. The failure of national institutions left the question of legacy unanswered, which would seem to make some sense of human immortality a more likely choice. The loss of institutions also left multiple options in terms of free will and determinism. The failure may have been the result of human sin infecting the institutions, the view of the Dead Sea sect, which required separation and withdrawal of the righteous. Others may have understood the problem to be the stance toward the groups occupying Israel, leaving the choice between resistance and accommodation. The former raised questions about the divine character similar to those who withdrew. Both responded to the problem of divine reticence, either with claims that an abrupt change was coming in which the ancient God would retake control of the world in a final battle, or that individuals would receive the gift of an afterlife in another realm as a reward for their faithfulness and suffering.

A God for the World

The previous discussion of sectarian Judaism has been an attempt to establish a context for both the production of the literature treated in this study and the competition that led to some of it being abandoned. It is important to return to two issues in the main body of discussion in this final chapter, and the first of these is the central aim of the book, the attempt to trace the development of the divine character in the Jewish literature of the last three centuries before the Common Era. The second will provide the outline of the discussion here. As we have examined that literature throughout this study certain issues have emerged as core concerns, some of which deal, directly or indirectly, with the portrayal of the divine being. What follows is an attempt to offer a synthetic presentation of these issues, especially in relation to the work of biblical theology.

The conclusion that the origin of evil and its continuing presence in the world was the central theological question of this era is difficult to avoid. In some cases we may need to separate this into two issues, origin and persistence, but ideas about the two of them are typically connected. The most important dividing point on this issue is the degree to which human beings are responsible for evil in the choices they make and thus are able to exert some control over its effect on the world. The group of texts treated in this study that tell stories of virtuous young people living in the Jewish diaspora do not answer this question directly, but that is typically the nature of stories. There is among some theologians of the Hebrew Scriptures a tendency to reject a narrative approach to theology precisely for that reason.[9] The expectation that theology can or should be stated in clear, propositional forms is true neither to human experience nor to much of the literature examined in this study. The stories of Esther, Daniel, Tobias, and Susanna might be answers to many different questions, but they certainly address this question of human moral agency. What biblical theologians need to do carefully is consider the answers such stories might provide without reducing the stories themselves to a "moral," something that the best stories resist. The worlds of all of these young people have evil in them, and that evil impinges upon their lives. Typically, the source of this evil is the choices of other human beings, whether it be foreign kings like Nebuchadnezzar or Ahasuerus, or other Jewish persons like the two men who seek to entrap Susanna. This is not always the case, however, as Tobias and his family suffer both because of the cruelty of nature and supernatural forces like the demon that keeps on killing the husbands of Sarah. If there is anything on which they all agree it might be that a combination of divine assistance, human virtue, and cleverness can effectively combat the power of evil in the world, even if they cannot fully overcome it.

---

9. Such a claim can be found in James Barr, *The Concept of Biblical Theology: An Old Testament Perspective* (Minneapolis: Fortress Press, 1999), 354–56. Barr's claim is that the story itself is not theology but only the "raw material for theology," because stories are "theologically unclear or ambiguous." See my discussion of this claim and the issues surrounding it in McEntire, *Portraits of a Mature God*, 12–13.

Many of the literary works presented here demonstrate that the hiding of God at the end of the Tanak was not a universally satisfying way to understand divine behavior. One way to address the issue was to present a more consistent hiddenness. Jubilees portrays a God hidden from the beginning, represented on earth by angels. It is possible that the wisdom literature always took such an approach to leveling the story of God. The female figure of Wisdom in Proverbs 8–9 has much in common with the angelic beings of other works but lacks a more explicit connection to the story of Israel beyond creation. The missing connection is the task Sirach and the Wisdom of Solomon address with great vigor and creativity. This choice raised the question of whether God's removal from the world of humans would come to an end abruptly, or whether the responsibility of humans was to learn to function within the system and to adapt it to the realities of different contexts.

Another option was to focus on a coming end to God's hiddenness, found most explicitly in the chronological dualism of apocalyptic literature. The very different choice of open revolt presented two difficulties. First, it did not offer the same benefits to Jews in the diaspora. Second, it might have to explain the eventual failures of its own attempts to overthrow oppressors. The comparison of 1 and 2 Maccabees revealed the struggle to find the right theological language to talk about such efforts. The challenge of finding the right theological language is one that persists. Whether to talk about divine presence in the world in direct, active, and dynamic language or in more subtle tones is a question that still confronts those who claim belief in the God who first emerges in the texts of ancient Israel.

Bibliography

Abegg, Martin, Jr. "The War Scroll." In Wise, Abegg, and Cook, *The Dead Sea Scrolls: A New Translation*, 150–71.

Adams, Samuel L. *Social and Economic Life in Second Temple Judea*. Louisville, KY: Westminster John Knox, 2014.

Argall, Randall A. *1 Enoch and Sirach: A Comparative Literary and Conceptual Analysis of the Themes of Revelation, Creation and Judgment*. Atlanta: Scholars Press, 1995.

Assmann, Jan. "Martyrdom, Violence, and Immortality: The Origins of a Religious Complex." In *Dying for the Faith, Killing for the Faith: Old-Testament Faith-Warriors (1 and 2 Maccabees) in Historical Perspective*, edited by Gabriela Signori, 39–60. Leiden: Brill, 2012.

Barr, James. *The Concept of Biblical Theology: An Old Testament Perspective*. Minneapolis: Fortress Press, 1999.

Barstad, Hans. *The Myth of the Empty Land: A Study in the History and Archaeology of Judah in the "Exilic" Period*. Oslo: Scandinavian University Press, 1996.

Bartlett, John R. *1 Maccabees*. Sheffield: Sheffield Academic Press, 1998.

Baumgarten, Joseph M., and Daniel R. Schwartz. "Damascus Document." In *The Dead Sea Scrolls: Hebrew, Aramaic, and Greek Texts with English Translations*, edited by James H. Charlesworth, 2:1–79. Tübingen: J. C. B. Mohr, 1995.

Bedenbender, Andreas. "The Place of the Torah in the Early Enoch Literature." In *The Early Enoch Literature*, edited by Gabriele Boccaccini and John J. Collins, 65–79. Leiden: Brill, 2007.

Bembry, Jason. *Yahweh's Coming of Age*. Winona Lake, IN: Eisenbrauns, 2011.

Berquist, John L. *Judaism in Persia's Shadow: A Social and Historical Approach*. Minneapolis: Fortress Press, 1995.

Boccaccini, Gabriele. "Introduction: From the Enoch Literature to Enochic Judaism." In *Enoch and Qumran Origins: New Light on a Forgotten Connection*, edited by Gabriele Boccaccini, 1–16. Grand Rapids, MI: Eerdmans, 2005.

———. *Roots of Rabbinic Judaism: An Intellectual History, from Ezekiel to Daniel*. Grand Rapids, MI: Eerdmans, 2002.

Borchardt, Francis. *The Torah in Maccabees: A Literary Critical Approach to the Text*. Berlin: Walter de Gruyter, 2014.

Breed, Brennan W. *Nomadic Text: A Theory of Biblical Reception History*. Bloomington, IN: Indiana University Press, 2014.

Brueggemann, Walter. *Theology of the Old Testament: Testimony, Dispute, Advocacy*. Minneapolis: Fortress Press, 1996.

Burnett, Joel S. *Where Is God? Divine Absence in the Hebrew Bible*. Minneapolis: Fortress Press, 2010.

Caird, G. B. *The Language and Imagery of the Bible*. Grand Rapids, MI: Eerdmans, 1997.

Calduch-Benages, Nuria. "The Hymn to Creation (Sir 42:15–43:33): A Polemic Text?" In *The Wisdom of Ben Sira: Studies on Tradition, Redaction, and Theology*, edited by Angelo Pessario and Giuseppe Bellia, 119–38. Berlin: Walter de Gruyter, 2008.

Charles, R. H. *The Apocrypha and Pseudepigrapha of the Old Testament*. Vol. 2. Oxford: Clarendon, 1913.

Charlesworth, James H. "Introduction for the General Reader." In *The Old Testament Pseudepigrapha: Apocalyptic Literature and Testaments*, edited by James H. Charlesworth, 1:xxi–xxxiv. Garden City, NY: Doubleday, 1983.

———. "The Messiah in the Pseudepigrapha." In *Religion (Judentum: Allgemeines, Palästinisches Judentum)*, edited by Wolfgang Haase, 188–218. Berlin: Walter de Gruyter, 1979.

Cheon, Samuel. *The Exodus Story in the Wisdom of Solomon: A Study in Biblical Interpretation*. Sheffield: Sheffield Academic Press, 1997.

Chialá, Sabino. "The Son of Man: The Evolution of an Expression." In *Enoch and the Messiah Son of Man: Revisiting the Book of the Parables*, edited by Gabriele Boccaccini, 159–63. Grand Rapids, MI: Eerdmans, 2007.

Clines, David J. A. *The Esther Scroll: The Story of the Story*. Sheffield: JSOT Press, 1984.

Cohen, Shaye J. D. *The Beginnings of Jewishness: Boundaries, Varieties, Uncertainties*. Berkeley: University of California Press, 1999.

———. *From the Maccabees to the Mishnah*. 3rd ed. Louisville, KY: Westminster John Knox, 2014.

Collins, John J. *The Apocalyptic Imagination: An Introduction to the Jewish Matrix of Christianity*. New York: Crossroad, 1984.

———. *Daniel: A Commentary on the Book of Daniel*. Minneapolis: Fortress Press, 1993.

———. "Introduction: Towards the Morphology of a Genre." *Semeia* 14 (1979): 1–20.

———. *Jewish Wisdom in the Hellenistic Age*. Louisville, KY: Westminster John Knox, 1997.

———. "What Was Distinctive about Messianic Expectation at Qumran." In *The Bible and the Dead Sea Scrolls*, edited by James H. Charlesworth, 2:71–92. Waco, TX: Baylor University Press, 2006.

Cook, Edward. "The Damascus Document." In Wise, Abegg, and Cook, *The Dead Sea Scrolls: A New Translation*, 49–73.

Coxon, Peter W. "Daniel III 17: A Linguistic and Theological Problem." *Vetus Testamentum* 26 (1976): 400–409.

Crenshaw, James L. "Method in Determining Wisdom Influence upon Historical Literature." *Journal of Biblical Literature* 88 (1969): 129–42.

———. "Sirach: Introduction, Commentary, and Reflections." In *The New Interpreter's Bible*, edited by Leander E. Keck, 5:601–867. Nashville: Abingdon, 1994.

Croy, N. Clayton. *3 Maccabees*. Leiden: Brill, 2006.

Davies, Philip R. "The Biblical and Qumranic Concept of War." In *The Bible and the Dead Sea Scrolls*, edited by James H. Charlesworth, 1:209–32. Waco, TX: Baylor University Press, 2006.

———. "Dualism and Eschatology in the Qumran War Scroll." *Vetus Testamentum* 28 (1978): 28–36.

DiTommaso, Lorenzo. *The Book of Daniel and the Apocryphal Daniel Literature*. Leiden: Brill, 2005.

Doran, Robert. "The First Book of Maccabees: Introduction, Commentary, and Reflections." In *The New Interpreter's Bible*, edited by Leander E. Keck, 4:1–178. Nashville: Abingdon, 1996.

———. "The Second Book of Maccabees: Introduction, Commentary, and Reflections." In *The New Interpreter's Bible*, edited by Leander E. Keck, 4:179–299. Nashville: Abingdon, 1996.

Duhaime, Jean. "The War Scroll." In *The Dead Sea Scrolls: Hebrew, Aramaic, and Greek Texts with English Translations*, edited by James H. Charlesworth, 2:80–203. Tübingen: J. C. B. Mohr, 1995.

Elliott, Mark Adam. *The Survivors of Israel: A Reconsideration of the Theology of Pre-Christian Judaism*. Grand Rapids, MI: Eerdmans, 2000.

Fishbane, Michael. *The Garments of Torah: Essays in Biblical Hermeneutics*. Bloomington, IN: Indiana University Press, 1989.

Fitzmyer, Joseph A. *The Genesis Apocryphon of Qumran Cave 1 (1Q20): A Commentary*. Rome: Biblical Institute Press, 2004.

———. *Tobit*. Berlin: Walter de Gruyter, 2003.

Flesher, Paul V. M., and Bruce Chilton. *The Targums: A Critical Introduction*. Waco, TX: Baylor University Press, 2011.

Fried, Lisbeth S., ed. *Was 1 Esdras First? An Investigation into the Priority and Nature of 1 Esdras*. Atlanta: Society of Biblical Literature, 2011.

Friedman, Richard Elliott. *The Bible with Sources Revealed: A New View into the Five Books of Moses*. San Francisco: HarperCollins, 2003.

———. *The Disappearance of God: A Divine Mystery*. New York: Little, Brown, and Co., 1995.

García Martínez, Florentino, and Eibert J. C. Tigchelaar. *The Dead Sea Scrolls Study Edition*. Leiden: Brill, 1997.

Gilders, William K. "The Concept of Covenant in Jubilees." In *Enoch and the Mosaic Torah: The Evidence of Jubilees*, edited by Gabriele Boccaccini and Giovanni Ibba, 178–92. Grand Rapids, MI: Eerdmans, 2009.

Glicksman, Andrew T. *Wisdom of Solomon 10: A Jewish Hellenistic Reinterpretation of Early Israelite History through Sapiential Lenses*. Berlin: De Gruyter, 2011.

Goldstein, Jonathan A. *1 Maccabees: A New Translation with Introduction and Commentary*. Anchor Bible 41. Garden City, NY: Doubleday, 1976.

———. *2 Maccabees: A New Translation with Introduction and Commentary*. Anchor Bible 41A. Garden City, NY: Doubleday, 1983.

Grabbe, Lester L. "Chicken or Egg? Which Came First, 1 Esdras or Ezra-Nehemiah?" In *Was 1 Esdras First? An Investigation into the Priority and Nature of 1 Esdras*, edited by Lisbeth S. Fried, 31–44. Atlanta: Society of Biblical Literature, 2011.

———. *A History of Jews and Judaism in the Second Temple Period*. Vol. 1, *Yehud: A History of the Persian Province of Judah*. New York: T&T Clark, 2004.

———. *A History of Jews and Judaism in the Second Temple Period*. Vol. 2, *The Early Hellenistic Period (335–175 BCE)*. New York: T&T Clark, 2008.

Griffin, Patrick J. *The Theology and Function of Prayer in the Book of Tobit.* Washington, DC: Catholic University of America, 1984.

Hacham, Noah. "3 Maccabees and Esther: Parallels, Intertextuality, and Diaspora Identity." *Journal of Biblical Literature* 4 (2007): 765–85.

Hamori, Esther. *"When Gods Were Men": The Embodied God in Biblical and Near Eastern Literature.* Berlin: de Gruyter, 2008.

Hann, Robert R. *The Manuscript History of the Psalms of Solomon.* Chico, CA: Scholars Press, 1982.

Hanneken, Todd R. *The Subversion of the Apocalypses in the Book of Jubilees.* Atlanta: Society of Biblical Literature, 2012.

Hartman, Louis F., C.SS.R., and Alexander A. Di Lella, O.F.M. *The Book of Daniel: A New Translation with Introduction and Commentary.* Anchor Bible 23. Garden City, NY: Doubleday, 1978.

Hayward, Robert C. T. "El Elyon and the Divine Names in Ben Sira." In *Ben Sira's God: Proceedings of the International Ben Sira Conference,* edited by Renate Egger-Wenzel, 180–98. Berlin: Walter de Gruyter, 2001.

Henten, Jan Willem van. *The Maccabean Martyrs as Saviours of the Jewish People: A Study of 2 and 4 Maccabees.* Leiden: Brill, 1997.

Henze, Matthias. "Enoch's Dream Visions and the Visions of Daniel Reexamined." In *Enoch and Qumran Origins: New Light on a Forgotten Connection,* edited by Gabriele Boccaccini, 17–22. Grand Rapids, MI: Eerdmans, 2005.

Holladay, William L. *The Psalms through Three Thousand Years: Prayerbook of a Cloud of Witnesses.* Minneapolis: Fortress, 1993.

Humphreys, W. Lee. *The Character of God in the Book of Genesis: A Narrative Appraisal.* Louisville, KY: Westminster John Knox, 2001.

Isaac, E. "1 (Ethiopic Apocalypse of) Enoch: A New Translation and Introduction." In *The Old Testament Pseudepigrapha,* edited by James H. Charlesworth, 1:5–89. Garden City, NY: Doubleday, 1983.

Jackson, David R. *Enochic Judaism: Three Defining Paradigm Exemplars*. New York: T&T Clark, 2004.

Jellicoe, Sidney. *The Septuagint and Modern Study*. Oxford: Oxford University Press, 1968.

Jobes, Karen H., trans. "Esther." In *A New English Translation of the Septuagint*, edited by Albert Pietersma and Benjamin G. Wright, 424–40. New York: Oxford University Press, 2007.

Jobes, Karen H., and Moisés Silva. *Invitation to the Septuagint*. Grand Rapids, MI: Baker Academic, 2005.

Kolarcik, Michael, S.J. "The Book of Wisdom: Introduction, Commentary, and Reflections." In *The New Interpreter's Bible*, edited by Leander E. Keck, 5:434–600. Nashville: Abingdon, 1994.

Kugel, James L. *The Bible as It Was*. Cambridge, MA: Belknap Press, 1997.

———. *Traditions of the Bible: A Guide to the Bible as It Was at the Start of the Common Era*. Cambridge, MA: Harvard University Press, 1998.

———. *A Walk through Jubilees: Studies in the Book of Jubilees and the World of Its Creation*. Leiden: Brill, 2012.

Kvanvig, Helge S. "Jubilees—Read as a Narrative." In *Enoch and Qumran Origins: New Light on a Forgotten Connection*, edited by Gabriele Boccaccini, 75–83. Grand Rapids, MI: Eerdmans, 2005.

Law, Timothy Michael. *When God Spoke Greek: The Septuagint and the Making of the Christian Bible*. Oxford: Oxford University Press, 2013.

Lee, Thomas R. *Studies in the Form of Sirach 44–50*. Atlanta: Scholars Press, 1986.

Levenson, Jon D. *The Hebrew Bible, the Old Testament, and Historical Criticism*. Louisville, KY: Westminster John Knox, 1993.

Levinson, Bernard M. *A More Perfect Torah: At the Intersection of Philology and Hermeneutics in Deuteronomy and the Temple Scroll*. Winona Lake, IN: Eisenbrauns, 2013.

Lim, Timothy. *The Formation of the Jewish Canon*. New Haven, CT: Yale University Press, 2013.

Lopez, Kathryn M. "Standing before the Throne of God: Critical Spatiality in Apocalyptic Scenes of Judgment." In *Constructions of Space II: The Biblical City and Other Imagined Spaces*, edited by Jon L. Berquist and Claudia V. Camp, 139–55. New York: T&T Clark, 2008.

Machiela, Daniel A. "The Genesis Apocryphon (1Q20): A Reevaluation of Its Text, Interpretive Character, and Relationship to the Book of Jubilees." PhD diss., University of Notre Dame, 2007.

Maier, Johann. *The Temple Scroll: An Introduction, Translation & Commentary*. Sheffield: JSOT Press, 1985.

McEntire, Mark. *The Function of Sacrifice in Chronicles, Ezra, and Nehemiah*. Lewiston, NY: Mellen Biblical Press, 1993.

———. "The God at the End of the Story: Are Biblical Theology and Narrative Character Development Compatible." *Horizons in Biblical Theology* 33 (2011): 171–89.

———. "The Graying of God in Daniel 1–7." *Review and Expositor* 109 (2012): 569–79.

———. *Portraits of a Mature God: Choices in Old Testament Theology*. Minneapolis: Fortress Press, 2013.

———. *Struggling with God: An Introduction to the Pentateuch*. Macon, GA: Mercer University Press, 2008.

McGlynn, Moyna. *Divine Judgment and Divine Benevolence in the Book of Wisdom*. Tübingen: Mohr Siebeck, 2001.

McLay, R. Timothy, trans. "Daniel." In *A New English Translation of the Septuagint*, edited by Albert Pietersma and Benjamin G. Wright, 991–1027. New York: Oxford University Press, 2007.

McLay, Tim. *The OG and TH Versions of Daniel*. Atlanta: Scholars Press, 1996.

Meadowcroft, Tim. "Who Are the Princes of Persia and Greece (Daniel 10)? Pointers toward the Danielic Vision of Heaven and Earth." *Journal for the Study of the Old Testament* 29 (2004): 99–113.

Middlemas, Jill. *The Templeless Age: An Introduction to the History, Literature, and Theology of the "Exile."* Louisville: Westminster, 2007.

Miles, Jack. *God: A Biography.* New York: Vintage, 1995.

Milik, J. T., and Matthew Black. *The Books of Enoch: Aramaic Fragments of Qumran Cave 4.* Oxford: Clarendon Press, 1976.

Mobley, Gregory. *The Return of the Chaos Monsters—and Other Backstories of the Bible.* Grand Rapids, MI: Eerdmans, 2012.

Moore, Carey A. *Daniel, Esther, and Jeremiah: The Additions; A New Translation with Introduction and Commentary.* Anchor Bible 44. Garden City, NY: Doubleday, 1977.

———. *Judith: A New Translation with Introduction and Commentary.* Anchor Bible 40. New York: Doubleday, 1985.

———. *Tobit: A New Translation with Introduction and Commentary.* Anchor Bible 40A. New York: Doubleday, 1996.

Moss, Candida. *Ancient Christian Martyrdom: Diverse Practices, Theologies, and Traditions.* New Haven, CT: Yale University Press, 2012.

Mulder, Otto. "Two Approaches: Simon the High Priest and YHWH God of Israel / God of All in Sirach 50." In *Ben Sira's God: Proceedings of the International Ben Sira Conference,* edited by Renate Egger-Wenzel, 224–32. Berlin: Walter de Gruyter, 2001.

Najman, Hindy. *Losing the Temple and Recovering the Future: An Analysis of 4 Ezra.* Cambridge: Cambridge University Press, 2014.

Neusner, Jacob. *Judaism when Christianity Began: A Survey of Belief and Practice.* Louisville, KY: Westminster John Knox, 2002.

Newsom, Carol A., with Brennan W. Breed. *Daniel: A Commentary.* Old Testament Library. Louisville, KY: Westminster John Knox, 2014.

Nickelsburg, George W. E. *1 Enoch 1: A Commentary on the Book of 1 Enoch, Chapters 1–36; 81–108*. Minneapolis: Fortress Press, 2001.

———. *Jewish Literature between the Bible and the Mishnah*. 2nd ed. Minneapolis: Fortress Press, 2005.

Nickelsburg, George W. E., and James C. VanderKam. *1 Enoch: The Hermeneia Translation*. Minneapolis: Fortress Press, 2012.

———. *1 Enoch 2: A Commentary on the Book of 1 Enoch, Chapters 37–80*. Minneapolis: Fortress Press, 2011.

Nicklas, Tobias. "'Food of Angels' (Wis. 16:20)." In *Studies in the Book of Wisdom*, edited by Géza G. Xeravits and József Zsengellér, 83–100. Leiden: Brill, 2010.

Nowell, Irene, O.S.B. "The Book of Tobit: An Ancestral Story." In *Intertextual Studies in Ben Sira and Tobit*, edited by Jeremy Corley and Vincent Skemp, 3–13. Washington, DC: Catholic Biblical Association of America, 2005.

———. "The Book of Tobit: Introduction, Commentary, and Reflections." In *The New Interpreter's Bible*, edited by Leander E. Keck, 3:973–1071. Nashville: Abingdon, 1999.

Otzen, Benedikt. *Tobit and Judith*. London: Sheffield Academic Press, 2002.

Perdue, Leo G. *The Collapse of History: Reconstructing Old Testament Theology*. Minneapolis: Fortress Press, 1994.

———. *The Sword and the Stylus: An Introduction to Wisdom in the Age of Empires*. Grand Rapids, MI: Eerdmans, 2008.

Portier-Young, Anathea E. *Apocalypse against Empire: Theologies of Resistance in Early Judaism*. Grand Rapids, MI: Eerdmans, 2011.

———. "'Eyes to the Blind': A Dialogue between Tobit and Job." In *Intertextual Studies in Ben Sira and Tobit*, edited by Jeremy Corley and Vincent Skemp, 14–27. Washington, DC: Catholic Biblical Association of America, 2005.

Priest, J. "Testament of Moses: A New Translation and Introduction." In *The Old Testament Pseudepigrapha*, edited by James H. Charlesworth, 1:919–34. Garden City, NY: Doubleday, 1983.

Rad, Gerhard von. *Wisdom in Israel*. Translated by James D. Martin. Nashville: Abingdon, 1972.

Reed, Annette Yoshiko. *Fallen Angels and the History of Judaism and Christianity: The Reception of Enochic Literature*. Cambridge: Cambridge University Press, 2005.

Reese, J. M. *Hellenistic Influence on the Book of Wisdom and Its Consequences*. Rome: Biblical Institute Press, 1970.

Reiterer, Friedrich V. *"All Weisheit stammt vom Herrn…": Gesammelte Studien zu Ben Sira*. Berlin: Walter de Gruyter, 2007.

Russell, D. S. *The Method and Message of Jewish Apocalyptic*. Philadelphia: Westminster, 1964.

Sacchi, Paolo. "Qumran and the Dating of the Parables of Enoch." In *The Bible and the Dead Sea Scrolls*, edited by James H. Charlesworth, 2:377–92. Waco, TX: Baylor University Press, 2006.

Saldarini, Anthony J. "The Book of Baruch." In *The New Interpreter's Bible*, edited by Leander E. Keck, 6:927–82. Nashville: Abingdon, 2001.

Sanders, James A. "What's Up Now? Renewal of an Important Investigation." In *Jewish and Christian Scriptures: The Function of 'Canonical and 'Non-Canonical' Religious Texts*, edited by James H. Charlesworth and Lee M. McDonald, 1–7. London: T&T Clark, 2010.

Schiffman, Lawrence H. *Reclaiming the Dead Sea Scrolls: The History of Judaism, the Background of Christianity, the Lost Library of Qumran*. Philadelphia: Jewish Publication Society, 1994.

———. "The Theology of the Temple Scroll." *Jewish Quarterly Review* 1–2 (1994): 109–23.

Schmid, Konrad. "The Canon and the Cult: The Emergence of Book Religion in Ancient Israel and the Gradual Sublimation of the Temple Cult." *Journal of Biblical Literature* 131 (2012): 289–305.

Schwartz, Daniel R. *2 Maccabees*. Berlin: Walter de Gruyter, 2008.

Schwartz, Howard. "Does God Have a Body?" In *Bodies, Embodiment, and Theology of the Hebrew Bible*, edited by S. Tamar Kamionkowski and Wonil Kim, 217–23. New York: T&T Clark, 2010.

Scolnic, Benjamin Edidin. "Mattathias and the Jewish Man of Modein." *Journal of Biblical Literature* 129, no. 3 (2010): 463–83.

Scott, James C. *Domination and the Arts of Resistance: Hidden Transcripts*. New Haven: Yale University Press, 1990.

Scott, James M. *On Earth as in Heaven: The Restoration of Sacred Time and Sacred Space in the Book of Jubilees*. Leiden: Brill, 2005.

Segal, Michael. *The Book of Jubilees: Rewritten Bible, Redaction, Ideology and Theology*. Leiden: Brill, 2007.

Skehan, Patrick W., and Alexander A. Di Lella, O.F.M. *The Wisdom of Ben Sira: A New Translation with Introduction and Commentary*. Anchor Bible 39. New York: Doubleday, 1987.

Smith-Christopher, Daniel. *A Biblical Theology of Exile*. Minneapolis: Fortress Press, 2002.

Sommer, Benjamin D. "Dialogical Biblical Theology: A Jewish Approach to Reading Scripture Theologically." In *Biblical Theology: Introducing the Conversation*, edited by Leo G. Perdue et al., 1–54. Nashville: Abingdon, 2009.

Stocker, Margarita. *Judith: Sexual Warrior; Women and Power in Western Culture*. New Haven: Yale University Press, 1998.

Stone, Michael E. *Ancient Judaism: New Visions and Views*. Grand Rapids, MI: Eerdmans, 2011.

Sweeney, Marvin A. *Reading the Hebrew Bible after the Shoah: Engaging Holocaust Theology*. Minneapolis: Fortress Press, 2008.

Tabor, James D. "Martyr, Martyrdom." In *The Anchor Bible Dictionary*, edited by David Noel Freedman et al., 4:575–76. New York: Doubleday, 1992.

Talshir, Zipora. *1 Esdras—From Origin to Translation*. Atlanta: Society of Biblical Literature, 1999.

———. *1 Esdras: A Text Critical Commentary*. Atlanta: Society of Biblical Literature, 2001.

Taylor, Joan E. *The Essenes, the Scrolls, and the Dead Sea*. New York: Oxford University Press, 2012.

Tiller, Patrick A. *A Commentary on the Animal Apocalypse in I Enoch*. Atlanta: Scholars Press, 1993.

Tov, Emmanuel. *Textual Criticism of the Hebrew Bible*. Minneapolis: Fortress Press, 1992.

VanderKam, James C. *The Book of Jubilees*. New York: T&T Clark, 2001.

———. *Enoch and the Growth of an Apocalyptic Tradition*. Washington, DC: Catholic Biblical Association, 1984.

———. "The Manuscript Tradition of Jubilees." In *Enoch and the Mosaic Torah: The Evidence of Jubilees*, edited by Gabriele Boccaccini and Giovanni Ibba, 3–21. Grand Rapids, MI: Eerdmans, 2009.

———. "Mapping Second Temple Judaism." In *The Early Enoch Literature*, edited by Gabriele Boccacini and John J. Collins, 1–20. Leiden: Brill, 2007.

Watts, James W. *Ritual and Rhetoric in Leviticus: From Sacrifice to Scripture*. Cambridge: Cambridge University Press, 2007.

Wheaton, Gerry. "The Festival of Hanukkah in 2 Maccabees: Its Meaning and Function." *Catholic Biblical Quarterly* 74 (2012): 247–62.

White, Sidnie Ann. "In the Steps of Jael and Deborah: Judith as Heroine." In *"No One Spoke Ill of Her": Essays on Judith*, edited by James VanderKam, 5–16. Atlanta: Scholars Press, 1992.

Williams, David S. *The Structure of 1 Maccabees*. Washington, DC: Catholic Biblical Association of America, 1999.

Williamson, H. G. M. *Ezra-Nehemiah*. Waco, TX: Word, 1986.

Winston, David. *The Wisdom of Solomon: A New Translation with Introduction and Commentary*. Anchor Bible 43. Garden City, NY: Doubleday, 1979.

Wintermute, O. S. "Jubilees." In *Old Testament Pseudepigrapha*, edited by James H. Charlesworth, 2:35–142. Garden City, NY: Doubleday, 1985.

Wise, Michael O. "Apocryphal Psalms of David." In Wise, Abegg, and Cook, *The Dead Sea Scrolls: A New Translation*, 447–52.

———. "Charter of a Jewish Sectarian Association." In Wise, Abegg, and Cook, *The Dead Sea Scrolls: A New Translation*, 123–42.

———. "The Eschatological Vision of the Temple Scroll." *Journal of Near Eastern Studies* 49 (1990): 155–72.

———. "The Temple Scroll." In Wise, Abegg, and Cook, *The Dead Sea Scrolls: A New Translation*, 457–93.

Wise, Michael, Martin Abegg Jr., and Edward Cook. *The Dead Sea Scrolls: A New Translation*. San Francisco: Harper Collins, 1996.

Wright, Benjamin G., III. *Praise Israel for Wisdom and Instruction: Essays on Ben Sira and Wisdom, the Letter of Aristeas and the Septuagint*. Leiden: Brill, 2008.

Wright, Jacob L. *David, King of Israel, and Caleb in Biblical Memory*. London: Cambridge University Press, 2014.

———. "Making a Name for Oneself: Martial Valor, Heroic Death, and Procreation in the Hebrew Bible." *Journal for the Study of the Old Testament* 36 (2011): 131–62.

Wright, R. B. "Psalms of Solomon: A New Translation and Introduction." In *The Old Testament Pseudepigrapha*, edited by James H. Charlesworth, 2:651–70. Garden City, NY: Doubleday, 1985.

Wyrick, Jed. *The Ascension of Authorship: Attribution and Canon Formation in Jewish, Hellenistic, and Christian Traditions*. Cambridge, MA: Harvard University Press, 2004.

Yadin, Yigael. *The Temple Scroll: The Hidden Law of the Dead Sea Sect*. New York: Random House, 1985.

Index of Subjects

4QEng, 168
4Q Sapiental Work A, 122n49

Aaron, 48, 103, 196, 217
Abel, 173, 232
Abram/Abraham, 39, 41, 42, 43, 57, 72, 87, 103, 114, 126, 162–63, 172, 232
Achior, 69–70, 69n4, 73
Acts of the Apostles, 141n26
Adam, 38, 114, 172–73, 176, 232, 234
Ahasueras, 89, 237
Alcimus, 136, 138
Alexander the Great, 126
Alexander (Seleucid ruler), 138
Alexandria, 89, 91
Angel of Darkness, 210
Angel of the Presence, 37, 39, 40, 41, 42, 43

angels, 39, 41, 46, 52, 53, 54, 55, 62, 78, 162, 173, 181, 183–84, 189, 202, 204, 207
Antiochus III, 90
Antiochus IV, 68, 125, 126, 127, 135, 136, 144–45, 149, 151–52, 154, 182, 190, 230
apocalyptic, 29, 31, 32–33, 57, 64, 108, 110, 111, 161, 162–66, 167–91, 193, 223, 227, 230, 238
Apocrypha, 7, 8, 25, 64, 67, 80, 96, 148, 226
Aramaic, 82, 83, 164n5
Aramaic Levi, 105
Ark of the Covenant, 164
Aristobulus, 142
Arpachshad, 232
Artaxerxes, 87–88
Ascension of Isaiah, 8n12
Asmodeus, 76, 78

Assyria, 63, 63n71, 67, 70, 72, 73, 75, 76, 129, 150, 153, 176, 233
authorship, 18–19
Awan, 38
Azaraiah (Maccabean character), 135
Azazel, 52, 52n46, 77n22, 204
Azura, 38

Babel, 232
Babylon/Babylonian empire, 15, 27, 32, 58, 61, 63, 67, 79, 85, 91, 107, 108, 150, 179, 185, 190, 233
Bacchides, 138
Bar Kokhba revolt, 158
Baruch, book of, 28, 107–11, 112
Baruch, son of Neriah, 20, 107
Batenosh, 56
Bel and the Dragon, 80, 85, 178, 185
Belial, 209
Belshazzar/Baltasar, 179

Cain, 38, 114, 173, 231
Cairo Genizah, 197n8, 210
calendar, 47, 220, 221
Callisthenes, 151
Canaan, 41, 44, 69
canon, 3, 7, 57
children, 78

Children of Light, 211
Christianity, 4–5, 8, 10, 25–26, 29–30, 34, 213, 225
Chronicles, book of, 9n14, 11, 27n59, 34, 58, 59, 150, 166, 194
Codex Alexandrinus, 89, 213
Community Rule, 195–96, 197, 208–10, 217
covenant, 46–47, 47n32, 85, 109, 169
creation, 36, 54, 55, 101, 102, 115, 117, 119
Cyrus Cylinder, 15n24
Cyrus the Great, 15n24, 62, 85, 86, 144, 183, 194

Damascus Document, 197, 197n8, 209, 210–13, 217, 221
Daniel (book of), 8, 22–23, 24–25, 33, 68, 80–86, 88, 108, 161, 166, 169, 189, 190, 194, 226, 227
Daniel (character), 19, 20, 64, 80, 82, 87, 92, 96, 144n32, 148, 180, 184, 237
Darius I, 32, 58, 63, 144
Darius the Mede, 179, 182
David, 16, 17, 133, 137, 164, 213
Davidic monarchy, 16n29, 17, 64–65, 216

INDEX OF SUBJECTS

Dead Sea Psalms scroll, 3, 4
Dead Sea Scrolls, 2, 25, 34, 50, 56, 75, 122, 127, 157, 158, 169, 175, 178, 188, 195–212, 213, 217–23, 234, 236
Deborah, 71
Demetrius, 138
demons, 39, 42, 78, 237
Deuteronomic theology, 136, 145–46, 156–57, 182, 230
Deuteronomy, book of, 163, 164, 219, 221
diaspora, 64–65, 75, 86, 92, 108, 152, 157, 229, 236
Dinah, 72
Dionysus, 91
Diptych, 115–16
divine characterization, 22–23, 32–34, 36–38, 40, 43–44, 45, 46, 47, 51, 63, 64, 70, 74, 81–82, 88, 92, 98–99, 102, 104–5, 109, 110, 113, 115, 127, 129, 132, 139, 154, 157, 162, 176, 185, 187, 191, 193, 198, 203, 219, 226, 227
divine designations, 77–78, 105, 107, 132, 140, 169, 200
divine embodiment, 42, 179–80
divine emissaries, 20–21
divine forgiveness, 121

divine judgment, 177, 199, 200, 202, 205, 212, 213, 215, 216
divine mediation, 46, 49, 53, 55, 184, 189, 193, 202, 204, 207, 217, 219, 222, 227
divine presence/absence, 19–21, 29, 100, 110, 128, 163–64, 165, 182, 187, 223, 225, 230, 238
divine speech, 37, 47, 201
divine warrior, 72–73
Dositheus, 90
dreams, 57, 87, 172
dualism, 32–33, 56, 64, 110, 165, 169, 171, 177, 186–87, 189–90, 193, 208, 218n60, 230

Eber, 232
Ecbatana, 76
Ecclesiastes, 96, 97, 98, 120
Egypt/Egyptians, 40, 41, 45, 46, 47, 69, 89, 91, 114, 115, 116, 117, 118, 119n45, 142
Eleazar (character in 2 Maccabees), 146–47, 152
Eleazar (character in 3 Maccabees), 92
Emmaus, 132, 133
Encomium, 103
Enoch (character), 19, 20, 55, 56, 162, 168, 174, 190, 199, 201
Enochic Judaism, 26–27, 50

257

Esau, 44, 44n29, 45
eschatology, 111, 112, 122, 123, 165, 199, 208, 216, 221, 223
Essenes, 198, 208
Essene Hypothesis, 198
Esther (book of), 8, 22–23, 64, 68, 86–89, 93, 96–97, 140, 157, 226, 227
Esther (character), 86–89, 96, 237
Ethiopic, 34, 168, 234
Eve, 38, 120, 173, 176, 232, 234
exile/deportation, 15, 80, 86, 109, 142–43, 233
exodus, 114–20, 232
Exodus, book of, 35, 47, 48, 49, 54, 156, 162
Ezekiel, book of, 16n29, 106, 109, 164, 200, 212
Ezra (character), 20, 59
Ezra-Nehemiah (book of), 8, 9n14, 11, 15, 16n29, 22–23, 27n59, 34, 57, 58, 59, 62, 64, 74, 88, 141n26, 143n29, 187, 190, 226, 233

fantasy, 208, 222
festivals, 220
First Enoch (book of), 9, 11, 24–25, 26–27, 28–29, 33, 34, 49–57, 64, 105, 120, 156, 156n53, 158, 161, 166, 188, 190, 196, 220
First Esdras (book of), 8, 9n14, 27, 31, 57–62, 64
First Kings, 126
First Samuel, 126, 162
First Maccabees, 27–28, 125–41, 143, 144, 149, 154–58, 187, 215n54, 230
flood, 38, 39, 44, 52–53, 55, 56, 171, 199
Fourth Ezra, 188
free will vs. determinism, 101, 235

Gabriel, 52, 182, 183, 202, 204, 207
Galilee, 134–35
Genesis, book of, 35, 43, 45, 46–47, 48, 49, 54, 79n27, 162, 171
Genesis Apocryphon, 56–57
Gentiles, 130, 131, 149
Gideon, 133
Gilead, 134–35
Gnostic Christianity, 50
Goliath, 133
Gomorrah, 43
Greek/Hellenistic Empire, 18, 32, 79, 95, 96, 100, 110, 120, 123, 138, 148, 184, 187, 190

INDEX OF SUBJECTS

Habakkuk (character), 85–86, 185
Habakkuk, book of, 194
Hagar, 43, 43n28, 44, 162–63
Haggai, book of, 16n29
Hannah, 78
Hannukah, 142, 143, 152, 152n44
Haran, 41, 72, 162–63
Hasmoneans, 128, 138, 139, 140, 155, 158, 215n54, 216
Hebron, 41
Heliodorus, 143–44, 151
Hellenism, 14, 24, 47, 112, 120, 122, 226, 229
Herod, 221
Hezekiah, 59n63, 150, 153, 233
Holofernes, 69–70, 69n4, 73, 74, 92

immortality, 122, 154–55, 235
Isaac, 43, 45, 72, 79, 103, 126
Isaiah (character), 150
Isaiah, book of, 16n29, 194
Ishmael, 43, 43n28

Jacob, 43, 44, 44n29, 45, 48, 57, 72, 79, 103, 114, 126
Jael, 71
Jason (character in 2 Maccabees), 144
Jason, son of Simon the high priest, 106–7

Jason of Cyrene, 141
Jeconiah, 107
Jeremiah, 60, 107, 109, 142, 154, 166, 183, 212
Jerome, 80, 87, 179
Jerusalem/Zion, 2–3, 10, 15, 31, 58, 89, 90, 96, 99, 105, 107n22, 111, 126, 128, 134, 135, 136, 137, 138, 142, 143, 144, 151, 152, 164, 165, 215
Jesus Ben Sira, 106
Joash (king of Judah), 138
Job, book of, 79, 96, 97, 98, 120
Joktan, 232
Jonathan (son of Saul), 133, 137
Jonathan (Maccabean character), 138
Jordan River, 99
Joseph, 45, 57, 87, 114
Joseph (Maccabean character), 135
Josephus, 10, 57, 127, 158, 198, 208, 234
Joshua (character), 133
Joshua, book of, 74, 188, 232
Josiah, 59, 60
Jabal, 231
Jubal, 231
jubilee, 186
Jubilees, book of, 27n59, 28–29, 31, 34–48, 51, 52, 54, 55, 57,

62, 64, 158, 166, 185–87, 220, 227, 234, 238
Judah (character), 44n29, 49, 60, 61, 63
Judah/Judea, land of, 11, 15, 63, 69, 85, 129, 142, 157, 229
Judaism, 4–5, 6–7, 10, 20, 24, 25–26, 29–30, 34, 50, 96, 101, 140, 154–55, 193, 225, 227
Judas Maccabeus, 130, 132, 134, 137, 138, 149, 150–53, 156–57, 187, 188
Judges, book of, 74, 156
Judith (book of), 27, 67, 68, 69–74, 88, 132
Judith (character), 70–75, 76

Keturah, 44
King James Bible, 7
Kings, book of, 61

Lamech, 56, 231, 232
Lamentations, book of, 194, 215
law, 130, 132, 169, 182, 209
Levi, 44n29, 48
Levites, 49
Leviticus, book of, 48, 194
Lot, 43, 114
Lot's wife, 114
Luke, Gospel according to, 141n26

Lysias, 133

Maccabees/Maccabean Revolt, 89, 100, 127, 170, 187, 188, 229, 230, 234,
Mahalel, 171
Malachi, 195
Man of Mockery, 211
Manasseh, 44n29
martyr/martyrdom, 84, 146–49, 153, 154–57, 230
Masoretic text, 34n4, 61, 83, 84, 89, 178
Mastema, 39, 40, 46, 228
Mattathias, 128, 129, 130, 135, 155
Media, 76, 181
Merkabah, 165
Mesopotamia, 69, 89, 92, 167
messiah, 54, 166, 180, 194–223, 231
Methuselah, 171
Micah, book of, 16n29
Michael, 52, 181, 183–84, 202, 204, 207
Midianites, 133
miracles, 139
Modein, 129
monarchy/kingship, 113, 194
Mordecai, 87

INDEX OF SUBJECTS

Moses 36–37, 39, 40, 48, 76, 79, 99–100, 103, 107, 114, 122, 129, 163–64, 174, 201, 217, 219
Mount Sinai, 37, 46, 72, 122, 162, 163, 201, 219

Naamah, 231
Nag Hammadi library, 50
Nahor, 232
Nebuchadnezzar, 67, 68, 69n4, 74, 80, 92, 237
Neco (Pharaoh), 60
Nehemiah (character), 59, 142–43, 143n29
New Testament, 2, 141, 165
Nicanor, 136, 137, 143, 149, 151–53
Nineveh, 67
Noah, 52–53, 56, 57, 114, 167n7, 171, 172, 173, 174, 190, 199, 212, 232
Northern kingdom, 233

Old Testament (Protestant), 1, 31
Old Testament theology, 2, 21–22, 96n1, 236
Onias III, 106, 143, 153
Orthodox Christianity, 89

Papyrus 967, 81n33, 179n33

Passover, 46, 59
Paul the Apostle, 141
Peleg, 232
periodization, 166, 169, 170–71, 190
persecution, 146–48
Persia/Persian Empire, 14–15, 32, 88, 135, 136, 151, 166, 181, 183, 184, 190
Persian period, 17–18, 24, 195, 226
Phanuel, 202, 204
Pharaoh, 132, 207
Philip of Macedon, 126
Philistines, 133, 135
Philo, 10, 198, 208
Philopater, 89–90, 91
Phinehas, 48–49, 103, 106n18, 129, 130
plagues, 117, 118
Pliny the Elder, 198
prayer, 70–71, 76, 77n23, 82, 87, 90, 99, 108, 110, 113, 118, 151, 171, 175, 182, 183, 190, 210, 216
Prayer of Azariah and the Song of the Three Jews, 80, 82, 84, 178, 228
priesthood, 16, 48, 90, 103, 105–6, 127, 128, 153
Prince of Light, 210

261

prophetic literature, 176, 212
Proverbs, book of, 96, 97, 98, 107, 120, 238
Psalms, book of, 2, 16n29, 194, 213
Psalms of Solomon, 195, 214–17
Pseudepigrapha, 7, 31, 67, 148, 226
pseudepigraphy, 21
Ptolemy, 149
Ptolemies, Ptolemaic Empire, 90

Rachel, 78, 79
Raguel, 77
Raphael, 52, 76, 202, 204, 207
Razis, 153, 157
Rebekah, 45, 78, 79
Red Sea, 132, 207
Remiel, 52n46
Restoration, 134, 233
Reu, 232
Reuel, 52n46
Revelation/Apocalypse of John, 189
Romans, 128, 137, 138, 151, 196, 215
Rule of the Community, 195
Ruth, 78

Sabbath, 38, 46, 130, 155
sacrifice, 47, 59, 62, 90

Samuel, book(s) of, 194
Sarai/Sarah, 41, 42, 43, 44, 78
Sarah (wire of Tobias), 77, 79, 237
Sariel, 52, 207
Saul, 137
Second Enoch (book of), 9
Second Kings, 126
Second Maccabees, 27–28, 125–27, 139, 141–58, 187, 215n54, 230, 238
Second Samuel, 126
Sectarian Judaism, 12, 233, 235
Seleucids/Seleucid Empire, 90, 97, 106–7, 129, 130, 136, 147, 149, 152, 155, 181
Sennacherib, 91, 150
Septuagint/ Greek text, 8, 12–13, 61, 73, 80, 81, 83, 84, 87, 88, 93, 114, 178, 179, 183, 213, 228
Serug, 232
Seth, 38
Shechem, 48, 232
shekinah, 164, 164n5
Shem, 232
Shemihazah, 51, 52, 228
Simon (character in 1 Maccabees), 138, 139
Simon (character in 2 Maccabees), 154
Simon II, 90, 91

INDEX OF SUBJECTS

Simon (high priest, son of Onias), 98, 102, 103, 105, 106
sin, 120, 121–22, 145, 177, 215, 216, 229, 236
Sirach (book of), 24, 28, 97–106, 120, 125, 238
Sodom, 43, 114, 171
Solomon, 24, 113, 134, 164, 221
Son of Man, 54, 181, 199, 200, 203–4, 206
Song of the Three Jews, 80
Sons of Darkness, 206
Sons of Light, 206, 207
Spartans, 128, 138
suffering, 92–93, 125–26, 146–47, 154, 166, 177, 182, 191, 212, 216, 230
Susanna, 80, 80n32, 85, 178, 185, 237
Syballine Oracles, 189

Tamar, 78
Tanak, 1, 4–5, 6, 8, 11, 12–13, 19, 23–24, 26, 31–32, 34, 40, 49, 51, 54, 58, 61, 61n67, 71, 78, 95, 96, 97, 99, 100, 102, 127, 139, 144, 145, 154, 155, 164, 176, 189, 195, 199, 200, 201, 212, 226, 227, 231, 232
Targumim, 13
Teacher of Righteousness, 211

temple, 17, 58, 62, 63, 76, 79, 90–91, 100, 107, 113, 128, 134, 137, 142–43, 144, 151, 164, 165, 169, 220, 221, 222, 226, 233
Temple Scroll, 197, 217, 218–23, 231
Testament of Moses, 188
Testaments of the Twelve Patriarchs, 10
theodicy, 33–34, 39, 51, 165, 177, 210, 227, 229, 230, 236, 237
Theodotian text (of Daniel) 80–81, 80n32, 83, 179, 184, 185
theophany, 42, 163, 205, 228
Third Enoch (book of), 9
Third Maccabees, 27–28, 68, 89–92, 93
Tigris, 77
Time, 47
Tobias, 76–79, 96, 237
Tobit (book of), 27, 64, 67, 68, 75–80, 88, 228
Tobit (character), 76–77
Torah, 48, 50, 107, 122, 131, 132, 136, 202–3, 218–23, 234
translation, 7, 131
Trypho, 138
Tubal-Cain, 231

263

Uriah, son of Shemaiah
Uriel, 52n46, 167
Uzziah, 72

vision, 165, 172, 176, 185, 199
Vulgate, 79, 79n29

War Scroll, 197, 206–8, 211
warfare, 134–35, 137, 155, 171, 207–8, 236
Watchers, 51, 51n41, 56, 173, 212, 227
wilderness, 117, 118
Wisdom (personified), 99, 100, 107, 108, 110, 112–13, 114, 119, 202–3, 238
Wisdom of Solomon, 24, 95, 96, 111–20, 125, 202, 229, 238

Wisdom literature, 23–24, 28, 95–123, 229, 230

Yehud, province of, 14

Zadok/Zadokite priesthood, 16–17
Zadokite Judaism, 50
zealotry, 154–55, 209
Zeboim/Zeboyim, 43, 43n27
Zechariah, book of, 16n29, 166, 195
Zechariah, son of Jehoiada, 147–48
Zerubbabel, 16, 58, 58n61, 59, 64–65, 194
Zeus, 180
Zimri, 129
Zipporah, 79, 79n27

Index of Authors

Abegg, Martin, Jr., 158n57, 206n31, 207n36
Adams, Samuel L., 18n36, 177
Argall, Randall, 167–68
Assmann, Jan, 154–55

Barstad, Hans, 15
Barr, James, 237n9
Bartlett, John R., 126n1, 140
Baumgarten, Joseph M., 211n42
Bedenbender, Andreas, 50n39
Bembry, Jason, 180, 200n17, 203n24
Berquist, John L., 14
Black, Matthew, 167n8
Boccaccini, Gabriele, 9n13, 16–17, 17n32, 27n58
Borchardt, Francis, 128, 129n11, 130n13
Breed, Brennan W., 3n4, 68n3, 226n2

Brueggemann, Walter, 21–22, 49
Burnett, Joel S., 163

Caird, G. B., 184n46
Calduch-Benages, Nuria, 100n8
Charles, R. H., 7, 174
Charlesworth, James, 7–8, 20, 195, 205
Cheon, Samuel, 115n37, 119n43
Chialá, Sabino, 200
Clines, David J. A. 86n43, 87–88
Cohen, Shaye J. D., 6, 101, 129, 129n10, 234n6
Collins, John J., 23–24, 81n34, 85n42, 98n5, 101, 112, 121, 121n46, 122n48, 122n49, 171n16, 172, 178n31, 180–81, 182–83, 195, 202
Cook, Edward, 158n57
Coxon, Peter W., 83, 83n37
Crenshaw, James, 96n1, 99

Croy, N. Clayton, 89, 90n55, 91n56

Davies, Philip R., 208, 208n37
Di Lella, Alexander A., 80n32, 102n12, 181n38, 183n43, 204n26
DiTommaso, Lorenzo, 178n32
Doran, Robert, 131, 131n15, 143n29, 144, 152n43
Duhaime, Jean, 207n33, 207n36

Elliott, Mark Adam, 25, 42

Fishbane, Michael, 217
Fitzmyer, Joseph A., 57, 75n19, 76n21
Friedman, Richard Elliott, 23n48, 36n10, 232n4

Gilders, William K., 46, 47n32
Glicksman, Andrew T., 113n33, 119, 119n45
Goldstein, Jonathan A., 126n2, 130n14, 131, 140, 146, 148nn37–38, 149, 149n40, 150n42, 153n45
Grabbe, Lester L., 14, 17, 57n59
Griffin, Patrick J., 77

Hacham, Noah, 89
Hamori, Esther, 42

Hann, Robert R., 214n48
Hanneken, Todd, 55
Hartman, Louis F., 80n32, 83, 84, 181n38, 183n43, 204n26
Henze, Matthias, 50
Holladay, William L., 3n2
Humphreys, W. Lee, 46n30

Isaac, E., 205n28

Jackson, David R., 51
Jobes, Karen H. 86n44

Kolarcik, Michael, S. J., 113n33, 114
Kugel, James L., 35–36, 39n17, 117n39
Kvanvig, Helge S., 17n34, 37–38

Law, Timothy Michael, 139n21, 140n23, 178n31
Lee, Thomas R., 102n13, 103, 104–5
Levenson, Jon D., 21n44
Levinson, Bernard M., 219
Lim, Timothy, 226n1
Lopez, Kathryn M. 181n39

Machiela, Daniel A., 56
Maier, Johann, 218n59
Martinez, Florentino García, 207n36

INDEX OF AUTHORS

McEntire, Mark, 21n43, 37n11, 38n14, 40n21, 41n23, 42n26, 46n30, 48n37, 53n48, 55n50, 59nn62–63, 61n67, 63n70, 81n35, 96n1, 150n41, 163n3, 180n37, 201n19, 203n25, 217n56, 227n3

McGlynn, Moyna, 115, 118, 118nn41–42

McLay, R. Timothy, 81n34, 179nn33–34, 182n40, 184n45

Meadowcraft, 184

Middlemas, Jill, 16

Miles, Jack, 16

Milik, J. T., 167n8

Moberly, Gregory, 97

Moore, Carey A., 67n1, 68n2, 74, 78, 78n24, 79n28, 108n23, 110n27

Moss, Candida, 156–57

Mulder, Otto, 106n18

Najman, Hindy, 216–17

Neusner, Jacob, 5–6

Newsom, Carol A., 68n3, 84

Nickelsburg, George W. E., 1n1, 7–8, 7n11, 52n45, 54n49, 56, 71n6, 72, 84, 87, 87n45, 90n53, 130n12, 132n18, 167n7, 171n16, 172, 174nn22–23, 175, 177n30, 188, 196n5, 199, 202–3, 206n29, 207n35, 209n39, 214n49, 215, 220n67, 221n68

Nicklas, Tobias, 118n40

Nowell, Iren O.S.B., 78

Otzen, Benedikt, 71n6, 72n11, 74n15, 88

Perdue, Leo G., 21–22, 98n4, 107n19, 111n28

Portier-Young, Anathea, 19, 19n38, 24–25, 79n29, 80, 156n53, 168–69, 171n15, 172n19, 175, 188

Priest, J., 188n55

Reed Annette Yoshiko, 39n16

Reese, J. M., 112n30

Reeves, John C., 56

Reitener, Friederich V., 101

Russell, D. S., 171n17, 184n46

Sacchi, Paolo, 197n7

Saldarini, Anthony J., 107n22, 110n26, 111n29

Sanders, James A., 3n2

Schiffman, Lawrence H., 195, 218n60, 221

Schmid, Konrad, 3n3

Schwartz, Daniel R., 142n28, 143, 144n32, 152n44, 157n56, 211n42
Schwartz, Howard, 53n48
Scolnic, Benjamin Edidin, 129, 129n10
Scott, James C., 19n38
Scott, James M., 186
Segal, Michael, 35–36, 38n15, 39n18, 185–86
Skehan, Patrick W., 102n12
Smith-Christopher, Daniel L., 15n26, 24
Stocker, Margarita, 71
Stone, Michael E., 159n58, 166, 233–34
Sukenik, Eleazar, 198

Tabor, James D., 148
Talshir, Zipora, 32n1, 58n60, 61n64
Taylor, Joan E., 198, 198n9
Tigchelaar, J. C., 207n36
Tiller, Patrick A., 172, 174n22, 175n27
Torrey, Charles Cutler, 57n58

VanderKam, James, 3n5, 34n5, 40, 40n19, 167n9, 185–86, 199n11, 202–3
van Henten, Jan Willem, 156n52
von Rad, Gerhard, 96n1

Watts, James W., 222n75
Wheaton, Gerry, 149n39, 152, 152n44
White, Sidnie Ann, 71n9
Williams, David, 127, 140
Williamson, H. G. M., 63n7
Winston, David, 115n36
Wintermute, O. S., 36n9, 186n50
Wise, Michael O., 158n57, 208n38, 209, 214n50, 218n61, 219, 221
Wright, Benjamin G., III, 105–6
Wright, Jacob L., 127n3, 135n19, 233n5
Wright, R. B., 215n52

Wyrick, Jed, 18–19

Yadin, Yigael, 218, 219

Index of Ancient Texts

Genesis
1–2......114
1......38, 39, 100, 201
2:6......99
2:9......33
2:10-14......99
4:1-31......232
4:17-22......231
5:1-32......231
6–11......51
6......51
6:1-4......31, 34, 51, 228
9:8-17......205
9:20......53
10:21-32......232
11:1-9......232
11:4......135
11:10-32......231, 232
12......162–63
15......47
16......43, 162–63
16:4-14......43
17......47
18:1-15......42, 43
18:16-33......43
19......171–72
21......43
22......39–40, 228
24......79
32:22-32......42–43
34......72
35:29......45
36:6......44–45
39:21-23......45
45:7-8......45
46:2-4......45
48:1-22......44n29
49......72
49:5......48

Exodus
2......79
3......37, 228

4:24-26......40
12......37
12:38......232
13......164
15......73
15:3......73
19–20......49
19......163
20......217
25:8......164n5
32:25-29......48, 154
34......201
34:6-7......109, 212
34:10-16......219
40......164

Leviticus
16......52
25:3-5......136

Numbers
11......164
11:1-9......118
21:4-9......117
24:17-19......207
25......48, 154
25:6-13......48–49
25:10-13......129, 130
25:14......129
30:3......219

Deuteronomy
7:25-26......219
12–26......221, 223
12:26......218
31:4-22......36
32:8-9......174n23
33......72

Joshua
6......164
24:1-13......232
24:18......232

Judges
4–5......71

1 Samuel
3......164

2 Samuel
1......137
8:17......16
24......40n22

1 Kings
8......106, 134, 164
8:33......90
9:3......90
12......233

2 Kings
19:35-37......150

INDEX OF ANCIENT TEXTS

Isaiah
11......199
37:36-38......150
40–55......154, 190
45:7......33–34

Jeremiah
24:1-10......233
25:11-12......174
26......147–48
26:23......147–48
31:27-34......109
31:29......212
31:33......109

Ezekiel
1......165
1:5-14......165
8–10......165
18......145
18:1-32......109
18:2......212
18:4......109, 212
18:20-21......190–91
18:25-29......212
18:32......145, 212
40–48......165, 221

Haggai
1:1......58n61

Psalms
2......199
106......102

Proverbs
1:7......110
8–9......114, 202, 238
8......24, 99, 114, 120
10–29......24
30......102n12

Job
1–2......39, 228
38–41......100, 102n12
38–39......24

Esther
6:1......88
8:11......88
8:13......88
9:16......88
11:12......87
16:16......88
16:21......88

Daniel
1–6......80, 81, 84, 86, 157, 178, 180, 185
1:2......81
1:9......81
1:17......81

1:21......183, 183n44
2:23......81
3......80, 178
3:16-18......70
3:17-18......82–84, 228
3:17......82, 83–84, 93
3:18......84
3:28......82
4:34-37......144
4:34......82
4:35......82
5:18......32
5:21......82
5:31......179
6:17......82
6:23......82
6:27......144
7–14......161, 178–85
7–12......80, 86, 108, 178
7–8......182
7......179, 181, 199, 203, 204
7:1......179
7:9-14......180
7:9-10......181
7:9......179, 181n39, 203
7:10......179
7:13......200, 204
7:14......181
7:15-22......181
7:22......181, 181n39
7:23-27......181

7:28......182n40
8......182
8:9......182
8:17......182, 200
8:19......182
8:27......182
9......108
9:1-19......182
9:2......183
9:4......182
9:5......182
9:7......182
9:8......182
9:9......182
9:11......182
9:13......182
9:15......182
9:18......182
9:23......183
9:24......183
9:25-27......183
10......183, 184
10:2......183
10:5-6......183, 184
10:13-21......184
10:21......184
12......185
12:1......195
12:12......185
13–14......80, 86, 178, 184

Prayer of Azariah and the Song of the Three Jews
4......82
5–9......82
11–22......82
30–34......84

Susanna
44–45......85

Ezra
3......134
4:3......233
6......134
6:14......63
6:21......233
6:22......63, 134
7:27......63

Nehemiah
9......57
9:6-37......63

1 Chronicles
7......134
21......40

2 Chronicles
7......106, 164
10......233
24:21-22......147–48
30......233
32:20-23......150
35–36......57
35:7-9......59
35:21......60
36:17......61, 62
36:21......174
36:22-24......144

Tobit
1:3-9......76
1:3......75
1:13......78
3:3-4......76
3:6......76
3:7-9......76
3:17......77
4:11......78
6:18......78
7......77
7:16......78
8......77
10:11......78
12:14-15......77
13:4......78
13:6......77
13:7......78
13:10......78
13:11......78
14:1-11......79

Judith
4:3......67
5:5-21......69
5:12......69
5:17-21......69–70
8:9—9:14......70
8:11-17......72
8:15-17......71
8:16-17......70
8:18-20......71
8:18......70-71
8:25-27......72
8:25-26......72
9:2......72
9:7......72
9:11......73
9:13......73
9:14......73
11:17......73
13:11......73
13:14......73
13:15......73
14:10......73
15:8......73
15:10......73
16:2......73
16:17......73

Wisdom of Solomon
1–6......112–13

1:1—6:21......112
2:23......112
3:1......112
4:15......112
6:22—11:1......112–13
6:22—9:18......113n33
6:22......113n33
7:1-14......113
8:1......114
9:1-4......113
9:8......113
10......114
10:1-21......114
10:1-11......114
10:1-2......114
10:3......114
10:4......114
10:5......114
10:6......114
10:7-8......114
10:10-12......114
10:15-21......119
10:16......114
10:17-21......114
11–19......113, 115, 119
11......115, 116
11:1—19:22......115
11:1-14......115
11:1......115
11:2—19:22......119
11:4-5......115, 116

11:4......116
11:7......116
11:8......116
11:9......116
11:10......115
11:17......116
11:20......116
11:23......116, 117
11:24......116, 117
11:25......117
11:26......116
16:1-3......117
16:5-15......117
16:6......117
16:9......117
16:16-29......117–18
16:20......118
16:26-28......118
17:1—18:4......118
17:3......118
17:20......118
18:5-25......118

Sirach
1:1......98
2:11......121
15......101
15:11-20......120
15:12-14......101
22:27—23:6......98
23:1......99

23:4......99
23:6......99
24......114
24:1-34......99, 120
24:3......99
24:8-12......99, 202
24:12-34......203
24:23-29......99
24:23......99–100, 122
25:24-26......120–21
25:24......121, 229
24:25-27......122
36:1-22......98
36:1......99
36:3......99
36:6......99
36:13......99
36:18......99
42:15—43:33......100, 101, 102n13, 120
42:15-25......102
42:15......101
42:18-20......100
42:18......100
43:13-26......102
43:27-33......102
43:33......102
44–50......103, 107, 122
44–49......105
44–45......103
44:1—50:24......102

44:2......104
44:4......122
44:17......104
44:18......104
44:21......104
44:22......104
44:23......104
45:1......104
45:2......104
45:3......104
45:4......104
50......105
50:1-29......102n13
50:1-24......104
50:1-21......98
50:11......106
50:20-24......106
50:21......105
50:22-24......105
50:27......98

Baruch
1:1—3:8......109
1:1-9......107
1:15—3:8......108
1:15......108
2......110
2:6-8......109
2:11-26......110
2:16......110
3:1-8......109

3:4......109
3:5......109
3:7......110
3:9—4:4......108
4:1......108
4:5—5:9......108, 109, 111
4:5-6......111

1 Maccabees
1–6......137
1:1—6:17......127, 136
1:1......126
1:15-26......128
1:20-23......128
1:56......128
1:63......128
2......129
2:1......128
2:20-21......128
2:23......129
2:26......129
2:27-28......130
2:39-41......155
2:41......130
2:44-48......130, 130n13
2:48......130
3–4......149
3:19......131
3:22......138
3:44......130
3:48......131

3:49......141
3:50......132
3:53......132
3:59-60......132
4......133
4:1-25......132
4:7......132
4:9-11......132
4:24......133
4:25......133, 141
4:26-35......133
4:30......133
4:31-33......134
4:36-61......134
4:40......134
4:55......134
4:58......134
5......134
5:31......136
5:55-68......140
5:55-62......135
5:56-57......135
5:57......135
5:65-68......135
6:1-17......135
6:11......155
6:12-13......135
6:17......127, 128, 136
6:18—14:15......127
6:18-63......136
6:18......136

6:19—14:15......136
6:53......155
7......152
7:39-49......137
8......137
8:3-4......156
9......137
9:1-22......137
9:5......137
9:10......137
9:19-22......137
9:28-31......137
9:46......136, 137
10......138
12:6-18......138
12:15......138
14—16......128
14:4-15......127, 138
14:13b......138
14:15......138
14:16—16:24......139

2 Maccabees
1:1-9......126
2:16-18......143
2:23......141
3:1......143
3:11......143
3:22......143
3:30......144
3:36-39......151

5:2-4......144
5:4......144
5:7......144–45
5:11-20......145
6–7......147, 149, 152, 153, 156, 157
6:1-11......149
6:7-11......145
6:12-17......145, 146
6:12......145
6:18—7:42......146
6:26......146
6:30......146
7......153
7:1-42......147
7:6......147
7:11......147
7:17......148
7:18......147, 230
7:19......147
8......152
8:1......149
8:4......149
8:5......149
8:11......149–50
8:13......150
8:15......150
8:18......150
8:19......153
8:20......150
8:21-29......150
8:28......150–51
8:33......151
8:36......151
9–10......151
9:1-12......151
9:1-4......151
9:4......151
9:5......151
9:14-17......151
9:19-29......152
9:28......152
10:1-8......143
10:9......152
10:29-30......144
11:8-11......144
14–15......152
14:12......142
14:34......153
14:37-46......153
15:16......153

1 Esdras
1–2......59, 62
1:6......60
1:7-9......59
1:24......60
1:27......60–61
1:28......60–61
1:32-33......60
1:50......60
1:51......60

INDEX OF ANCIENT TEXTS

1:52......61
1:53......60
2......62
2:2......60
2:3......60
2:8......60
3–4......9, 58, 59, 64–65
4:36-40......58
4:42-46......58
4:58-63......58
4:58......62
6:5......63
6:33......63
7:4......63
7:15......63
8:25......63

1 Enoch
1–36......27, 28–29, 51, 54, 167, 168, 196
1–5......51
6–11......51, 53
6–10......53
6......51
6:3......51
8–9......52n46
9......172
9:3......172
10......52, 55, 170
10:1-2......52
10:4......77n22

10:17-19......52
10:19......53
10:20—11:2......53
11:2......53
12–16......53
12:3......53
14:3......53
14:21......53
22......53
25......54
33–36......167
36:4......54
37–71......54, 167, 195, 196, 197, 198–206
37:1......199
37:4......200
38......204
38–44......199
38:1......198
38:3......201
39:2......201
39:3-8......201
39:9-14......201
39:11......201
40:1-10......202
41:8-9......202
42......202
42:1-2......202
42:3......202
43:1-4......202
45–57......199

279

45:1......198
45:3......203
46–48......200
46......203, 204, 205
46:1......203
46:3......199
47......204
47:3—48:6......200
47:4......204
48......204
50–51......204
53–53......204
54:7—55:2......204
55:1-2......204–5
58–69......199
58:1......198, 205
61:8......205
62:1-2......205
64:64–69......205
65:1-12......205
68:1......198
69:27......205
71......200
71:9-14......200
71:10......205
71:14......205
71:17......206
72–108......161, 167–77
72–82......161, 167, 220
72:1......167
75:3......167

82:6......172
83–90......167, 171
83–84......171
84:2-6......171, 172
85–90......172
85:3—89:8......172
85:3-10......173
86:1-6......173
87:1-4......173
88:1-3......173
89:1-9......173
89:9—90:27......172
89:14......173
89:15-27......173
89:28-40......173
89:41-50......173
89:51-67......173
89:57......173
89:58......174
89:59......173
89:71......174
89:72......174
89:73-74......174
89:75......174
89:77......174–75
90......175, 187
90:9......175
90:14......175
90:17-19......175
90:18......175
90:19......175

90:20-37......175–76
90:22......176
90:24-26......176
90:24......175
90:30......176
90:34......176
90:35......176
90:36......176
90:37-39......176
90:40......176
91–105......161, 167
91......167n7
91:11-17......168, 222
91:14......169
92......176
92:2......176
93......186
93:1-10......168, 176, 222
93:2......169
93:4......169
93:5......169
93:6......169
93:9-10......168
93:10......169
93:12......169
93:14......169
93:16......169
93:22......186
100:4-5......177
106–108......167n7

Jubilees
1......52, 55, 59, 185–87
1:5-17......36
1:13......36
1:17......36–37
1:18-20......36
1:18......36
1:26-28......37
1:29......35
2......37, 39
2:2-17......36
2:14......38
2:17......38
2:18-33......36
4:1-11......38
5:11-12......39
5:12......38, 44
6:17......35
10:8......39
10:9-13......39
12......41
12:3......41
12:19......41
12:23......41
13:10-12......41
15......47n34
15:23-24......41
15:31-32......41, 42
15:33-34......42
16......42
16:1......42

16:5-6......43
16:6-7......43
17:16......39
18......39
18:9-12......39
19:15—22:30......43–44
19:15-29......44
20–21......44
22:10-24......44
22:28-30......44
23......11, 44, 161, 185–87
23:1-7......44
23:9-10......44
23:29......186
23:30-31......186
23:32......186
24......44
29:13......42–43
29:14-20......44
29:18......44–45
30:6......48
30:7-17......48
30:18......48
31:11-20......44
31:11-17......49
35–36......45
35:17......45
35:18-27......45
36:1-20......45
37–38......45
39:12-14......45

43:18-19......45
44:5-6......45
48:1-3......40
49......37
50......37

Psalms of Solomon
2......215
2:22......215
2:34-36......215
3......215
3:7-8......215–16
4......215
4:3-13......216
4:14-22......216
5:1-4......216
6......216
6:8......216
7......216
7:4......216
7:5-8......216
16......216
17......213
17:6-15......216
17:23......216–17

3 Maccabees
1:1-7......90
1:8—2:24......90
1:9......90
2:1-20......90

INDEX OF ANCIENT TEXTS

2:9......90
2:13......90
2:15......90
2:22......91
3:11......91
5:11......91
5:28......91
6:10-12......91
6:18......92
6:24-28......92
7:2-9......92

Revelation
4:6-8......165

11Q5
27......214n50

Community Rule
9:11-12......195–96

Damascus Document
1......211
2:6-13......211
2:13......211

Temple Scroll (**11Q19**)
2......219
3–13......220
29:3-4......221
29:7-10......222
30–45......220
52–66......223
53:14......219

War Scroll
1:13-15......206
3:23......210
4......210
4:18-19......210
5:1......207
9:10-16......207
10......207
11......207
11:2......210
11:6......207
11:9-10......207
11:12......210
11:17-18......210
17......206

Antiquities of the Jews (**Josephus**)
Book 11......16
Book 18:1......235